85 -0828

Petroleum
and
Economic
Development

Petroleum and Economic Development

The Cases of Mexico and Norway

Ragaei El Mallakh
University of Colorado
Øystein Noreng
Norwegian School of
Management
Barry W. Poulson
University of Colorado

LexingtonBooks
D.C. Heath and Company
Lexington, Massachusetts
Toronto

Library of Congress Cataloging in Publication Data

El Mallakh, Ragaei, 1925-
    Petroleum and economic development.

    Includes index.
    1. Petroleum industry and trade—Government policy—Mexico.
2. Mexico—Economic policy—1970-   . 3. Petroleum industry and
trade—Government policy—Norway. 4. Norway—Economic policy.
I. Noreng, Øystein, 1942-   . II. Poulson, Barry Warren, 1937-
III. Title.
HD9574.M6E4   1983   330.972'083   83-12044
ISBN 0-669-07002-5

Copyright © 1984 by D.C. Heath and Company

Published simultaneously in Canada

Printed in the United States of America

International Standard Book Number: 0-669-07002-5

Library of Congress Catalog Card Number: 83-12044

This volume is dedicated to Carl McGuire, professor emeritus of economics at the University of Colorado, Boulder, who has trained thousands of American and foreign economists in the intricacies of international trade; has administered the department with concern, fairness, and undeniable success; and who now continues to offer his expertise in the classroom and as book review editor of the Journal of Energy and Development.

Contents

Figures and Tables

Foreword

This volume deals with two major petroleum producers and exporters: Mexico and Norway. While the body of literature on the member states of OPEC (Organization of the Petroleum Exporting Countries) has burgeoned in recent years, publications dealing with non-OPEC sources have not kept pace. Among the non-OPEC oil and gas exporters, Mexico and Norway are of growing significance, the former because of its vast reserves and proximity to the energy-hungry United States and the latter because of its proximity to industrialized Europe and its high degree of supply security.

Mexico's expanding oil-reserve estimates in the last half decade place that nation second to Saudi Arabia—holder of the world's largest oil reserves and the largest oil exporter. And although Norway's output remains comparatively modest, new discoveries—particularly in natural gas—mark Norway as a major and secure source of energy for Europe in the years to come. Because of European commitment to the USSR's gas-pipeline project and Europe's increasing dependence on Russian gas, Norway offers a critical way to diversify petroleum sources.

This study of petroleum in the Mexican and Norwegian economies was carried out under the auspices of the International Research Center for Energy and Economic Development (ICEED). The center has a long record of research in the areas of energy and development, and publishes the *Journal of Energy and Development.*

Mexico and Norway were two of the petroleum-exporting countries selected for examination in a major, multiyear ICEED study begun in 1979 and supported by a grant from The Rockefeller Foundation on New Constraints on Absorptive Capacity and the Optimum Rate of Petroleum Output. It was my privilege to serve as director of and principal investigator for that project along with the other principal investigators, Dr. Øystein Noreng and Dr. Barry Poulson. The study, which contributed in large measure to this book, benefited from a wide range of contacts, discussions, interviews, research work, and assistance in data collection from numerous persons participating in ICEED conferences, meetings, and other related activities. Of particular value were the seventh annual international energy conference (October 1980) on Absorptive Capacity and the Supply of Petroleum, and the second annual international area conference on Mexico: Energy Policy and Industrial Development (August 1981).

We wish to express our appreciation to some of those, such as Mason Willrich (formerly with The Rockefeller Foundation), and including, in Mexico: Lic. Arturo del Castillo, Dr. Gustavo Garza T., Ing. Guillermo de la Mora, and Ing. Enrique Vazquez D. of the Mexican Petroleum Institute; Dr. Rene Villarreal Arrambide (Deputy Director General of Planning) and

Ms. Victoria Sordo of the Ministry of Finance; Gilberto Escobedo, Deputy Director (Commercial) of Petroleos Mexicanos; Juan Eibenschutz, Director of the Federal Commission of Electricity (former Director General of the National Energy Commission); Drs. Clemente Ruiz Duran and Angel de la Vega Navarro of the National Autonomous University of Mexico; Drs. Francisco J. Cardenas C. and Mario Coria Salas, Carlos Betancourt M., and Octavio Luis Pineda of the National Polytechnic Institute; Miguel Wionczek and Mrs. Marcella Serrato of the College of Mexico; Drs. Jaime Corredor Esnoala and Manuel Zepeda Payeras of the Economic Advisors to the President; Javier A. Barrientos, Jr. of ICATEC S.A.; Fernando Uro (Engineers' College); and Felipe Ramon y Castaneza (National Commission of Electric and Gas Tariffs).

In Norway we would like to thank Dr. Petter Nore, Johan Nic. Vold, Erik Johnsen, and Terje D. Skullerud of the Royal Ministry of Petroleum and Energy; Arve Johnsen, Svein Rennemo, Terje Vareberg, and Kjell Stautland of Statoil; Tore Tonne and Harald Aasheim from the Norwegian Embassy in Washington, D.C.; Dr. Pal Erik Holte of the Royal Ministry of Environmental Affairs; and Dr. Paul L. Eckbo of Petroplan. We are also indebted to Dennis Miller, ICEED Senior Research Fellow and a doctoral candidate at the University of Colorado, Boulder, as well as former and present graduate students in the Department of Economics at the University of Colorado, Boulder: Drs. Francisco Carrada Bravo and Jacques Rogozinski, Juan Amieva Huerta, Jose Parra Sanchez, Guillermo Robles Martinez, Juan M. Saldivar Canto, Helios Cesar Torres, and Gabriel Haddad. Typing, editing, and the manuscript tending have been handled with the usual efficiency and good spirits by Glenda Bolin, Dr. Dorothea El Mallakh, Kim Giovacco, Nancy Nachman Hunt, Barbara Heroy John, and Kathleen O'Brien.

Ragaei El Mallakh

1 Introduction

Another title for this book could appropriately have been *Petrolization and Economic Development*. The term *petrolization* was probably first coined by Mexican economists to describe the impact of rapid growth in petroleum output on their nation's economy. Although the term suffers somewhat in translation it may be generalized to describe any economy experiencing structural change as a result of the rapid growth of the petroleum sector. Much has been written in recent years about the impact of such petrolization on the economies in developing nations such as those belonging to the Organization of the Petroleum Exporting Countries (OPEC).

Norway and Mexico are special cases in the sense that both countries are further along in the process of industrialization compared with the OPEC nations, and the rapid growth of petroleum output has had quite a different impact on the process of modern economic development in these countries. Norway represents a developed economy with one of the highest levels of income per capita in the world, whereas Mexico has a level of income per capita that places it among the developing nations. In 1981 Norway ranked third internationally in per-capita gross national product.[1] Yet both countries have experienced rapid growth of petroleum output in the context of a substantial industrial base accompanied by major structural changes in the industrial and nonindustrial sectors of their economies. We shall see important parallels in the structural changes resulting from the petrolization of the Norwegian and Mexican economies. Nonetheless, two separate national case studies will be presented rather than a comparative examination.

It might be argued that the institutional arrangements in the petroleum sector differ substantially in Norway and Mexico. Norway has continued to rely on private multinational firms in addition to a national petroleum company in the production and sale of petroleum, whereas Mexico has completely nationalized the domestic production and distribution of petroleum, permitting multinational firms a role only in exploration and drilling. Despite these differences in institutional arrangements, petrolization is linked to the domestic economy in much the same way in both countries. Revenue generated from the oil sector has come to play an increasingly important and, to some extent, dominant role in both economies.

Oil revenue enters the economy as public-sector revenue that in turn provides the financial resources for government investment and consumption. In the case of Norway, oil revenue accrues to the government in the form of shares in the profit of the multinational and national operating companies, and those shares have increased substantially over the last decade. In Mexico, the oil revenue accrues to the government through shares in the revenues over and above the operating costs of Pemex (Petroleos Mexicanos), the company that was formed after Mexico nationalized oil production in the 1930s. In terms of flows of revenues generated, the differences in institutional arrangements are more a matter of form than substance. In effect both countries have successfully transferred property rights in petroleum from the multinational operating companies to their own governments.

Mexico was a relatively large-scale producer and exporter in the 1930s, but Norway did not become a net exporter until 1975. Moreover, present and potential domestic consumption in Mexico and Norway differ widely. In 1981 Norway's offshore production amounted to seven times the domestic consumption of petroleum. Norway's population of about 4.1 million should be contrasted with that of Mexico—some 68.2 million in early 1981, with estimates of 100 million by the year 2000. Given the level of industrialization and the population base in Mexico, it may be expected that present domestic oil consumption of approximately one-third of production will not fall appreciably throughout this century and instead will probably expand.

The shift in petroleum property rights has received some analysis with respect to the pricing of oil. The sharp increase in petroleum prices in 1973-1974 can be explained at least in part by the transfer of property rights in oil from multinational operating companies to the producing countries. Indeed, the expectations of that loss in property rights induced the operating companies to produce and export petroleum at a high level in the late 1960s and early 1970s, which had a depressing effect on petroleum prices. When property rights shifted to the producing countries, the producer nations reduced output to levels consistent with their longer time horizon and lower discount in the future production of petroleum, resulting in sharp increases in oil prices.

The shift of property rights in petroleum to the producing countries has had a broader range of effects than in oil production, export, and pricing. The increase in the price of petroleum has resulted in a significant shift of resources from the oil-importing countries to the oil-producing nations. Because of the change in property rights and new institutional arrangements among the producing countries and multinational petroleum firms, most of those resources accrue to the producer governments. Over the last decade petroleum revenues have become the major source of government revenues in both Norway and Mexico. Petroleum has emerged as the dominant influence not only in terms of economic growth and development but also in terms of the social and political institutions of these countries. Again, *petrolization* refers to this broad range of effects of petroleum production on the political economy of the producing nations.

Most non-oil-exporting countries look upon petrolization in Norway and Mexico with envy. The production and export of petroleum by these two nations have transferred resources away from the petroleum-importing countries and have generated significant increases in revenue available to their respective governments. As a result, those countries have not been subject to the external and internal constraints that have limited economic growth in the oil-importing nations. In the latter, higher oil prices have increased the costs of petroleum imports, bringing trade deficits and disequilibrium in the balance of payments. That external constraint has forced these oil-importing countries to reduce imports and limit domestic expenditures in order to reduce their trade deficits. Despite such efforts, the oil-importing countries continue to be plagued by disequilibrium in the balance of payments and depressed domestic economic conditions.

In oil-exporting nations such as Mexico and Norway, increased oil revenues have offset the constraints imposed by external and internal economic disequilibria. They have been able to expand imports and domestic expenditures at a rapid pace in the face of slower growth and depressed economic conditions worldwide. Yet within Norway and Mexico the petrolization of their economies is often looked upon in negative terms as introducing a new set of problems for and constraints on their economic development.

As petroleum production expanded, both Norway and Mexico found that their trade was increasingly dominated by and sensitive to the world petroleum market. The vicissitudes of that market brought wide swings in their export revenues, introducing an element of instability that had not existed prior to petrolization. Sharp increases in oil prices generated revenues that were then pumped into the domestic economies at a faster rate than anticipated. Inflationary pressures brought dislocation and crowding out of the non-oil economy. Traditional sectors experienced declining output and exports, further increasing dependence in the petroleum sector. Periods of excess supply in world petroleum markets with depressed oil prices have been accompanied either by sharp decreases or substantially lower-than-projected increases in petroleum revenues, suddenly imposing constraints on development that were unanticipated in both Norway and Mexico.[2]

Using Norway as an example of the structural change in the economy wrought by petrolization, the sectoral contribution to the gross national product (GNP) offers a vivid picture. In 1972 the share of oil and gas (the petroleum sector) in Norway's GNP was 0.2 percent; just ten years later, in 1982, its share was 17 percent. In that same decade, the share of oil and gas in investment leaped from 4.5 to 20 percent and, in exports, similarly rose from 0.5 to 34 percent. During the latter year in that period (1982), total exports (excluding ships) were $15.2 billion, of which $7.4 billion emanated from traditional goods and services.[3] Imports for 1982 totaled some $13.3 billion, which included $500 million for ships and offshore equipment. Clearly, a sizable deficit in the trade balance existed in the area of traditional goods and services.

One question that arises is why Norway and Mexico have not been more successful in establishing a buffer to safeguard their domestic resources from the fluctuations of the world petroleum market. One option would be to maintain a fund of petroleum revenues that would be expanded with higher petroleum prices and revenues and depleted in periods of depressed prices and petroleum revenues. To understand why this option has not existed, we must understand the difference between oil-producing countries such as Norway and Mexico that are further along in industrialization and development and the so-called low-absorber nations within OPEC. Countries such as Saudi Arabia, Kuwait, Qatar, and the United Arab Emirates have utilized a significant portion of their oil revenues to accumulate foreign assets. Those assets have been accumulated primarily for utilization in a post-oil period. It seems that all major petroleum-exporting nations during the 1970s and, indeed, until the early 1980s, expected oil prices to continue rising and did not adequately relate business cycles to either demand for or prices of their oil exports. Yet those so-called low-absorber Arab countries are low absorbers only in the sense that the resources required to meet their needs for imports and domestic investment and consumption spending are less than the amount of revenue generated from petroleum exports.

In contrast, the resources required to finance imports and domestic expenditures (including the financing of oil development) in Norway and Mexico have exceeded the amount of accrued revenue generated by oil exports. In this sense we refer to these countries as high absorbers. In fact, they have both borrowed heavily against future oil revenues in order to finance a higher level of current expenditures. This borrowing against future oil revenues has occurred in both Norway and Mexico, despite the substantial differences in their levels of development.

Mexico's debt burden is far greater than that of Norway. The total public and private foreign debt of Mexico escalated from $40.2 billion in 1979 to $50.7 billion in 1980, and is estimated to reach $80 billion in 1982. By contrast, Norway's foreign debt in the spring of 1978 amounted to $20 billion, equivalent to half its gross national product. Nonetheless this gave Norway the highest debt ratio attained by any country in the Organization for Economic Cooperation and Development (OECD). By 1981 foreign borrowing was equivalent to some 14 percent of Norway's GNP. Of course, the deepening global recession along with the continuing decline in oil demand and relatively high interest rates significantly added to each country's foreign-debt burden in 1982.

In other words, high-absorber countries tend to adjust their expenditures to match or exceed the amount of petroleum revenues generated, regardless of their level of economic development. The only high-absorber nation attempting to establish a buffer fund of oil revenues has been Venezuela; that fund was rapidly dissipated among the various demands on its government revenues and the experiment was abolished.

The experience in Norway, Mexico, and other high-absorber countries over the last decade shows why petrolization creates a new set of problems and why these nations are urgently attempting to decrease their dependence on petroleum. Dependence on oil revenues introduces new sources of external and internal instability. Before the shift in property rights, changes in world demand for petroleum and the vicissitudes of oil prices were absorbed in the changing volume of production and revenue of the multinational petroleum companies. This was reflected in some changes in royalties and taxes paid by multinational firms to the host governments in those countries. With the shift in property rights to the governments of the producing nations, oil became the major source of government revenue, and variations in oil prices had to be absorbed by the governments.

The governments of Norway and Mexico have had difficulty absorbing and adjusting to the abrupt changes in oil revenues over the past decade. Periods of sharp increases in oil prices and revenues, such as those which occurred in 1973-1974 and in 1979-1980, produced revenues far exceeding those anticipated in government plans. Immediate pressures from various interest groups forced the governments to increase levels of expenditures to more than match the high levels of revenue. In periods of depressed prices, especially in the mid-1970s, late 1980, 1981, and 1982, revenues fell far short of government plans. Efforts to respond to lower revenues by adjusting expenditures downward met with resistance, and that failure was accompanied by disequilibrium in both the external balance of payments and the internal budgeting process.

This economic instability was closely tied to political instability. In both Norway and Mexico, individual leaders and their political parties have been judged in terms of their success or failure in managing oil revenues. The loss of the election by the liberal party to the conservative party in Norway was directly linked to the perceived failure of liberal energy policies. In Mexico the major political party, PRI (Partido Revolucionario Institucional), continues to dominate the political system. However, the director of Pemex, Jorge Diaz Seranno, who had been considered a leading candidate in the presidential election, was removed from his position by President Lopez Portillo because of a perceived failure relating to energy pricing. Seranno responded to decreased demand for Mexican oil in world markets by cutting the price of petroleum by $4. It is important to note that Mexico subsequently adjusted its price to almost exactly the level that Seranno had set in order to sell its petroleum in the depressed market of 1982 and early 1983. This incident illustrates the internal political as well as economic conflicts that emerge in countries such as Mexico where the government is heavily dependent on petroleum revenues.

The economic potential and future of Mexico and, to a lesser but still significant degree, of Norway will depend on the prices and demand for oil and natural gas. Here there is a clear difference between two schools of thought: the "gloom and doom" forecasters predict a deepening recession into depression in 1983, leading to a scramble for the diminished markets among major exporters and a break in oil prices—plummeting to as low as $15 per barrel. This group of prognosticators contend that an oil-price break could even bring on depression as oil-revenue-dependent nations fall into bankruptcy and default on United States and European creditor banks.[4]

The second view looks at declining demand for petroleum as caused by two factors: structural (fuel switching and the like, which tend to be permanent) and temporary (recession-induced; for example, the decline in factory utilization in the industrialized countries as in the United States, which was running about one-third below capacity in 1982). Additionally it should be recalled that energy-intensive industries such as steel, aluminum, and petrochemicals have been among the hardest hit. With lower inflation pressures and lower interest rates, improvement in such weathervane industries as construction should be reflected in rising demand for energy. The high unemployment rates in the major industrialized nations have become a compelling element in governmental action to stimulate the respective economies and accelerate economic recovery.[5]

In a larger context and longer timeframe, the financial borrowing of Norway and Mexico is less alarming. The debt-burden mortgages are but an extremely small portion of the value of their petroleum reserves. In terms of the longer-range capabilities of their economies, and with the austerity programs now in place in Norway (early 1983), and De la Madrid's new administration in Mexico, the present cash-flow pinch is not only temporary but may prove short-lived, again depending on the rapidity of worldwide economic recovery.

Mexico's austerity program is tough by any standards, particularly when contrasted with the boom mentality that prevailed until recently. Cuts in government expenditures of more than 15 percent are envisaged in 1983, plus slashes in public subsidies for food and gasoline (causing gas prices to double), and an end to subsidization of the peso (devalued 53 percent in December 1982 for the third time in that year).

Both Norway and Mexico are searching for ways to diversify their economies to insulate them from the vagaries of the world petroleum market and to maintain greater stability in their political and economic systems. Petroleum revenue is seen as a source of instability, introducing a new set of problems into political economy as well as offsetting the external and internal constraints on economic development. This book examines petrolization or the pervasive impact of the petroleum sector on the political economies of Norway and Mexico.

Notes

1. Norway's gross national product (GNP) in 1981 was some 328,000 million Norwegian krones, giving a per capita GNP of 79,900 krones. Den norske Creditbank, "Look to Norway," Denver Representative Office, 1983.

2. The aggregate value of oil and gas exports from Norway in 1982 was $7.6 billion, a rise of only $0.7 billion over that of 1981. Norwegian Information Service in the United States, *News of Norway*, vol. 40, no. 2 (February 4, 1983), p. 1.

3. Total exports (excluding ships) in 1981 totaled $14.2 billion, of which $7.2 billion came from traditional goods and services. Ibid.

4. "The Gloomy View," *Wall Street Journal*, December 31, 1982, pp. 1 and 20.

5. The second view is presented in some detail in Ragaei El Mallakh, "Hydrocarbons in a Changing World: Some Future Strategies," *OPEC Review* (Autumn 1982), pp. 287-294.

2 The Case of Mexico

Overview of the Mexican Economy

Mexico is the third largest nation in Latin America, consisting of 761,895 square miles. The nation is comprised of thirty-one states and a Federal District that contains Mexico City, the nation's capital. The country shares borders with the United States to the north, Guatemala and Belize to the south, and has numerous ports on both the Gulf of Mexico and the Pacific Ocean. Geography has played a significant role in economic and political change in Mexico. The shared 2,000-mile border with the United States has resulted in an interdependence that has historically created conflicts as well as opportunities for the Mexican people. Trade, capital flows, and migration flows with the United States have played a crucial role in Mexican economic development. The close link between the northern Mexican border states and the U.S. Southwest has emerged as a major public policy issue for both countries. Geography has placed Mexico in a unique position as a center of trade for the Caribbean, Central America, and Latin America. The Mexican government plans to use this strategic location to become a major conduit for world trade in the Western Hemisphere. Mexico can be expected to pursue a more independent course in its economic and foreign policy, conflicting in important respects with that pursued by the United States.

Mexico has substantial and varied mineral resources in addition to oil and gas. Mexico is the world's largest producer of silver and fluorite. The country is also a significant producer of barite, antimony, sulfur, lead, and bismuth. The production volume of Mexico's principal minerals satisfies most of its industrial requirements and also enables it to export silver, barite, sulfur, and zinc. Mining accounted for 1.1 percent of its gross domestic product in 1979.

Mexico is the second most populous nation in Latin America with an estimated population of 68.2 million in early 1981.[1] The population is expected to increase to 100 million by the year 2000.[2] Mexico City is the country's largest municipality with an estimated population of 14 million.[3] The next two largest cities are Guadalajara and Monterrey, with estimated populations in 1981 of 2.5 million and 2.0 million, respectively.[4]

Improved economic and social conditions and better medical care have extended the average life expectancy and have decreased the infant mortality rate by nearly two-thirds over the last four decades. This in turn has

9

resulted in an average annual rate of population growth of 3.4 percent over the last ten years. Like other developing countries, Mexico has a very young population; 67 percent are under thirty years of age and 29 million have not reached their fifteenth birthday. Declining birth rates in urban areas, where approximately 65 percent of the population is concentrated, and among women under thirty-five years of age, are expected to result in a moderation of the rate of population increase during the 1980s.

The demographic statistics indicate pressing problems. Mexico's rapidly increasing population ensures that the average age will be young and largely dependent, requiring heavy human capital outlays in education and other social services. Age distribution also is a factor in Mexico's poor income distribution since the young have considerably lower incomes than older members of society. Massive migration from rural to urban areas will require effective action and large expenditures to accommodate these new urban dwellers.

Mexican immigration to the United States is of concern to both governments. An estimated 800,000 Mexicans illegally crossed the United States-Mexico border in pursuit of better employment opportunities in 1980.[5] This approximately equals the annual increase in Mexico's labor force, making it an important safety valve for Mexico's unemployment pressure.

Recent Economic Performance

Mexico's GDP (gross domestic product) has grown at extremely high rates. Between 1940 and 1960 Mexico's GDP increased from 21.7 billion pesos to 74.3 billion pesos.[6] For the three years 1978 through 1980, the GNP grew 8 percent per annum in real terms;[7] however, the growth rate has declined sharply with the glut of oil in the 1980s.

Mexico now confronts a serious problem in dealing with inflation. Rapid growth in money supply and government deficits have raised Mexico's inflation rate to an expected average of 28 percent for 1981.[8] The 30-percent devaluation of the peso in February 1982 caused experts to predict that inflation could reach 40 to 50 percent in that year. In fact, by August 1982 inflation was running at about 60 percent; however, there is evidence of moderation in the rate of inflation following the presidential inauguration and extending into 1983. Furthermore, the Mexican government's emphasis upon rapid industrial growth has caused severe supply problems for certain sectors of the economy because capital-intensive projects have had priority in access to limited resources. This, in addition to a worsening of Mexico's external financial position, has forced policymakers to reduce GDP growth-rate goals to only a 6.5-percent rate.[9]

In Mexico, about 800,000 new jobs must be created per year just to keep up with demographic increases in the labor force. The United States has served as an outlet for this increasing work force and a solution to limited job availability in Mexico. To shut off this alternative, as many Americans favor, would add to an already serious unemployment problem in Mexico. The pressure of an expanding labor force upon a limited supply of available jobs is not likely to abate in the short run nor in the relevant future. Mexican population growth appears likely to continue at rates above 3 percent per annum. Moreover, refugees from politically disrupted El Salvador, Guatemala, and Nicaragua compound the problems of the employment situation.

Much criticism is directed at the Mexican government's tendency to stress capital-intensive investment projects while neglecting perhaps more appropriate labor-intensive investment projects. It is clear that capital formation has taken place at very high rates. From 1970 to 1979, capital formation has increased by an average of 8.9 percent per annum.[10] However, real GNP increases have occurred at an average rate of 6.88 percent. The average of marginal increases in gross fixed capital during these ten years has been larger than the average of the marginal percentage increases in GDP. During 1978 and 1979 the gross fixed capital to output ratios have been larger than the average for the ten-year period of 1970-1979. This suggests an inappropriate deepening of capital in a capital-scarce and labor-rich country.

The private sector and the government are apparently at odds over the issue of labor-intensive versus capital-intensive development as explained by analyst Robert H. McBride: "Among the private sector there seems to be a willingness and even desire to stress labor-intensive industry for a variety of reasons (including, possibly, mitigating the migration problem). Official policy, to the contrary, has stressed the desire for the most modern type of industry, even if creating fewer jobs."[11]

In September of 1981, inflation brought about a clear demonstration of the Mexican government's desire to continue its own development policies while restricting the private sector through a tightening of credit when the central bank, Banco de Mexico, bought 10 billion pesos ($404.8 million) of government treasury bills.[12] This occurred in an already tight credit market.

As a percentage of GDP, sectoral contributions changed very little between 1975 and 1979 as can be seen in table 2-1. Agriculture declined during this period by nearly one percentage point. Forestry, fishing, and of course petroleum, coke, and basic petrochemicals all made sizable increases in absolute terms of output, as well as in their shares of the GDP.

In summary, Mexico's recent economic performance has been impressive by any standard. Mexico's oil bonanza holds much promise for future prosperity. However, this hope has been partially tempered by press

Table 2-1
Contribution to Gross Domestic Product by Major Sectors, 1975-1979
(years ended December 31; million pesos)

Sector	1975	1976	1977	1978	1979[a]	Percentage of GDP	
						1975	1979
Agriculture	70,399	89,907	118,020	147,186	172,434	7.1	6.2
Livestock	24,539	32,036	48,489	63,417	85,552	2.5	3.1
Forestry	3,189	4,269	5,917	7,625	12,497	0.3	0.5
Fishing	1,800	2,371	4,156	5,246	7,262	0.2	0.3
Mining	10,701	13,802	21,284	23,159	31,518	1.1	1.1
Petroleum, coke, basic petrochemicals	31,304	37,431	64,141	83,119	132,371	3.2	4.8
Manufacturing[b]	227,147	289,827	405,696	513,033	658,692	23.0	23.8
Construction	63,290	78,121	99,106	134,561	186,580	6.4	6.7
Electricity	11,171	14,891	23,628	25,400	32,563	1.1	1.2
Transportation and communications	29,013	36,197	52,968	68,916	87,760	2.9	3.2
Commerce	288,249	334,536	447,689	573,361	744,390	29.2	26.9
Services	238,423	308,847	398,910	500,005	645,577	24.1	23.3
Subtotal	999,225	1,242,235	1,690,004	2,145,028	2,797,196	101.1	101.1
Less adjustment for banking services	10,925	14,235	15,304	22,228	30,196	1.1	1.1
Total gross domestic product	988,300	1,228,000	1,674,700	2,122,800	2,767,000	100.0	100.0

Source: "Prospectus: United Mexican States," *Financial Times* (London), September 15, 1982, p. 32.
[a]Preliminary.
[b]Manufacturing sector includes secondary petrochemicals.

ing developmental problems and by the dampened world demand for petroleum in the early 1980s. The age structure of the population requires that the economy provide both jobs for an expanding work force and accomodations for the dependent young and old. The capital-intensive emphasis of the past is beginning to bend toward labor-intensive projects, but it is not clear that this is occurring fast enough. Agricultural output has not kept pace with domestic requirements, causing Mexico to import increasing quantities of foodstuffs. Inflation has become a major problem. Mexico began to encounter problems in later 1981 in selling sufficient quantities of petroleum on a glutted world oil market to support its ambitious development goals.

International Trade and Finance

Because of its huge oil reserves, increasing oil-production rates, and industrialization program, Mexico's foreign trade will certainly be expanding. From 1975 to 1979 imports of goods were about 8.6 percent of the GDP compared with exports, which made up about 5.7 percent.[13] Historically the United States has been Mexico's largest trading partner, purchasing 62 percent of Mexico's exports in 1980, while in that year 58 percent of Mexico's imports were from the United States.[14] In addition to the United States, Mexico's principal export markets are Spain, Israel, France, Japan, and Brazil.

The sectoral proportions of total foreign trade will certainly change in the future. Predictably, crude-oil exports have been growing at rapid rates in recent years. Between 1975 and 1980 crude-petroleum exports grew from 7.3 percent of total exports to 61.6 percent. Preliminary estimates for 1980 indicate that the total volume of exports of crude oil grew nearly ninefold, from 94,180 barrels per day in 1976 to 827,750 barrels per day in 1980. Exports of refined products increased by almost fourteen times over the same period (see table 2-2).[15]

In value terms, petroleum-export increases were even more impressive. By 1980 the value of crude-oil exports in nominal terms increased by about sixteen times over its 1976 value, while refined and other petroleum products increased by seventeen times (table 2-3). Half of these increases were the result of a doubling in the world market price of crude petroleum in 1979. Mexico, nevertheless, imported some petroleum products with a heavy emphasis on petrochemicals, as can be seen in table 2-3.

Table 2-4 depicts the rapidly changing structure of Mexico's foreign trade. Imports have increased in each given category. Metal products, machinery and equipment imports rose rapidly. This reflects Mexico's heavy industrial emphasis in its development planning. (It also gives sub-

Table 2-2

Volume of Mexican Petroleum Exports and Imports, 1976-1980

(*years ended December 31*)

	1976	1977	1978	1979	1980[a]
Exports					
Crude oil (*b/d*)	94,180	202,016	365,060	672,200	827,750
Refined products (*b/d*)	3,335	4,525	1,844	10,141	46,403
Petrochemicals					
(*tons per day*)	—	83	1,920	2,055	2,063
Natural gas					
(*thousands of ft³/day*)	—	—	—	—	280,900
Imports					
Refined products (*b/d*)	25,371	9,493	29,088	27,054	14,831
Petrochemicals					
(*tons per day*)	865	1,261	1,330	1,386	2,082

Source: "Prospectus: United Mexican States," *Financial Times* (London), September 15, 1981, p. 33.

[a]Preliminary.

Table 2-3

Value of Mexican Petroleum Exports and Imports, 1976-1980

(*millions of pounds*)[a]

	Year Ended December 31				
	1976	1977	1978	1979	1980
Exports					
Crude oil	246.9	514.2	861.8	1,717.6	3,952.0
Natural gas	—	2.8	—	—	187.3
Refined and other petroleum products	9.3	11.9	4.6	30.5	160.7
Petrochemicals	0.2	1.7	33.1	48.4	50.4
Total	256.4	530.6	899.5	1,796.5	4,350.4
Imports					
Refined and other petroleum products	74.1	26.9	70.5	94.0	101.6
Petrochemicals	61.0	81.5	80.1	149.4	218.7
Total	135.1	108.4	150.6	243.4	320.3
Net exports	121.3	422.2	748.9	1,553.1	4,030.1
Percentage increase from previous year	38.4	248.1	77.4	107.4	159.5

Source: "Prospectus: United Mexican States," *Financial Times* (London), September 15, 1981, p. 33.

[a]Exchange rates of pesos per dollar were: 1976, 15.426; 1977, 22.573; 1978, 22.767; 1979, 22.805; 1980, 22.951. Exchange rates of dollars per pound were: 1976, 1.8062; 1977, 1.7455; 1978, 1.9195; 1979, 2.1216; 1980, 2.3263. International Monetary Fund, *International Financial Statistics* (June 1982).

Table 2-4
Mexican Exports and Imports by Major Groups, 1978-1980
(*millions of pounds*)[a]

	Year Ended December 31[b]		
Commodity	1978	1979	1980[c]
Exports (f.o.b.)[d]			
Agricultural	734.9	801.5	645.8
Crude oil and natural gas	868.4	1,696.6	4,131.5
Other extractive materials	104.0	142.9	210.4
(Total extractive materials)	(972.4)	(1,839.5)	(4,341.9)
Food	360.7	360.2	323.3
Textiles	92.7	94.2	84.2
Metal products, machinery, and equipment	332.8	340.2	396.9
Other manufactured goods	474.0	528.5	608.8
(Total manufactured goods)	(1,260.2)	(1,323.1)	(1,413.2)
Unclassified products	1.0	0.8	1.2
Total exports	2,968.5	3,964.9	6,402
Imports (f.o.b.)			
Agricultural	448.4	438.2	841.4
Chemicals	385.5	497.6	621.1
Iron and steel products	443.1	507.8	763.0
Metal products, machinery, and equipment	1,814.9	2,800.2	3,727.2
(Total manufactured goods)	(3,325.1)	(4,760.3)	(6,728.9)
Unclassified products	3.2	93.7	90.2
Special border-zone products	99.7	109.2	107.0
Total imports	3,876.4	5,401.4	7,767.5

Source: "Prospectus: United Mexican States," *Financial Times* (London), September 15, 1981, p. 35.

[a]Exchange rates of pesos per dollar were: 1978, 22.767; 1979, 22.805; 1980, 22.951. Exchange rates of dollars per pound were: 1978, 1.9195; 1979, 2.1216; 1980, 2.3263.

[b]Pre-1978 information is not included because of changes in reporting classification.

[c]Preliminary.

[d]The export values of the items in this table are based on prices declared in export invoices, except that such values for certain items are adjusted to reflect the average prices reported in United States import statistics and the export value of cotton is based on the quotations for Mexican cotton in the Liverpool market, after deducting freight and other transportation charges.

stance to criticism concerning Mexico's overwhelming emphasis on capital-intensive industry in a labor-abundant country.)

Agriculture export and import statistics suggest other trends. Exports of agricultural products decreased 12 percent from 1978 to 1980. And imports of agricultural goods rose by nearly 88 percent over the same period. Several explanations are often given for these trends. First, during 1979 Mexico was stricken with drought conditions that severely limited agricultural output for that year and into the next. Second, higher incomes cause greater expenditures on food, particularly in a society in which much of the population is either underfed or malnourished. Third, and perhaps most alarming, the rural sector is getting, both absolutely and comparatively, less federal-government financial support than are higher-priority sectors such as industry and refining. Even if the absolute allocations to agriculture have increased, the relatively larger allocations to the industrial (and usually urban) sectors far outweigh allocations for agricultural development.[16]

Also noteworthy is the slight increase in exports of metal products, machinery, and equipment. Mexico has spent much to develop its steel-producing capabilities. It plans to invest $17.2 billion during the 1980s to increase total output from 4.5 million tons in 1980 to 20.3 million tons in 1990.[17] One of Mexico's goals is to increase its production of steel threefold by 1990.[18] But because of heavy protectionist policies, many critics believe that Mexico will have difficulty producing salable steel that is competitive on the world market. This may be a somewhat irrelevant point, since most of Mexico's steel production is for internal consumption and its production cannot now keep pace with expanding domestic demands.[19] Even if Mexican steel is not salable on the world market at competitive prices, however, domestic users who must purchase it may find their efficiency decreased by an expensive and low-quality product.

For many years Mexico has had a current-account deficit in its balance of trade. This deficit situation is largely the result of Mexico's stress on industrialization and its lack of domestic supplies to support this emphasis. The 1977 current account deficit was considerably lower than the preceding year's. This could be traced to a large devaluation in 1976 when President Portillo first came to power. Pressure against the peso brought another devaluation in February of 1982 in the last year of Portillo's tenure in office.

A small proportion of Mexico's trade was with members of the Latin American Free Trade Association (Association Latino-Americano de Libre Comercio, or ALALC). The reasons for this relatively small proportion of trade with member nations may have been because member countries failed to achieve the ALALC goal of significantly reducing tariffs. As manufacturing played an important role in the members' economies, the clamor for protection was loud. ALADI, the Association Latino-Americano de Integracion, came into effect in March 1981 to replace ALALC. It has the same basic goals but seems to have less influence.

Mexico's tendency toward protection is affirmed by its unwillingness to become a member of the General Agreement on Tariffs and Trade (GATT). Mexico did agree in principle to the purposes of GATT, but by refusing to join GATT Mexico has created more uncertainty in the trading community. Mexico is not required, as a nonmember of GATT, to inform its trade partners of any action that might adversely affect them.

Mexican foreign trade is robust and with increases in petroleum production or higher oil prices is likely to expand even more. However, a few dangers loom on the horizon. A policy of protectionism may permanently disable domestic industries from effective competition on world markets. Mexico's rapid pace of oil exploration and development might tend to divert resources away from its traditional export leaders in agriculture, constricting Mexican export options. Continued large trade deficits, such as its $2.67-billion merchandise trade deficit in the first eight months of 1981,[20] have adversely affected the exchange rate of the peso, decreasing its purchasing power worldwide.

Only about 3 percent of total investment in Mexico is foreign.[21] Accumulated foreign investment in Mexico reached $8.46 billion at the beginning of 1981.[22] Nearly 70 percent of this was from the United States.[23] During the first half of that same year, foreign investment rose significantly. In fact, foreign direct investment in Mexico has been increasing at an unprecedented rate. New foreign investment inflow increased by 40.3 percent in the first half of 1981 to $496.4 million.[24] The Ministry of Industry will approve projects with foreign investment worth $3 billion in 1981. New foreign investment totaled $1 billion in 1980, $781 million in 1979, and $385 million in 1978.[25]

One of the greatest attractions of Mexico for foreign investors is its lack of restrictions on remittances of profits, replication of capital, and convertibility of exchange. Yet the rules of foreign investment are more complicated in Mexico than in many other countries. Foreign investors are barred from direct investment in oil (but not from its supplies or services), basic petrochemicals, electricity generation, telecommunications, railways, radioactive minerals, banks, bonding and investment companies, television and radio stations, and freight transport. Manufacturing, commerce, and services are open to foreign investment, while in mining foreign investment is limited to 34 percent. Foreign companies can have 100-percent ownership of in-bond companies and assembly plants that export their total output. Majority ownership is sometimes achieved through pyramiding ownership of different companies, but this is frowned upon by the government. Before 1973 companies could be established with 100-percent foreign ownership in some sectors such as automobiles. Since 1973 companies are limited to 49 percent and 51 percent Mexican ownership. The problem for many foreign investors has been finding suitable Mexican partners for such joint ventures. Coinvestment funds have been set up between Nacional Financiera, the state development bank, and several countries to help finance and establish joint ventures. But the funds are underused partly because of infighting among Mexican government agencies and partly because of the reluctance of foreign investors to enter joint ventures with government bodies. The problem of inadequate supply of suitable partners has led to speculation that Mexico might relax these restrictions but such changes appear to be far in the future.

Since the Mexican Revolution in the early years of this century, that nation has been quite cautious concerning foreign investment. The Mexican Revolution was partially caused by a strong sentiment against the large foreign ownership of capital in the country. The nationalization of the oil industry was one of the manifestations of this sentiment. Today, foreign investment is allowed only if it is necessary as a complement to Mexico's own basic industries or if it aids in export or import substitution. Of course, a great deal of foreign investment has occurred to help advance Mexico's technological base. But even this is subject to great stringency under the Law to Promote Mexican Investment and Regulate Foreign Investment enacted in 1973.

Mexico's foreign debt is now second only to that of Brazil, the largest debtor in the Third World. Table 2-5 shows the rapid growth in Mexican debt during the past seven years. Since 1975 ($12.8 billion) it will have grown more than three times to an estimated $45 billion. But the debt service is predicted to grow by nearly a factor of six, from $1.8 billion per year in 1975 to $10.4 billion per year in 1981.[26] This is only referring to public debt. If private debt, both short and long term, is included, the total by one estimate jumps to more than $62.1 billion, and even as high as $80.1 billion by year-end 1982.[27]

The weakening of the world market price of petroleum in the early

Table 2-5
Growth of Mexico's Foreign Debt, 1975-1981
(*billions of dollars*)

Year	Government Debt	Service on Government Debt
1975	12.8	1.8
1976	21.7	3.7
1977	25.5	5.2
1978	29.5	7.0
1979	29.8	7.8
1980	33.8	7.7
1981[a]	45.0	10.4

Source: "Mexico: Dangers of Petrolization," *Energy Detente*, August 20, 1981, p. 4.
[a] 1981 government debt figure from Peter Montagnon and William Chislett, "Mexico's Lenders Get Indigestion," *Financial Times* (London), December 9, 1981, p. 17.

1980s will make this debt much harder to withstand. Petroleum makes up about 74 percent of Mexico's total export earnings, and much of the planned government expenditure and indebtedness was based upon escalating prices of petroleum at conservative production levels. The productivity of other sectors of the Mexican economy has not matched the levels of productivity in the petroleum sector. This extreme debt situation is one of the reasons we predict that Mexico will increase its level of oil production in the near future.

Sectoral Analysis

Petroleum. The emergence of Mexico as a major producer and exporter of petroleum is not without precedent. In fact, in the 1920s Mexico was the second largest world producer of petroleum, after the United States. Mexico was the largest exporter of petroleum in that period; in 1921 Mexico was exporting 531,000 barrels per day (b/d).[28]

Following the nationalization of the petroleum industry and the creation of Pemex in the 1930s, oil production and exports declined sharply. In the following years Mexico produced enough petroleum to be self-sufficient with a small amount of exports. By the early 1970s rapid economic growth had shifted Mexico from a net exporter to a net importer of petroleum. Imports of petroleum reached a peak of 65,000 b/d in 1973. Because of these imports, the sharp increase in the price of petroleum in that year had a significant negative effect on the Mexican balance of payments during the Echeverria government (1970-1976).

The new era in Mexican energy development was launched by major oil discoveries in the south of the country in 1974, and further discoveries in subsequent years. Mexican authorities estimated that proven reserves of oil increased from 6.3 billion barrels in 1975 to 70 billion barrels in 1981. The *Oil and Gas Journal* provides a more conservative estimate of proven oil reserves at 57 billion barrels and natural gas at 75.4 billion cubic feet.[29] Comparison is difficult because the Mexican estimates combine oil and gas reserves. Some Mexican authorities estimate the potential reserves of oil and gas as high as 250 billion barrels.[30]

Production of hydrocarbons has expanded rapidly since the mid-1970s. From 1975 to 1981 petroleum production expanded from 800,000 b/d to 2.7 million b/d, natural-gas production increased from 2.2 to 4.0 billion cubic feet, petrochemical output expanded from 3.6 to 10 million tons, and output of refined products increased from 0.6 to 1.2 million b/d. From a global perspective, Mexico was producing about 3.3 percent of total world crude-oil production in 1980. Most important from the standpoint of Mexico's external imbalance problem was the growth in exports from 90,000 b/d to 125 million b/d over that period. In 1938 oil exploration was at an extremely low rate; only three wells were drilled in that year with only one find. The sizable increase in drilling activities during the past decade is shown in the table 2-6.

During most of the twentieth century, Mexico has been producing petroleum mainly for its own internal consumption. In 1938 under Lazaro Cardenas, Mexico expropriated all foreign companies' holdings. Not until 1941 were the terms of compensation finally reached.

With the 1938 nationalization, policies regarding oil exploration, production, and export shifted from the operating companies to the Mexican government. A national petroleum company, Petroleos Mexicanos (Pemex), was established to implement those policies. The fundamental directive to Pemex was to develop the petroleum industry in the interests of national objectives of the Mexican government, "Al Servicio de la Patria." Those goals turned out to be quite diverse and often conflicting.

The first objective was to meet the petroleum needs of the domestic economy and, most importantly, domestic industry. However, this petroleum was to be supplied at subsidized prices in order to stimulate rapid industrialization. The result was a bias in Mexican industry toward energy-intensive technology and energy-intensive industries that caused a misallocation of resources in the economy. The initial decision to maintain downstream petroleum prices below the world-market price of petroleum would come back to haunt the Mexican government.

Table 2-6
Petroleum Exploration in Mexico, 1938-1979

Year	Holes Drilled	Productive Holes	Dry Holes	Percentage of Success
1938	3	1	2	33
1948	28	10	18	35
1958	76	17	59	22
1968	154	41	113	27
1969	134	40	94	30
1970	130	28	102	22
1971	134	31	103	23
1972	144	30	114	21
1973	103	20	83	19
1974	100	21	79	21
1975	87	13	74	15
1976	78	24	54	31
1977	79	30	49	38
1978	83	28	55	34
1979	83	30	53	36

Source: Jaime Corredor, "Oil in Mexico: Summary of Relevant Information and Some Comparisons with Other Oil-Producing Countries," informative appendix prepared for The Oxford Energy Seminar, Oxford University, Oxford, England, September 1980.

In recent decades when oil prices were rising rapidly and Mexico was forced to import significant quantities of oil, the disparity between domestic oil prices and world oil prices was a major handicap in the efficient allocation of resources in Mexico. Although this problem was recognized by each administration, a policy of adjusting prices upward toward the world-market prices proved to be politically infeasible. Finally, in 1982, the last year of the Portillo government, energy prices were adjusted in one discontinuous change to parity with world-market prices. The shock of this adjustment will be felt for years to come as some industries abandon older energy-intensive technologies and substitute newer energy-conserving technologies. Consumers also must veer away from energy-intensive goods and services. Clearly such a sharp increase in domestic petroleum prices after decades of subsidized prices will lower the productive capacity of the Mexican economy compared to what would have existed if domestic energy prices were determined by world-market prices, or if domestic prices were permitted to adjust to world-market prices in a more gradual manner over a longer time period.

A second objective of Pemex, coincidental with the decision to develop petroleum resources to meet the needs of the domestic economy, was to reduce exports of petroleum to a minimum. That decision reflected the nationalistic motives that led to the expropriation of the assets of the multinational petroleum companies in 1938 and the continued pressure of the political left in subsequent years to limit exports in the name of Mexican nationalism. The result was a sharp drop in the volume of petroleum exports from Mexico in the decades following nationalization.

The combination of low levels of petroleum exports and controlled petroleum prices below market prices provided little incentive for Pemex to undertake new exploration activities in Mexico. The exploration activities undertaken by Pemex between 1938 and 1955 increased proven reserves from 835 million to 2,800 million barrels. Circumstantial evidence suggested reserves far in excess of these proven reserves. A report by the United Nations Economic Commission for Latin America (ECLA) in 1957 stated that

> According to some foreign expert sources, Mexico counts with sedimentary zones whose total extension compares with those in Texas and it is possible that the country happens to be endowed with oil resources as large as any other Latin American Republic, including Venezuela. Moreover it is quite possible that the extensive continental shelf along the Gulf of Mexico contains very sizeable hydrocarbon resources. It is worth mentioning that only in the Middle East, Venezuela and Mexico wells producing 3,000 barrels a day were drilled in the past few years.[31]

Even more surprising is evidence that knowledge of large reserves was available in Mexico throughout this period. The Pemex company records and diplomatic correspondence in the 1920s refer in great detail to the location of the reserves that were rediscovered by Pemex in the 1970s. Despite this evidence, Mexican officials continued to promote the idea of limited reserves and energy scarcity in the country.

It is often argued that Pemex failed to undertake a long-term exploration program in the decades following nationalization because it lacked the financial resources and technological capability. However, those constraints reflected the policy decisions regarding oil pricing and oil exports. With oil prices set below those prevailing in the market and with low levels of oil exports, the funds generated internally by Pemex as oil revenues were insufficient to implement a larger exploration program, and the federal government was not in a position to finance such a program. In 1948 and 1949 the Mexican government did seek a loan of $475 million from the Export-Import Bank to finance development of petroleum resources by Pemex, including exploration for new reserves, expansion of production capacity, and diversification of refined products to include refining and other downstream operations. Negotiations for the loan broke down, in part because of the opposition by leftist political groups in Mexico, and the ambitious program for development of Mexico's petroleum resources was scrapped. Indeed, the technical and financial conditions of Pemex deteriorated after World War II.

The national objectives assigned to Pemex at the time of nationalization also included improvements in the working conditions and welfare of oil workers. The oil workers' union emerged with powerful government backing to place demands on Pemex for increased employment and improvements in workers' welfare. In effect Pemex was asked to assume the function of a public welfare agency as well as an operating petroleum company. The operations of Pemex were dominated by an excess number of employees, inefficiency, incompetence, and corruption. Pemex became known as one of the worst-managed energy companies in the world. As Pemex and the petroleum workers' union became more firmly entrenched in the Mexican political system, their operations became more insulated from public scrutiny. There was virtually no attempt to integrate policies regarding development of petroleum resources into an energy policy or to a broader scope of public policy. Pemex policies often conflicted with those of other energy sectors in Mexico, most notably the electric industry, particularly in competition for limited investment resources provided by the government.

The powerful position of Pemex in Mexican politics permitted it to pursue autarchic policies that limited the growth and development of the petroleum sector. Investment in exploration and long-term development of the industry was curtailed in order to allocate more resources to oil processing and distribution in order to meet the swift growth of demand in the domestic market. Low prices for petroleum products stimulated a rapid growth in domestic demand, and Pemex was hard pressed to expand output in order to keep up.

These problems continued to plague Pemex during the post-World War II period: conflicting objectives imposed by the Mexican government; inadequate technology and financial resources; inefficient management; and lack of coordination in terms of overall energy development. In 1956 the Mexican government did increase energy prices close to world-market prices. And in the 1960s the Mexican government successfully secured loans abroad and began to allocate more investment into the petroleum sector. But these efforts failed to expand petroleum output to match the growth in domestic consumption. Despite these shifts in government policies, by the early 1970s the Mexican petroleum sector was in a crisis. Domestic demand outstripped supply so that in 1971/72 Mexico became a net importer of petroleum for the first time in its history. The sharp increase in the price of imported petroleum in 1973/74, combined with steadily increasing imports, created a disequilibrium in the Mexican balance of payments.

It is important to contrast the trends in the petroleum industry with those in natural gas. In the early 1950s the natural-gas industry in Mexico was in a similar position to that of petroleum. Large reserves of gas in the Reynosa fields remained undeveloped because of the domestic policies of the Mexican government. Domestic gas prices were maintained at levels far below those in the world market. Production of gas for the domestic market absorbed only a small share of proven reserves, and the revenue generated by that output was insufficient to finance a larger scale of output.

The low levels of gas production and exports changed radically in 1955 when Pemex successfully negotiated a contract to export a maximum of 200 million cubic feet per day of natural gas to the Texas Eastern Transmission Company. Pemex received an initial price of 14.2 cents per cubic foot, which was higher than the price prevailing in the North American market and significantly higher than the domestic market price at that time. The contract also called for an annual price increase of 0.2 cents per cubic foot with prices renegotiable every five years over the twenty-year life of the contract. Actual production and export under the contract did not begin until 1958, but the experience of the gas industry as a result of this contract was considerably better than that of the petroleum industry in this period.

The contract opened up a new market for natural gas that generated substantial revenues for the Mexican government. Those revenues provided the financial resources needed for the investment program to explore and develop the Reynosa gas fields. The expanded production capacity for gas permitted a rapid growth in output for the domestic market as well as the foreign market, and the availability of natural gas at low prices in the domestic market stimulated rapid growth in industries dependent on gas, particularly in northern Mexico. The expanded exports helped to offset an unfavorable balance of trade and generated increased foreign exchange earnings. The improved financial position of Pemex permitted the company to obtain the foreign credit in North America and in France needed to finance construction of refining and petrochemical plants in the 1960s.

It is not difficult to explain the successful development of the gas industry in contrast to the stagnation of petroleum in Mexico during the 1950s and 1960s. Successful development required access to foreign capital and technology to explore and develop the gas resources of the country, and given the constraints of the domestic market, it required access to the sale of gas in foreign markets. Both of these conditions were met in the contract with Texas Eastern Transmission Company, despite the fact that the political left in Mexico opposed this contract just as they had opposed development of petroleum resources for export. The director of Pemex, Bermendez, offered a number of arguments in support of the development of gas for export and the decision went in his favor despite the political opposition.

The crises in the petroleum sector in the early 1970s finally induced the Mexican government to undertake an expanded program of exploration and development of petroleum resources. The rediscovery of large petroleum fields in Mexico in 1976 changed the Mexican perspective from one of oil scarcity to one of oil abundance. Suddenly Mexico was presented with the option of not only meeting her domestic energy needs but also of again becoming one of the major petroleum exporters in the world. Suddenly Pemex had access to foreign credit for a greatly expanded program of exploration and development. Petroleum exports appeared to be a panacea for the economic ills afflicting the Mexican economy. The country could continue to maintain domestic energy prices far below world-market prices in order to stimulate rapid industrialization. The revenue from petroleum exports could finance an expanded government program for industrialization and social welfare.

The Mexican government set a target rate of economic growth of 10 percent per year and launched an expansionary monetary and fiscal policy designed to achieve that target. Such a radical change in energy policy did not take place without a highly charged debate in the public and private sectors. Those supporting this reversal in policy, including President Lopez Portillo and the director of Pemex, Jorge Diaz Serrano, defended the new energy program on the grounds that this was a short-term program required to escape the financial trap imposed on Mexico by the disequilibrium in its balance of payments and limited foreign-exchange reserves. The argument was that in the long run, which was usually expressed in terms of the period after 1980, rapid industrialization and economic growth would generate the exports and foreign exchange required for Mexican development without such heavy reliance on petroleum and gas exports. A ceiling was placed on petroleum exports of 1.5 million barrels per day.

This export ceiling (1.5 million b/d) was based upon the assumption that the real price of petroleum would continue to rise in the 1980s as it had in the 1970s. The glut of oil in world markets and the drop in price have invalidated those assumptions, at least for the early 1980s. Exports of Mexican petroleum dropped sharply in 1981, forcing a reduction in crude-oil prices. The combination of lower levels of oil exports and of lower prices resulted in oil revenues far below those projected in development plans.

While oil exports were falling domestic consumption of petroleum soared in the 1980s at the rapid pace it had set in the preceding decade. The subsidized domestic prices had deviated even further from world-market prices in 1978 and 1980. By 1982 the distortions and burdens imposed on the Mexican economy by subsidized domestic petroleum prices became unacceptable, and the government responded with an abrupt adjustment, bringing domestic prices in line with world-market prices.

By the 1980s it was clear that the optimistic scenario projected for the Mexican economy was unrealistic, as the bubble burst on a sea of surplus oil. By 1981 Mexico was selling far less oil in international markets at far lower prices than had been projected. The old constraints that have plagued the Mexican economy reemerged with a vengeance. A balance-of-payments disequilibrium undermined confidence in Mexican loans, threatening to cut off Mexican access to foreign credit. Lower levels of oil revenues required sharp cutbacks in government spending for welfare and development programs. Resources provided for energy development have been sharply curtailed.

We maintain in this book that the mutability of Mexico's petroleum policies following nationalization of that industry has imposed a burden on the Mexican people that has been a major factor in the economic, political, and social instability of the country. Implicit in this thesis is the complementary thesis that a more stable development of the petroleum industry would have contributed to a more stable development of the Mexican economy, resulting in significant improvements in the welfare of the Mexican people. There are several alternative scenarios that could have satisfied this assumption.

One possible scenario is one in which the Mexican petroleum industry was not nationalized in the 1930s but continued to permit multinational petroleum companies to operate in the country as did the oil-producing countries of the Middle East in that period. We would expect the multinational petroleum companies to have continued the program of exploration and development of Mexico's petroleum resources with a continued expansion in output and exports as they had in the pre-1930s period. In another scenario, the Mexican government could have established a national petroleum company such as Pemex to work closely with multinational companies in developing the petroleum resources of the country, as did Venezuela in this period. A third scenario is one in which the Mexican petroleum-industry resources were nationalized but the national company, Pemex, was permitted to rely on foreign financial resources and technical skills to develop the petroleum resources and produce for an export market as well as the domestic market. The analogy here would be with the natural gas industry, which did pursue these policies following the negotiation of contracts for the sale of natural gas to Texas Eastern Transmission Company in 1955. A fourth scenario would have involved nationalization of the petroleum industry, with the Mexican government relying on its own internal resources to develop the industry. This scenario would have required quite different policies regarding oil pricing, exploration, production, exports, and investments.

Obviously these scenarios have quite different implications regarding the economic and political issues surrounding Mexico's petroleum industry. It might be argued that the first scenario would have resulted in the most efficient allocation of resources. The second alternative would have given Mexico greater control over petroleum revenues without sacrificing a great deal of efficiency; the third alternative would have sacrificed some efficiency by relying on Pemex to develop the petroleum resources of the country, but this would have been more consistent with the ideology and political sentiments of the country. The last scenario would have been the most palatable to the political left in Mexico but would have faced the most difficult financial and technical barriers to development of the industry.

Although these scenarios have different economic and political implications, they share one thing in common: they would have resulted in a more stable growth for the Mexican petroleum industry from the 1920s to the 1980s. In any one of these scenarios the growth of petroleum production and exports would have been more stable than the actual growth path in which the industry virtually stagnated from the 1930s to the mid-1970s, and then accelerated at a very rapid pace from the mid-1970s to the present. Further, it could be hypothesized that a more stable growth path for the petroleum sector would have contributed to a more stable development path for the Mexican economy than the one pursued. In order to test this hypothesis, a macroeconomic model for the Mexican economy will be developed and the model simulated under different assumptions regarding public policy in Mexico. The unique approach to macroeconomic modeling utilized in this study reveals in a dynamic way some basic problems in the Mexican economy that have important implications for energy policy, not only in Mexico but for other countries as well.

The estimated proven petroleum reserves of Mexico more than doubled from 1979 to 1981. Figure 2-1 shows this explosive growth. In 1981, with 106 billion barrels of announced proven reserves, Mexico held 9.2 percent of the world's total. With the November 1981 proven reserve calculation,[32] Mexico now holds as much as 15 percent of the world's proven reserves. These are only the proven (not probable) reserves, with only 10 percent of the petroliferous areas having been explored. With proven reserves of 106 billion barrels, Mexico could be blessed with as much as 200 billion barrels of potential reserves.[33]

Regarding the rate of oil output, Mexico has adopted a "go-slow, plan carefully" attitude. The examples of other oil-exporting countries' unbalanced approaches to economic development caused the Mexican government to temper their economic plans with considerable caution. In June of 1981 Mexico was producing 2.75 million barrels per day. This was close to Mexico's highest rate of production as can be seen from table 2-7.

Though not a member of OPEC, Mexico has taken advantage of OPEC's price rises by following suit. Its share of the world petroleum production has grown in relation to OPEC's share as table 2-8 shows. But in 1981 Mexico also encountered problems with the world oil glut.

Mexico has stipulated an export ceiling on their crude oil of 1.5 million b/d. Half of this is destined to go to the United States. This ceiling was set in conjunction with the false assumption that the real price of crude petroleum on the world market would climb by 5 to 7 percent annually.[34] The 1981 oil glut has invalidated that assumption. In 1981 the average export level was 1.098 million b/d. However, Mexico now intends to reach the 1.5 million b/d export level in 1982[35] partly because of a price reduction of

Table 2-7
Average Petroleum Production Rates in Mexico, 1973-1981
(*thousand barrels per day*)

Year	Production
1973	465
1974	571
1975	705
1976	831
1977	981
1978	1,209
1979	1,461
1980	1,937
1981 (January-September)	2,325

Sources: United States, Department of Energy, *Monthly Energy Review*, January 1982, p. 89. *Petroleum Intelligence Weekly* February 22, 1982, p. 5 estimates Mexico's production for 1981 to average 2,313 thousand barrels per day.

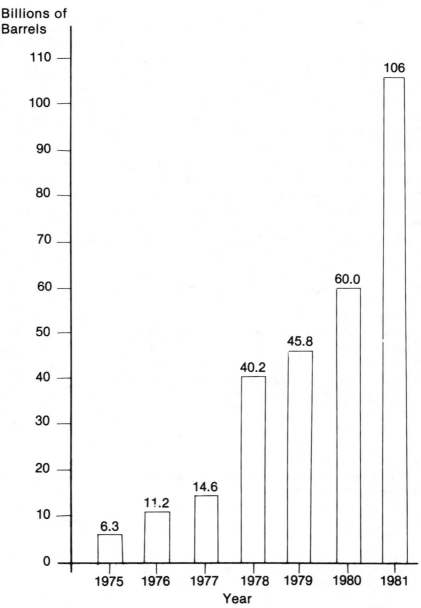

Sources: For 1975-1979 adapted from "Le Petrole, facteur d'Autonomie et d'Independence," *Le Monde Diplomatique*, June 1980, p. 23; for 1980 "Mexican Economy High on Oil," *The Economist*, September 20, 1980, p. 93; and for 1981, "Mexico Confirms 34 Billion BBL Jump in Proved Hydrocarbons," *Platt's Oilgram News*, vol. 59, no. 219 (November 13, 1981), p. 1.

Figure 2-1. Growth of Proven Petroleum Reserves in Mexico

Table 2-8
Percentage of Total World Crude-Oil Production for Major Petroleum-Exporting Countries, 1980-1981

Country	1980	1981 (October)
Algeria	1.7	1.3
Canada	2.4	2.1
China	3.6	3.7
Indonesia	2.7	2.9
Iran	2.8	1.8
Iraq	4.2	2.0
Kuwait	2.8	1.8
Libya	3.0	1.3
Mexico	3.3	4.6
Nigeria	3.5	2.3
Qatar	0.8	0.7
Saudi Arabia	9.9	17.8
U.S.S.R	19.8	21.7
United Arab Emirates	2.9	2.7
United Kingdom	2.7	3.4
United States	14.4	15.7
Venezuela	3.6	3.6
Other	8.6	9.9
OPEC	45.2	39.0

Total average barrels per day: 59,452,000

Source: United States, Department of Energy, *Monthly Energy Review*, October 1981, pp. 88-89, for 1980; and February 1982, pp. 90-91, for October 1981.

its Maya (23°) crude to $26.50 per barrel and a new price of Isthmus (33°) crude of $35.00 per barrel.[36]

The lower price of crude combined with selling at planned levels has particularly severe ramifications concerning Mexico's development program. The higher levels of petroleum revenues were to support the Mexican government's economic development plans. In April 1981 exports of petroleum were 1.36 million b/d and had earned in the previous year (1980) $9.5 billion in revenues. However, by July 1981 exports had fallen to only 457,000 b/d but picked up to 1 million b/d the next month.[37]

In June 1981 a political flurry was caused by Pemex director Jorge Diaz Serrano. He reduced the price of Mayan and Isthmus crude by $4 per barrel to retain customers who had begun to slow or halt buying. For this price lowering, Serrano was forced to resign. Julio Rudolfo Moctuzema Cid, Serrano's replacement, jacked the price back up but by only $2 per barrel. This was still insufficient to keep customers buying at high enough levels. Mexico has controlled the price of refined petroleum products sold domestically at very low levels. It is estimated that the cost of this policy was $10 billion in 1980 alone.[38] The Mexican government stood by this policy, arguing that

Mexico is a less-developed economy and that this pricing policy indirectly subsidized energy-using sectors of the economy, particularly Mexico's nascent industries. But the policy was reversed when the costs in terms of distortions were more closely considered. The policy tended to subsidize industries that were energy intensive and that were also usually quite capital intensive. This contributed to a capital structure that was increasingly dependent on cheap energy. In December of 1981 Mexico more than doubled the price of domestic petroleum. Mexico's huge foreign debt was cited as one of the major reasons for the price increase, as well as the need to dampen domestic demand for hydrocarbon products. For example, home demand for oil was growing 1.7 times more quickly than the gross domestic product.[39] Overall domestic energy demand has grown by 7 percent annually. Figure 2-2 shows the sources of energy and projections by Petroleos Mexicanos until 1990; figure 2-3 shows the 1979 use and projected use in 1990.

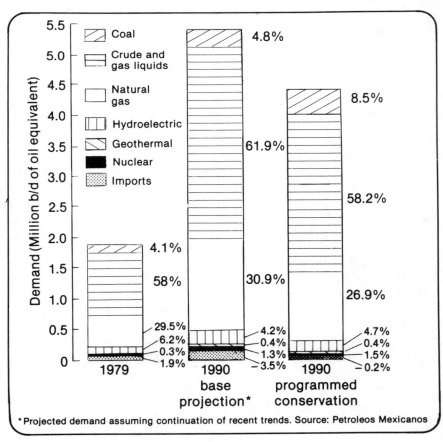

Source: *Oil and Gas Journal*, August 24, 1981, p. 82.

Figure 2-2. Pemex Projection of Energy Sources

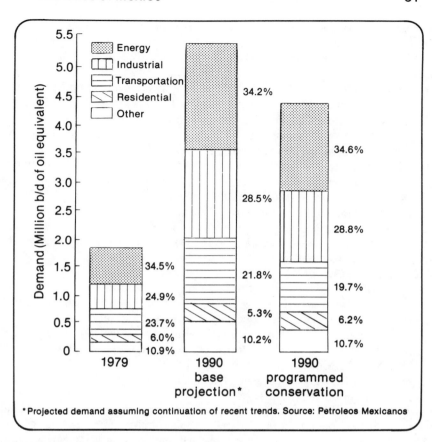

Figure 2-3. Pemex Projection of Lessening of Sector Energy Demand

In summary, Mexico's minimal economic-growth targets were based upon exports of petroleum not exceeding 1.5 million barrels per day and at a price in real terms that would grow at 5 to 7 percent per year. This is no longer feasible. The world petroleum glut has temporarily thwarted this scenario. Mexican internal consumption has raced upward at 7 percent annually, encouraged by prices of refined petroleum products at below-world-market prices. Furthermore, Mexico's option of borrowing in the world capital market is becoming a less likely one since its present indebtedness and declining oil revenues make it more risky from the lenders' point of view. In all probability, in coming years Mexico will increase its oil output and sell more oil internationally even at reduced prices. However, one constraint on production will be Mexico's limited present capability of utilizing associated gas. But because of the pressing need for revenue, this will likely be only a temporary constraint.

Agriculture.   Perhaps the most encouraging sign in Mexican economic development is the recent success in agriculture. In 1981 Mexico produced a record crop of 28.6 million tons, 4.3 million tons more than in 1980. In the production of corn, the staple of the Mexican diet, output rose 2.4 million tons to 14.7 million tons, close to self-sufficiency in meeting consumption needs. Agricultural production grew 6 percent in 1981 compared with only 1.6 percent between 1965 and 1976.[40] Despite this success Mexico's deficit in 1981 agricultural trade was between $650 million and $700 million, and slightly lower than the $858 million registered in 1980. Imports of foodstuffs were about 8 million tons in 1981 compared to 10.5 million tons in 1980. Imports are unofficially estimated at 2.5 million tons in 1982. The success of Mexican agriculture is in part due to better weather conditions, but is also a result of more rational government policies toward agriculture under SAM, the acronym for the Mexican Food System.[41] The continued success of Mexico in expanding food production more rapidly than population and in achieving greater self-sufficiency in foodstuffs is crucial to the success of their long-term planning.

It is difficult to tell whether this large agricultural output is a temporary aberration or the start of a new trend. The year 1981 was exceptionally favorable in terms of weather. Because of less frost and more rain, an extra 2 million hectares were harvested. This is abnormal, since 18 percent of the land under cultivation is usually lost every year and only 8 percent was lost in 1981. Also, Mexico experiences drought in nine out of ten years and none occurred in 1981. Only 15 percent of the land is cultivatable.[42]

More attention has been given to the Mexican Food System in recent years. The United States grain embargo against the Soviet Union created an impetus for Mexico to be more self-reliant in agricultural production. Many believed that the United States might be inclined to use its agricultural leverage to haggle for lower prices of Mexican petroleum. The agricultural sector is also receiving aid from the government via subsidized credit, cheap raw materials, high guaranteed prices, more crop insurance, and technical assistance.[43]

In addition to weather, the transportation system has been an impediment to agricultural expansion. A transportation infrastructure has lacked the ability to ensure quick and cheap movement of agricultural commodities to urban areas. This has often caused havoc with the Mexican government's efforts to restrain the price increases of food products. Inadequate port facilities and storage facilities have compounded distributional problems.[44]

It is hoped that agricultural performance in 1980 and 1981 is not an anomaly but the start of a continued trend. However, some have criticized Mexico for not having given enough attention to agricultural development: "Mexico has about 80,000 rural communities with fewer than 5,000 inhabitants, and they rank low on the government's list of priorities. Planners argue that it takes too much money to bring water, electricity, and roads to such small communities.[45] Emphasis upon industrialization has drawn resources from the rural areas. The rural-to-urban migration is a very real burden, and many of the resourceful and talented leave the countryside for cities. The burden of their accommodation is a heavy weight on economic development. During the decade of the 1960s, the rural areas gained 15.3 percent more inhabitants while cities gained 52.5 percent.

Mexican agriculture is typified by three different types of land holding: private, communal, and public. Unique to Mexico is its *ejidos* or system of communal land holding that dates back to before European conquest. There are at least 14,000 ejidos comprising 40 percent of the cultivated land.[46] Management of the ejidos is by election and they are recognized judicially as corporations. The *ejidarios,* or farm laborer on the ejidos, farms a maximum of 10 hectares of irrigated land and 20 hectares of dry land. Ejidos must be worked within at least two consecutive years or the ejidataro's assigned land is taken back by the ejidos administration and designated for another. This communal system of land holding is subject to much controversy as to its economic efficiency. Ejidos constitute approximately one-half of Mexico's arable land but produce only one-third of its total food production. Arguments against the system are based largely upon the tendency for considerable separation between efforts extended and rewards received. Also, some argue that not allowing private ownership tends to weaken individuals' attachment to the soil and, therefore, encourages lack of regard for careful soil husbandry. Proponents usually argue that the system is more egalitarian.

Private ownership of land is limited to a maximum of 100 hectares. However, a sizable number have managed to circumvent this limitation since there are about 500 private farms with over 50,000 hectares (123,550 acres), and more than 40,000 farms over 101 hectares (249.6 acres).[47]

Efforts at land reform have been met with rather poor or fleeting results. Distribution of production is still very unequal. "Of the more than 2.8 million farms, 4 percent account for 50 percent of agricultural production; about 1 percent produce all of the agricultural exports, and about 15 percent produce most of the food for urban areas."[48] Between 1965 and 1972, 31.1 million hectares (76.8 million acres) were distributed to 520,134 farmers.[49]

A major agriculture-support industry that has recently provided tangible results is fertilizer. Mexico's Fertilizantes Mexicanos built two urea plants in Falamanea and Pajaritos that have a combined annual capacity of 825,000 tons.[50] A second facility at Pajaritos will have an annual capacity of 495,000 tons.[51] Several other fertilizer complexes stand in line for construction, including two ammonium-sulfate plants at Queretaro with a capacity of 200,000 tons each per year.

Corn is Mexico's biggest food crop. Nearly one-half of all crop land is given to the production of maize. One-third of the land is pasture. Because of this vast pastureland, Mexico is one of the world's largest beef producers and beef exporters.

Mexico has a large potential in forestry as an estimated 20 percent of Mexico's land is forested, mostly in Chihuahua, Durango, and Michoacan. Only 25 percent of Mexico's potential 385 million cubic meters of timber is now exploited.[52]

Agriculture, livestock, and fisheries contributed 9.6 percent of Mexico's GDP in 1979 but employed one-third of the economically active population.[53] On average, from 1978 to 1981 agricultural exports made up 24.7 percent of Mexico's external trade.[54]

Mexico has instituted several programs to develop the rural sector and agricultural productivity. One nationwide program that was begun in 1973 is PIDER. It is a stop-gap program intended to redistribute income and production capacity to poor communities that have been neglected by other government programs.[55] COPLAMAR is a government commission that coordinates and integrates public activity to improve living standards in targeted areas. Programs begun by COPLAMAR during 1979 and 1980 are extensive. They include the establishment of government agencies to manage 2,000 new medical units in rural areas, provide basic foodstuffs to more than 10 million persons, construct school facilities in 4,500 communities, and establish adequate housing and a drinkable water supply in rural areas. These COPLAMAR activities are expected to create more than 200,000 permanent jobs in the rural areas. SAM, the Mexican Food Supply System, is concerned with the provision and distribution of food to lower-income groups.[56] This effort will tend also to stem the tide of rapid rural-to-urban migration.

Poor weather and concentration upon industrial development had depressed Mexican agricultural production prior to 1980. Good weather and the institution of several governmental agricultural support programs helped to reverse the general decline in agricultural output during 1980 and 1981.[57] Exceptionally good weather conditions were certainly a major factor during the 1981 agricultural turnaround. However, the Mexican agricultural output will have to keep up the momentum in years to come as population growth continues to exceed 3 percent per annum. The emphasis on reallocating petroleum revenues to the agricultural sector via various government programs will do much to help sustain the momentum and to reduce the rural-to-urban migration flow. The poor marketing-transportation system and the concentration and type of land ownership both deserve special attention. Much will depend upon propitious weather conditions and the continued flow of financial resources to the rural areas to ensure Mexico's desired level of agricultural self-sufficiency.

Industry. The structure of Mexican industry can begin to be seen by the proportion of GDP that each sector contributes and by the proportions of

the working population employed in each. Table 2-9 shows these proportions contributed by each sector to the GDP for averages of 1950-1960,
1960-1970, and 1970-1977 and the changes in these proportions. Increases
occurred in manufacturing, construction, public administration, and other
sectors. Decreases took place in mining, transportation, trade and finance,
and agriculture. The rural-to-urban migration might be partially account-
able for the decrease in the proportion contributed by agriculture.

Table 2-10 sheds light upon the relative sector employment responsible
for the above mentioned GDP contributions. Unfortunately, the two tables
do not chronologically coincide. But taken together, and assuming that
changes are not too significant in 1975 labor proportions compared with
those in 1977, they do suggest the relative productivity of each sector. Labor
employed in agriculture, livestock, forestry, hunting, and fishing would appear to be very low in overall productivity. Here approximately 40 percent
of the economically active population was contributing a mere 10 percent of
the GDP, an output-to-labor ratio of only 0.24. By comparison, the ratios
of manufacturing and mining, construction, and electricity, gas and water
are 1.6, 1.28, and 3.5, respectively.

The most obvious advances in industrial output have occurred in
petroleum and allied industries. Coal showed a sizable increase between
1976 and 1977, from 5.65 to 6.61 million metric tons, a 17-percent output
advance. Production of silver jumped by 10.4 percent and gold by a hefty
25.8 percent. The motor-vehicle industries also increased their output by a
sizable amount, passenger cars up by 26.5 percent and commercial vehicles
up by 39.5 percent.[58]

The rate of change in industrial production from year to year (table
2-11) from 1976 to 1981 displays a robust quality. In the years 1976 to 1979
only two changes in the indices for the various industrial sectors were

Table 2-9
Industrial Origin of Mexico's Gross Domestic Product, 1950-1977
(*percentage of GDP*)

Sector	1950-1960	1960-1970	1970-1977
Agriculture	17.3	13.4	10.2
Mining	2.1	1.4	1.2
Manufacturing	23.3	24.5	26.5
Construction	3.4	4.5	5.9
Electricity, gas, and water	0.9	1.3	1.3
Transport and communications	3.7	2.9	2.9
Trade and finance	39.0	39.4	28.7
Public administration and defense	4.4	5.7	8.3
Other branches	5.9	6.8	15.0

Source: World Bank, *World Tables*, 2d ed. (Baltimore: Johns Hopkins University Press,
1980), p. 141.

Table 2-10
Mexico: Economically Active Population, 1960 and 1975

	1960		1975	
	(thousands)	*(percentage)*	*(thousands)*	*(percentage)*
Total labor force	11,332	100.0	16,597	100.0
Agriculture, livestock, forestry, hunting and fishing	6,144	54.2	6,788	40.9
Mining and extractive industries	142	1.3	3,087	18.6
Manufacturing	1,556	13.7		
Construction	408	3.6	763	4.6
Electricity, gas	41	0.4	66	0.4
Commerce	1,075	9.5	1,660	10.0
Transport	375	3.1	498	3.0
Services	1,527	13.5	3,668	22.1
Nonclassified	82	0.7	763	0.4

Sources: Nacional Financiera, S.A. (Nafinsa), *Statistics on the Mexican Economy* (Mexico City: Nafinsa, 1964); Banco de Comercio (1975).

negative. The two downturns could have been in part results of the jarring effect of the peso devaluation of 1976. The largest single year-to-year change was recorded between 1977 and 1978 in the petrochemical sector, some 18 percent. Growth in petrochemicals is targeted to allow greater increases of output in the agriculture sector to feed Mexico's exploding population.

Table 2-11
Mexico: Industrial Production by Industry
($1970 = 100$)

	1976	1977	1978	1979	1980	1981
Manufacturers	142.9	147.8	162.5	174.3	183.7	202.3
(percentage of change)		3.6	10.0	9.8	5.8	6.6
Petroleum	153.6	178.8	200.3	222.7	271.0	335.6
(percentage of change)		16.4	15.1	15.9	17.8	19.0
Petrochemicals	192.9	185.1	218.5	223.2	280.9	304.8
(percentage of change)		−4.0	18.0	10.0	12.0	19.1
Mining	119.4	120.3	122.9	125.9	137.4	152.4
(percentage of change)		0.8	2.1	1.5	6.5	4.8
Electricity	169.2	184.9	200.1	210.7	233.0	267.6
(percentage of change)		9.3	9.0	8.6	6.5	8.3
Construction	147.5	144.5	163.7	176.6	211.2	232.1
(percentage of change)		−2.4	13.3	14.3	13.0	13.1

Source: United States, State Department, *Foreign Economic Trends and Their Implications for the U.S.* (May 1979; January 1980; February 1982).

Electricity production will likely continue its high rate of growth since the Federal Electricity Commission (CFE) "announced plans to accelerate the plant construction program in order to meet an anticipated growth in demand for electrical energy of 13 percent a year from 1979 to 1982."[59]

Mexico's auto industry has been booming. Production rose 33 percent during 1978 and had increased in the first six months of 1979 by 19 percent.[60] Among efforts to lessen its foreign debt, Mexico is purposely restricting auto production rates during 1982 since one-third of the components of autos are imported.[61] The production of automobiles rose by 23 percent during the first eight months of 1981 accompanied by a sizable increase in foreign components. Four of every ten parts in autos produced in Mexico are imported.[62]

Mexico has one of the oldest iron and steel industries in Latin America. Large increases in production have been fueled in part by the significant demands made upon the sector by petrochemical, petroleum, and manufacturing sectors. The steel industry does not produce at full capacity because of frequent labor problems at some locations and bottlenecks in receiving raw materials. In 1980, because of these bottlenecks, Mexico imported 1.5 million tons of raw materials.[63] Plans for expansion of the steel sector are ambitious. The state holding company of the three state steel companies, Sidermex, intends to triple output by 1990 to 24 million metric tons just to fulfill domestic demand and to reduce steel import levels. To fulfill this plan, a new $6.7 billion steel complex at Altamina on the Gulf of Mexico will be built in three stages, each capable of producing 2 million tons. Capacity at the Sicarsta steel plant at Lazaro Cardenas will be raised to 3.3 million tons by 1984 from the present 2-million-ton capacity.[64]

Mexico is protectionist. This is one of the main reasons it did not sign the General Agreement on Tariffs and Trade (GATT) in early 1980.[65] The Mexican government favored membership in GATT but strong anti-GATT lobbyists exerted influence to dissuade the government from joining. However, Mexico has participated in the Tokyo Round negotiations and is set upon abiding by the GATT though not acceding to the status of a signatory. Some of the effects of a protected economy are circumvented by the In-Bond Program which "permits foreign companies to import component parts free of duty if the assembled product is re-exported. This program has attracted over 530 United States firms."[66]

Mexico has an insignificant quantity of imported labor and welcomes new technology. Imported technology is permitted under the Law to Promote Mexican Investment and to Regulate Foreign Investment of 1973. Essentially, this law provides that

Foreign investments are welcome under certain conditions, such as when they complement domestic investments, introduce new technology, help to increase exports and import substitution, use a high percentage of local components, are labor intensive and are located in a depressed area of the country.[67]

One of Mexico's major stumbling blocks to smooth and continuous economic growth is its insufficient internal transportation system. Though extensive, it remains inadequate in view of present needs and anticipated future requirements. In 1975 the Mexican rail system totaled some 12,211 miles and consisted of six lines, only one of which was private-sector owned. Carrying almost 80 percent of the total traffic and operating about 70 percent of the total trackage, the National Railways is by far the largest line. Like the National Railways, the second largest system, the Pacific Railroad, is an autonomous government agency; it links Nogales with Guadalajara. The remaining government lines are the Chihuahua-to-Pacific Railroad, the Sonora-Baja California Railroad, and the United Railroads of the Southeast. The railroad system is linked with Central America through Guatemala, and with the United States at such points as Cuidad, Jurez, Naco, Nogales, Loredo, Pedras Negras, Regmosa, Matamoros, and Agua Priela. Only sixty-three miles of the railway line are electrified, although a subway/underground railway system began operation in Mexico City in 1969. In 1975, rail traffic totaled 4.198 billion passenger-kilometers and 32.542 billion net-ton-kilometers.[68]

The problems with insufficient railroads were made clear in 1979 at the Texas-Mexico border, when railway freight congestion became so bad that "every siding from Loredo to the Oklahoma border—a distance of some 500 miles—was backed up for a time with Mexican-bound cargo."[69]

The problems confronting Mexico's railroads are numerous. The more than 12,000 miles of track are outdated and, as noted earlier, not electrified for all practical purposes. The gradients are severe, the engines are not reliable, and freight is often difficult to track since the system is not computerized. Moreover:

A quarter of the workers are past the retirement age, but Ferrocarriles Nacionales, the state railway company, is already paying pensions of more than $1 billion and cannot pay any more. However . . . the government is supposed to assume the railway's pension obligations, thus enabling the company to retire its older employees.[70]

So, the Mexican government plans to invest considerable money and effort into renovating its railroad system. These plans include the electrification of the most heavily used routes and the laying of 375 miles of new track by the year 2000. A recently concluded contract between the state rail-construction company and General Electric (in the United States) calls for the delivery of up to 100 new locomotives annually over a ten-year period—a $480 million agreement. Mexico retained the option in this contract to assemble some of the locomotive components domestically. In 1979, the addition of some 3,500 freight cars was targeted.[71]

Mexico's internal transportation problems do not stop with the railroads. Trucking inefficiency poses another challenge. Since only one-quarter of Mexico's freight is moved by rail, and since no system of barge lines exists, a sizable part of the remainder must be moved by truck. But the trucking industry is ossified by special interests. Many politicians derive great benefit from the partial or complete ownership of government-fixed routes. These routes are not easily changed as this may infringe upon another's monopolized service area. Truck transportation is unable to suitably accommodate Mexico's rapid rate of economic growth.[72]

Previous plans to embark upon a very extravagant nuclear power program were increasingly questioned, and it is very likely that momentum in that direction will be slowed, if not completely stopped.[73] Many had criticized this program since Mexico's outstanding factor endowment is in petroleum. In the throes of financial difficulties, both domestically and externally, the nuclear power option appears to be too much of a luxury when many ready energy alternatives are available. Though Mexico has as much as 10,000 metric tons of uranium (and possibly 250,000 metric tons),[74] the cost of the program was estimated to eventually reach $30 billion in current prices for 20,000 megawatts (MW) of electrical output by the year 2000. Before possible cancellation, planners will have to estimate how much more must be spent to finish two light-water reactors at Veracruz now under construction and intended to begin supplying 654 MW by 1983. If a complete cancellation is not likely, at least a modification of plans appears to be in store.[75]

Mexican port facilities will have to be expanded to handle the tremendous increase in its share of world commerce brought about by its newly found petroleum wealth. Ocean port activity is very concentrated: "Five of Mexico's 49 ocean ports—Tampico, Veracruz, Guaymas, Mazatlan, and Manzanillo—handle 80 percent of the nation's ocean freight."[76] Though truck-freight transportation is hamstrung by certain privileges of an institutional nature, the road system itself is one of the best in Latin America. Mexico has over 185,000 kilometers (114,885 miles) of all-weather roads (about 60-percent paved) that reach 40 percent of the total territory of the nation.[77]

Mexico has a large number of domestic airlines, a total of seventy-seven including only two international lines, Aeromexico and Mexicana. The government owns 100 percent of Aeromexico and 10 percent of Mexicana. There are about 1,768 airfields, besides the hub of air operation, Mexico City.

Education. If taken over a long period of time, education in Mexico has made considerable strides. In 1910, just before the beginning of the Mexican Revolution, slightly under a quarter of the elementary-school-age children were in school. Two decades later in 1930, that enrollment had risen to 42 percent and to more than 80 percent by 1970. A reflection of this change can be gleaned from census figures that indicate a downward trend in illiteracy, from 76.9 percent in 1910 to 28.3 percent in 1970. This decline in illiteracy may not be as clearcut as it first appears. If a stricter definition of literacy is applied, less than 40 percent of the population over nine years of age can be considered functionally literate.[78]

Furthermore, the access to secondary, preparatory, and university levels of education is restricted, helping to

> . . . perpetuate class barriers. In 1926, 3,860 students were enrolled in secondary or high school track, probably no more than 4 or 5 percent of the relevant school age population. In 1970, the proportion had risen to no more than 20 percent.[79]

In 1975 there were 52,792 primary and secondary schools, with a combined enrollment of 14,187,600. In 1976 some 700,000 were enrolled in higher education. Approximately 3.2 percent of the GNP in 1974 was spent on education. Women were underrepresented in public school enrollment. In 1975 approximately 48 percent of primary school enrollment, 36 percent of secondary enrollment and 20 percent of post-secondary enrollment were girls.[80]

Public education is the basic responsibility of the Secretaria de Educacion Publica (SEP). No religious private schools are permitted to operate in Mexico. Any private schools must conform to the will of the State.

There are 42 universities, the largest of which is the Universidad Nacional Autonoma de Mexico where 222,982 of the total nationally enrolled university/college student population of 514,909 in 1975 were enrolled.[81]

Monetary and Fiscal Policy

Mexico has one of the most developed banking systems of Latin America. The central bank, the Banco de Mexico (Bank of Mexico), founded in 1925, started operations in 1932. It has the central responsibility of orchestrating monetary policy.

> It decides on the nominal and real levels of the rediscount rate, grants rediscounting facilities, operates the complicated system of reserve requirements imposed on financial intermediaries, sets maximum nominal interest rates for various deposits and loans, supervises foreign transactions, is the sole issuer of paper currency, and regulates the issues of certain government bonds. Because reserve requirements are imposed on nonbank financial intermediaries and because the central bank fixes the level of nominal rates for these institutions, its power vis-a-vis the financial sector is greater than it would be in many other countries.[82]

The Mexican banking system is rather complicated with numerous private intermediaries that are restricted to providing only one kind of financial service. These services include (1) deposit banks, (2) savings banks, (3) financiers, (4) mortgage-credit trust companies, (5) capitalization companies, (6) trust companies, and (7) savings-and-loan banks for family housing. Because private banks may offer only one of these services, there are a great number of banks in the private sector—more than 200 banks with over 2,500 branches.

A national commission supervises the private banking sector. It maintains close ties to the Bank of Mexico in order to coordinate private with public monetary goals.

> The Bank of Mexico's reserve requirements are quite large: The bank is obliged to hold reserves of a minimum of 25 percent of the money in circulation and its other liabilities; 80 percent of these reserves are in gold and foreign currency, the rest in silver. In practice the percentages in both cases are usually higher.[83]

Aside from the Bank of Mexico, the Nacional Financiera is probably the most important of the official banks. It has been, since its establishment in 1932, one of the prominent agents in the promotion of Mexico's industrialization.

In the years prior to 1972 the money supply in Mexico was growing at an average rate of about 10 percent per year. Real income was growing at a rate of approximately 6.5 percent per annum and the rate of inflation was maintained at less than 5 percent annually. After 1972 the Mexican monetary authorities expanded the money supply at a much higher rate, from 20 to 30 percent per year. This rapid expansion of the money supply was used to finance deficits incurred by the government as a result of substantially higher levels of government expenditure. From 1971 to 1975 domestic bank credit extended to the government increased at an annual rate of 29 percent. As this extension of credit to the government expanded, bank credit available to the private sector declined. Over this period credit extended to the private sector grew less than 1 percent annually so that by 1976 the credit extended to the public sector had tripled while that granted to the private sector remained virtually the same. A deficit on the current account had a depressing effect on the Mexican money supply; however, this was offset by an increase in external credit extended to the Mexican economy. As a result, the foreign base of the Mexican money supply remained roughly constant over this period. The entire increase in the Mexican money supply was a result of the growth in the domestic base tied to the extension of credit to the Mexican government.

The acceleration in the growth of the money supply after 1972 was accompanied by a significantly higher rate of inflation. The consumer price index in Mexico increased at an average annual rate of over 15 percent from

1972 to 1976. This rate of inflation was higher than that experienced in the United States and other industrialized nations; the average annual rate of inflation in the United States over those same years was about 8 percent. Higher rates of inflation were not, however, accompanied by higher rates of growth in real income. In fact, the average rate of growth in real income from 1972 to 1976 was 4.8 percent, substantially below the average annual growth rate in the prior decade.

As the Mexican price level increased at more than twice the rate of increase of the U.S. price level, the pressure on the exchange rate grew. Mexico found it increasingly difficult to obtain foreign credit to finance deficits on its current account. In August 1976 the Central Bank was forced to abandon the fixed exchange rate and adopt flexible exchange rates. The exchange rate rose to over 20 pesos per dollar. Table 2-12 gives the index of consumer prices in Mexico from 1969 to 1980.

Following devaluation in 1976 the money supply in Mexico increased even more rapidly to about 30 percent per year. Price increases in 1977 were about 30 percent but then fell below 20 percent in 1978 and the first part of 1979. Industrial production, which had declined sharply in 1976, accelerated in 1977 and 1978 over 10 percent per annum. The Mexican monetary authorities permitted the exchange rate for Mexico to fluctuate in 1976 after devaluation. But since 1976 they have attempted to peg the exchange rate. This pattern in which the exchange rate moves from fixed to flexible to managed makes the interpretation of the monetary changes in Mexico somewhat complex. We would expect that the shift from fixed to flexible exchange rates should increase the independent control of the Mexican monetary authorities. Theoretically they could pursue an expansionary

Table 2-12
Index of Consumer Prices in Mexico, 1969-1980

Year	Index	Percentage Change
1969	95.1	—
1970	100.0	5.2
1971	105.7	5.7
1972	111.0	5.0
1973	123.6	11.4
1974	151.3	22.4
1975	158.4	4.7
1976	162.7	2.7
1977	168.4	3.5
1978	185.2	10.0
1979	219.0	18.3
1980	269.1	22.9

Source: International Monetary Fund (IMF), *International Financial Statistics* (Washington, D.C.: IMF), April 1981, pp. 266-267.

monetary policy somewhat independent from world-market conditions. If Mexican prices accelerated more rapidly than world prices, this would result in exchange-rate adjustments, but Mexican prices could diverge from world-market prices. If this interpretation is correct, one would expect that under flexible exchange rates Mexican prices and industrial production would be more influenced by domestic monetary and fiscal policies as compared with the period under fixed exchange rates.

The problem with such an interpretation is the short span of time in which flexible exchange rates were permitted to operate in Mexico. The period of flexible exchange rates in 1976 was a time of instability because of the disequilibrium that had emerged in the previous period of fixed exchange rates. Devaluation permitted Mexican prices to adjust to an equilibrium relationship with world-market prices. During this lagged adjustment process world prices and market conditions would influence Mexican prices and industrial production as well as domestic monetary and fiscal policies. Over time one would expect that under a system of flexible exchange rates, domestic monetary and fiscal policies would exert more influence over prices and industrial production, but Mexico quickly reverted to a managed exchange rate so that it is not clear that these expectations have been fulfilled.

As a result of the crisis in the balance of payments and the devaluation of the peso in 1976, Mexico signed an agreement with the International Monetary Fund (IMF) as a condition for the extension of credit from that institution. This agreement, signed in September 1976, required that Mexico institute policy changes from 1977 to 1979 designed to reestablish equilibrium in the balance of payments. The agreement provided that (1) increases in nominal wages should not exceed those registered in the United States, which is Mexico's main trading partner; (2) tariffs and prices of the goods and services offered by public enterprises must reflect their actual costs; (3) external trade had to be totally liberalized; (4) inflation would be controlled by repressing the economy's rate of growth; and (5) the rate of exchange should be maintained under equilibrium by flotation.

Three other IMF provisions were designed to reduce government spending and aggregate demand. (1) With regard to monetary policy, limits would be set to the issue of money, the cost of credit must be raised, and deposits had to be secured. (2) Fiscal policy should integrate lessening public expenditure as well as increasing fiscal revenues. In addition, total public employment should not increase more than 2 percent during 1977. (3) Finally, with regard to the government's financing policies, three major limits would be set: to overall public deficit, to external public indebtedness, and to intensive borrowing.

The agreement worked out between Mexico and the IMF would have imposed constraints on the domestic economy in order to achieve external balance. The result of slower growth in government spending and monetary expansion would have been slower growth in aggregate demand and in total output. Structural changes would have reduced the access of the public sector to credit and decreased the share of the public sector in total output. Liberalization of trade involving reductions in tariff protection and subsidies to domestic industries would have exposed the Mexican economy to greater competition in world markets. A floating exchange rate would have eliminated the need to maintain an overvalued currency and would have given the Mexican monetary authorities greater leeway in pursuing domestic monetary policies.

As it turns out, the Mexican government never fully implemented the provisions of the agreement worked out with the IMF. From January 1977 to 1981, the Mexican government returned to expansionary monetary and fiscal policies accompanied by rapid economic growth. The exchange rate was again pegged through purchase and sale of foreign exchange by the Central Bank. Exports and imports accelerated rapidly over this period.

The discovery of significant resources of oil permitted the Mexican government to pursue alternative policies from those agreed to with the IMF. The expansion in oil exports permitted Mexico to escape the stringent requirements imposed by the IMF as a condition for extension of credit. The Mexicans used their actual and future oil revenues as the base for expanded credit from non-IMF sources, and international capital markets were quite willing to finance the increased borrowing. In 1979 Mexico's total debt increased by $4.3 billion, with $4.1 billion of that total accounted for by foreign debt. The foreign-debt accumulation was roughly equal to the $4 billion deficit in the Mexican current account. In 1980 indebtedness increased by $8.6 billion, including $1.5 billion in short-term indebtedness. The current-account deficit in that year was $6.6 billion, despite the fact that Pemex exported approximately $10 billion in crude oil and petroleum products.[84] Oil revenues provided the basis for expansionary fiscal and monetary policies that in turn stimulated a rapid rate of economic growth in Mexico from 1977 to 1980.

In mid-1980, a number of problems emerged in the Mexican economy, partly as a result of the domestic policies pursued over the previous years and partly because of changes in the international economy. Domestic policies focused upon rapid growth in production and export of oil had created what the Mexicans refer to as petrodependency.[85] Oil exports accounted for 67 percent of merchandise exports and 47 percent of foreign-exchange earnings. The share of public investment allocated to the petroleum sector grew from 19.5 percent in 1976 to 29 percent in 1979 and increased even further in 1980. The share of federal-government income generated by oil revenues increased from 5 percent in 1976 to 29 pecent in 1979. As in most other energy-producing countries, the rapid growth of the petroleum sector had a negative impact on growth in other sectors. The growth in the oil sector left other sectors of the Mexican economy behind. The growth in credit allocated to the public sector reduced the credit available to the private sector. Interest rates increased to over 30 percent per year, dampening private investment. The pace of industrial production and agricultural production slowed, and Mexico was forced to import approximately 10 million tons of grain.[86] The lack of investment in transportation infrastructure began to put a strain on the transportation and port facilities of the country.

The rapid growth in government spending and monetary expansion resulted in inflation with price levels increasing over 30 percent annually. The more rapid rate of inflation in Mexico compared with the United States and other countries, combined with a pegged exchange rate, caused the peso to be overvalued. Not surprisingly, nonoil exports declined by 15 percent in real terms. The deficit on the current account soared to $6.6 billion.

In 1981 and 1982 these sources of external and internal equilibrium in Mexico came to a head. A glut in the world petroleum market added to a worldwide recession undermined the Mexican development strategy based on rising oil prices and revenues. In July 1981 Mexico followed the lead of OPEC members by cutting the price of oil by $4 per barrel in response to depressed demand for oil in world markets. This price cut brought a political storm in which the director of Pemex was removed. Subsequently, Pemex raised its prices by $2 per barrel, at which point several countries suspended purchases. Faced with a potential loss of $3.5 billion in export earnings, Mexico reduced the price of Mayan crude by $2 to $26.50 per barrel in January 1982. Its Isthmus crude, a lighter, higher-quality grade, remained at $35 per barrel. Some oil-industry spokesmen predicted further cuts in petroleum prices because of the glut in the world oil market and the continued recession in Western economies. The lower oil prices generated revenues $7 billion below those projected in Mexican economic plans.

The sharp increase in U.S. interest rates created another problem for the Mexican government. They faced $3 billion in unbudgeted interest payments on foreign debt. These interest payments, combined with the lower level of oil revenues, resulted in a current-account deficit of $10.8 billion in 1981. Public-sector foreign indebtedness climbed $14.9 billion in 1981 to a total of $48.7 billion. Adding private-sector foreign indebtedness to the public-sector debt, the total foreign debt was estimated at $74.9 billion. During the summer of 1981 there was speculation against the peso resulting in an outflow of $4 billion in capital. The peso was devalued to approximately 25 pesos per dollar by mid-1981 and to close to 30 pesos per dollar by the year end. Estimates in December 1982 put total public and private foreign indebtedness at about $80 billion.[87]

The danger signals from external and internal deregulation led to a significant shift in public policy in Mexico in late 1981 and early 1982. The change in policy is evident in both short-term policies and in the long-term strategy for the energy sector and the development of the Mexican economy. In the short-term the Mexican government has moved to slow the pace of growth. The fiscal budget for 1982 is set at 3.28 trillion pesos with a projected deficit of $657 billion. In nominal terms the federal budget for 1982 is about 28 percent higher than in 1981; however, in real terms this will mean no increase in federal expenditures. Slower growth in federal spending will presumably be accompanied by a lower rate of monetary expansion although this has not been spelled out. The rationale for the slower growth in government spending is to bring the federal budget in line with the lower levels of revenue resulting from lower oil prices and exports in the current depressed oil market. The slower growth in expenditures and in monetary expansion will also reduce the rate of inflation and other distortionary impacts on the domestic economy.

In addition to the slower rates of growth in government spending there will be major reallocations within the federal budget. The allocations for the oil sector have been reduced 15 percent from previous budgets. Pemex will receive about $396 billion, that is, 30 percent of the total public-sector budget. This is much lower than the share allocated to Pemex in recent years when heavy investments were made to expand production capacity. The Mexican government believes that it can achieve the desired 1.5 million b/d in exports with little additional capital investment in the energy sector.

An increased share of the federal budget will be allocated to agriculture and traditional sectors of the economy. Agriculture will receive 303 billion pesos or 38 percent of the budget. The objective is to create 1 million new jobs in 1982 and to reduce some of the disparities that have emerged among economic groups and different regions of the country.

The most uncertain and risky elements in current Mexican policy relate to the foreign sector. The Mexican government attempted to gradually devalue the peso without the shock of a major devaluation and recession such as occurred in 1976. The crawling depreciation of the peso was stepped up in 1982 to a rate between 17 and 18 percent compared with 12 percent over 1981 as a whole. This policy changed abruptly in March 1982 when the peso was devalued by roughly 50 percent. Even that sharp devaluation did not halt speculation against the peso and a flight of capital from Mexico. In 1982 the public sector's gross borrowing was about $20 billion. Total external debt of the public sector was projected to climb from $48.7 billion to $59.7 billion, requiring a foreign funds flow into Mexico at the rate of $1.5 billion per month. The Mexican authorities were rather sanguine regarding the availability of foreign credit to finance this level of borrowing. By the autumn of 1982, Mexico was finding it increasingly difficult to meet its foreign debt obligations. It was forced to reschedule interest payments and to refinance the foreign debt in order to avoid defaulting on the debt.

There are several signs that Mexico will continue to have difficulties in solving its external imbalance problems in 1982. Most important is the evidence of increasing cost and limited availability of foreign credit. As early as 1981, Mexico's state development bank, Nafinsa, attempted to raise a $300-million, medium-term credit with only a 1/16 margin over the United States prime rate. The issue failed and Nafinsa has since been forced to borrow at a higher margin relative to interest rates in the United States. Experts estimate that these margins will increase even more in 1983. Another sign of problems is the increase in the share of short-term borrowing as a percent of Mexico's total outstanding public-sector debt.

The flight of capital last year caused the Mexican monetary authorities to increase the rate of interest paid on peso deposits to 34 percent compared with 14 percent on dollar deposits. Despite this differential, the rate of growth of foreign-exchange deposits last year increased by 53.2 percent compared with a 23.8-percent growth in peso deposits. There does not appear to be much room for further increases in the peso-deposit rate. The best industrial borrower now pays an interest rate of 43 percent at Mexican commercial banks, a level about 15 percent higher than the inflation rate. Further increases would stifle the rate of private investment and trigger a recession the new government could ill afford. In order to tighten peso credit and steer the outflow of capital, the Central Bank required that commercial banks purchase 5 billion pesos of three-month treasury bills known as *tetes*. Another 10 billion pesos of tetes that the banks were required to purchase in August have been kept on deposit for an additional three months. A total of 15 billion pesos was thus removed from the banking system.

Despite these measures taken by the Mexican government, the economy will be exposed to significant risk from the foreign sector. An increase in the United States interest rate will increase the burden of foreign debt, about three-quarters of which is at floating rates. Devaluation of the peso will accelerate the flight of capital. Finally, it is not clear which foreign banks and institutions will be willing to increase their exposure to Mexico. The government must repay $6 to $7 billion in short-term debt as well as $3.3 billion in long-term debt. An additional $11 billion in foreign debt has been incurred to meet the public sector's requirements in 1982, and many experts doubt that Mexico will find the foreign creditors to finance that level of indebtedness.

The Energy Program of the Mexican government explicitly recognizes the problems that have emerged from rapid growth of the energy sector in recent years and sets guidelines for energy policy designed to stimulate development of the Mexican economy in the long term. That program sounded a warning, projecting that a three- to four-fold increase in the 1982 export volume would be needed by 1990. The warning continued by predicting that the imbalances or malajustments in the nonpetroleum sectors of the economy by then "would be so deep and the requirements of foreign exchange so high, that limits would be met in the exploitable hydrocarbons *before the end of the eighties*. In other words, by then, production would have attained from 8 to 10 million of equivalent barrels of crude oil."[88]

In order to reduce this so-called export petrodependency, the Energy Program sets the following limits.

1. Exports will be limited to 1.5 million b/d of oil and 300 million cubic feet/day of natural gas. The effort to stimulate greater exports of goods and services other than hydrocarbons is implicit in this policy.
2. In order to reduce dependency on hydrocarbon exports as a source of foreign exchange in light of the risks associated with such dependency, hydrocarbon exports will not be permitted to generate more than 50 percent of current foreign-exchange earnings.
3. In order to diversify the export market several criteria are established. Mexico will try to avoid concentration of more than 50 percent of its oil exports to a single country. An attempt will be made to maintain the share of Mexican exports at less than 20 percent of the hydrocarbon imports of any nation, except for the cases of countries of Central America and the Caribbean in which Mexican oil could provide up to 50 percent of the requirements of a country.

It would appear that the crisis in Mexico's balance of payments will make it difficult to achieve these targets in the short term. In 1981 the dispute over prices resulted in exports of only 1.1 million barrels a day, far below the 1.5 million b/d target set in the Energy Program. The government is committed to exporting 1.5 million barrels a day in 1982, but the glut in world oil markets and depressed prices may again cause exports to fall below this target. As noted earlier, this shortfall in oil exports and lower prices for oil is a major factor in the huge current-account deficit and external-financing difficulties facing Mexico in 1982.

An indication that Mexico may forgo the targets contained in the Energy Program in order to solve the short-term crisis is the current negotiations between the Mexican government and the U.S. company, Border Gas, Inc., regarding increased gas exports. That group currently imports 300 million cubic feet of natural gas a day from Mexico at a price of $4.94 per cubic foot, which is the amount permitted by the Mexican Energy Program. The group is negotiating to double gas imports from Mexico to 600 million cubic feet/day. That would mean sacrificing the target of the Energy Program in order to generate the foreign-exchange requirements of Mexico's substantial import bill. These negotiations are politically sensitive in both the United States and Mexico. The Carter administration withdrew approval of an early contract negotiated between U.S. firms and the Mexican government on the grounds that the price for gas was inflationary. The

Mexican government, on the other hand, faces criticism from the political left for selling its scarce resources to the United States. Despite these risks, the current negotiations suggest that an agreement will be reached to ship more gas from Mexico to the United States. The completion of the new gas-gathering system in oil-rich Campeche Bay has expanded the gas production capacity to 400 million cubic feet/day.

One factor that will help ease the Mexican problem is the decision by the United States to purchase Mexican crude for the U.S. strategic reserve. The United States Department of Energy has signed a five-year contract with Pemex to purchase 110 million barrels of Mexican crude, with deliveries beginning at 200,000 b/d in 1981 and dropping to 50,000 b/d from 1982 to 1986. The price was set at $31.80/barrel, but it may be adjusted if world oil prices declined over the period. With the glut in world oil markets and declining prices in 1982, the United States has slowed its purchases for its petroleum reserve.

The Energy Program also sets guidelines concerning the relation between energy and the external sector. (1) Once internal demand is met, hydrocarbons will be exported only to the extent that the economy can productively absorb the additional resources from abroad. (2) Mexico will attempt to increase the aggregate value of energy exports. This means not only a commitment to higher prices for energy exports but also a policy of increasing the value added to Mexican energy exports through refining and other downstream operations. (3) Mexican trade has been dominated by the United States. The Mexicans want to use hydrocarbon exports to diversify their trade in order to attain greater independence from the U.S. economy. Hydrocarbon exports will be used to gain access to new markets for exports of manufactured goods. The goal is to make manufactured goods the major export by the year 2000. The development of the domestic capital-goods industry will be stimulated through subsidies as well as through trade policies. (4) Exports of petroleum and gas will be used to achieve better financial terms from foreign investors. (5) Mexico will cooperate with other countries in the development of oil supply as well as in research and exploration of local energy sources.

Mexico's recent decision to double the domestic price of petroleum in 1982 indicates that the Energy Program policies will be enforced in the 1980s. The price of ordinary-grade petroleum was raised 155 percent to close to $1 per gallon; high-grade petroleum was increased 42.5 percent to $1.60 per gallon; and diesel was raised 150 percent to 40 cents a gallon. This is the first increase in five years and will generate as much as 100 billion pesos in extra revenue a year. Mexico's domestic prices are still below world prices, but the increase is part of a long-term policy to equalize domestic and foreign oil prices. This will remove the distortionary effects of subsidized prices for consumers and industry in Mexico and slow the rapid increase in domestic consumption. It will also ease the cash-flow problems of Pemex and the Mexican government.

The fuel-price increase was part of a three-point energy-conservation program announced by the government. The automobile industry has been given three years to phase out production of eight-cylinder models and to improve mileage of models already in production. In addition, the tourism ministry imposed a new daylight-savings-time zone in the Mexican Caribbean region.

From 1969 to 1979, Mexico's rate of inflation, as indicated by the consumer price index (CPI), averaged 10.3 percent. The influence of subsidies upon the CPI is not clear. Data pertaining to the determination of the CPI were not found. However, for 1980 it is estimated that food subsidies would reach a total of $3.7 billion, up 25 percent over the previous year. Assuming that the GDP will grow by at least 20 percent from the 1978 level through 1980 (a 1980 GDP of $133 billion), food subsidies would account for 2.9 percent of the GDP of 1980. Or, if we make a simple projection of the government expenditure of $24 billion in 1977 at a 10-percent rate of increase, we get a budget of $31.9 billion for 1980 with food subsidies comprising nearly 12 percent of the federal budget. With such large proportions of the GDP and the federal budget made up of food subsidies, one would assume the CPI has a considerable downward bias that does not reflect the actual rate of inflation.

Economic Planning

In Mexican economic planning, each ministry historically has submitted its own plans without much regard for the relationship between its plans and those of other ministries. The rapid turnover of secretaries of ministries resulted in continual revision of plans that have little impact on actual policy or economic performance. However, the Global Plan, published at the end of 1980 and including the Energy Program for Mexico, was a serious effort at comprehensive planning conducted by De la Madrid while he was Secretary of Programacion de Presupuesto. The selection of De la Madrid as the presidential candidate by PRI (Institutional Revolutionary Party) assures that the Mexican policies will be strongly influenced by economic planning even though the plans will continue to be revised.

There are some indications that the Mexicans are attempting to implement the plan and are achieving some success. There has been a significant shift in the role of Pemex in the Mexican economy. The emphasis in the 1970s was rapid growth in exploration and production, requiring significant outlays for investment. The emphasis in the 1980s is on greater efficiency. The previous investment has expanded production capacity sufficiently to meet the production targets without significant amounts of new investment. As a result, some of Pemex's investment projects and operations have been cut back and salaries and expenditures reduced. Exploration will continue and more emphasis will be placed upon the quality and service of production. The Mexicans expect that the demand for heavy oil will increase relative to light oil and are shifting their production accordingly. Increased emphasis will be on downstream operations: processing the oil into gasoline, kerosene, other refined products, and petrochemicals. Increased attention will be focused upon linkages of Pemex to other sectors in the Mexican economy, especially to the capital-goods sector with priorities on pipe and other investment goods produced in Mexico. Pemex will attempt to reduce the import content of their expenditures to economize on scarce foreign exchange. It will enter into joint ventures with other sectors of the Mexican economy to invest in capital improvements including industrial ports and agricultural projects. Foreign investment that is consistent with these objectives will be welcomed.

The proportion of GDP given to government consumption has more than doubled in Mexico since 1952 when government outlays were only 4.1 percent of GDP. They were 11.5 percent in 1979.[89]

In comparison to other LDCs (less-developed countries) the proportion of government consumption is rather small. This relatively small weight of government taxation is best exemplified by the fact that Mexico ranked sixty-sixth of seventy-two countries in the ratio of tax revenues to GNP.[90]

> The aims of fiscal policy between 1940 and 1970 were fourfold: (1) to maintain the basic machinery of government and to procure such services as deemed desirable for the achievement of the country's basic socioeconomic objectives; (2) to promote economic development, either by direct government action, such as the construction of highways, or indirectly through the combined effort of taxation and expenditures on the economic system; (3) to improve social and cultural conditions, including not only specific purposes (such as education and public health) but also broad social objectives (such as a distribution of income) to insure a balanced growth of the economy (these goals have been pursued through the government's tax and expenditure policy); and (4) to stabilize the economy insofar as possible to offset fluctuations in general business activities and to maintain full employment.[91]

In the late 1960s taxes and fees accounted for 70 to 75 percent of government revenues, and other incomes, mostly from the so-called decentralized agencies and enterprises with state participation.[92] Table 2-13 depicts the sources of Mexico's federal-government tax revenues for 1955 to 1970. This should be compared with table 2-14 showing the national budget for 1975. In the course of only five years, 1970 to 1975, income tax has dropped as

Table 2-13
Mexico: Federal-Government Tax Revenues, 1955-1970
(millions of pesos)

Year	Income Tax	%	Import Tax	%	Export Tax	%	Sales Tax	%	Natural Resources Exportation Tax	%	Industry Commerce Production Tax	%	Other Taxes	%	Total
1955	1,985	32.3	915	14.8	1,446	23.5	642	10.4	299	4.9	796	12.9	73	1.2	6,156
1956	2,565	36.8	998	14.3	1,253	17.9	727	10.5	222	3.2	934	13.5	267	3.8	6,966
1957	2,720	39.7	1,013	14.8	1,045	15.3	775	11.3	131	1.9	937	13.8	215	3.2	6,836
1958	2,758	35.2	1,313	16.7	1,023	13.2	879	11.2	134	1.7	979	12.6	739	9.4	7,825
1959	3,056	37.9	1,554	19.2	946	11.9	973	12.1	214	2.6	1,188	14.7	129	1.6	8,060
1960	3,628	38.8	1,753	18.7	923	9.9	1,102	11.8	261	2.8	1,314	14.2	355	3.8	9,345
1961	4,070	40.5	1,641	16.4	807	8.0	1,286	12.8	296	2.9	1,466	14.6	484	4.8	10,050
1962	4,727	42.3	1,688	15.1	863	7.7	1,449	13.0	244	2.2	1,802	16.2	391	3.5	11,163
1963	5,475	41.0	1,949	14.6	872	6.4	1,532	11.5	263	2.0	1,934	14.5	1,335	10.0	13,360
1964	7,262	46.0	2,411	15.1	880	5.6	1,860	11.7	271	1.7	2,211	13.8	1,024	6.5	15,919
1965	8,630	47.9	2,651	14.7	876	4.8	2,108	11.7	325	1.8	2,463	13.7	974	5.4	18,018
1966	8,625	45.3	2,412	12.8	783	4.2	2,389	12.7	340	1.8	2,533	13.4	1,753	9.3	18,835
1967	10,170	49.9	2,630	12.9	565	2.8	2,627	12.9	338	1.6	2,892	14.2	1,154	5.7	20,376
1968	11,700	50.9	2,600	11.3	600	2.6	3,300	14.4	330	1.4	3,400	14.8	1,070	4.7	23,000
1969	13,700	51.3	2,500	9.4	500	1.9	3,800	14.2	350	1.3	3,700	13.9	2,150	8.1	26,700
1970	15,500	58.1	3,100	10.4	400	1.3	4,300	14.4	390	1.3	4,300	14.4	1,910	6.4	29,900

Source: Secretaria de Hancinda y Credito Publico, *The Federal Public Finance Account* (Mexico City, 1955 to 1970), annual issues.

Table 2-14
Mexico: National Budget Revenues, 1975
(millions of pesos)

Income	Amount	Percentage
Income Taxes	46,200	13.3
Tax on Exploitation of Natural Resources	1,925	0.6
Tax on Industry	32,550	9.4
Sales Tax	24,150	7.0
Stamp Tax	1,450	.4
Import Duties	11,726	3.4
Export Duties	4,400	1.3
Other Taxes	2,326	0.7
Social Security Quotas	19,954	5.8
Fees for Public Services	2,620	0.8
Proceeds	2,400	0.7
Other Non-tax Income	1,280	0.4
Income for Sale of Goods	150	(less than 0.1)
Capital Recuperation	750	0.2
Income from Borrowings	54,181	15.6
Other Income From:		
Autonomous Agencies	87,669	25.3
State Controlled Enterprises	20,621	5.9
Borrowings of State-Controlled Enterprises	32,306	9.3

Source: George Kurian, ed., "Mexico," *Encyclopedia of the Third World* (New York: Facts on File, 1978), p. 993.

a major component from 58.1 percent of total tax revenue to only 13.3 percent.

The significant decline of the importance of both import and export taxes as a source of government revenue is also noteworthy. In 1955 these taxes constituted 14.8 percent and 23.5 percent of total tax revenue, respectively. By 1975 they comprised only 3.4 percent and 1.3 percent, respectively.

The government trend in expenditures from 1941-1970 has been away from military expenditures and toward social and debt expenditures. Table 2-15 shows this relative decline in expenditures among very aggregated sectors.

The 1980 budget was expansionary. The Mexican government planned to make full use of Pemex's revenues to bolster economic development. A major revision that stands out in its revenue sources is the reduction of the tax burden on lower-income groups by 30 percent. This should help to correct, in part, Mexico's problem of unequal income distribution. Pemex revenues will no doubt fill in for this forgone revenue from the lower-income groups. Table 2-16 shows the large magnitude of budget increases from 1979 to 1980.

Table 2-15
Mexico: Federal Expenditures, 1940-1970
(*percentages*)

Year	President	Administrative	Military	Economic	Social	Debt
1941-1946	Avila Camacho	10.7	16.6	39.2	16.5	17.0
1947-1952	Aleman	9.7	9.7	51.9	13.3	15.4
1953-1958	Ruiz Cortines	8.7	8.0	52.7	14.4	16.2
1959-1963	Lopez Mateos	9.8	6.0	39.0	19.2	26.0
1964	Lopez Mateos	9.7	5.4	39.4	21.1	24.4
1965	Diaz Ordaz	8.1	4.3	42.5	18.2	26.9
1966	Diaz Ordaz	10.1	5.3	40.7	22.4	21.5
1967	Diaz Ordaz	8.8	4.4	37.6	20.3	28.9
1968	Diaz Ordaz	11.3	5.0	40.4	21.6	21.7
1969	Diaz Ordaz	10.9	5.1	42.3	21.3	20.4
1970	Diaz Ordaz	12.0	4.6	40.1	22.0	21.3

Sources: James W. Wilkie, *The Mexican Revolution: Federal Expenditures and Social Change Since 1910*, 2d. ed. (Los Angeles: University of California Press, 1970); Direccion General de Estadistica, *Anuario Estadistico* (Mexico City), annual issues 1959-1970.

Pemex will get the largest percentage increase of any single budget sector. The budget also reflects Mexico's determined efforts to remove supply bottlenecks by increasing allocations to communications and transportation. Recent problems with agriculture have made it unavoidable that more financial concern be shown this sector. A mixture of guaranteed prices for

Table 2-16
Mexico: Main Headings of Budget Expenditures, 1979-1980
(*billions of pesos*)

Expenditures	1979	1980	Percentage Change[a]
Federal departments	435.7	549.3	25.6
Finance & public credit	96.6	132.4	37.0
Agriculture & water resources	57.3	74.9	30.8
Communications & transport	31.3	37.4	19.7
Commerce	19.4	28.6	47.4
Education	105.2	125.4	19.1
Industrial development	42.6	50.4	18.1
Public works	21.8	26.2	20.3
Public debt	170.9	197.1	15.3
Semi-autonomous agencies	657.6	844.4	28.4
Pemex	289.8	399.6	37.8
Electricity	128.0	165.2	29.0
Railways	37.4	43.4	15.9
Conasupo	51.5	48.1	-6.7
Mexican fish products	13.0	19.1	46.3

Source: Economist Intelligence Unit, *Mexico, Annual Supplement* (London), 1979.
[a]Based on unrounded data.

farm produce and food subsidies will require that a sizable increase be made in expenditures on agriculture. In 1979 alone, subsidies for food were estimated to total $3.7 billion, over 24 percent higher than the total of 1978.[93]

In 1979 the Mexican government had planned to increase its expenditure by a rather large amount over 1978. The expenditure level was expected to rise from 912 billion pesos to 1,124 billion pesos, or an increase of 23.2 percent. The largest portion of this budget was slated to go to industry (300 billion or 26.7 percent), then debt services (252 billion pesos or 22.4 percent), health and social security (121 billion pesos or 10.4 percent), and agriculture (72 billion or 6.4 percent).[94]

Public investment is a large and growing sector of government expenditure. A part of total public investment is channeled to the industrial sector through the Nacional Financiera. This institution holds a controlling interest over the country's largest steel producer, Altos Hornos de Mexico. It also holds substantial financial stakes in pulp and paper, fertilizer, electrical equipment, electrolytic copper, sugar, films, textiles, food, beer, chemicals, cement, glass, metal working, and hotels.[95]

Official banks are also a conduit through which government investment flows. These banks are the Banco Nacional de Comercio Exterior, the Banco Nacional do Oboas Publicas, the Banco de Formento Co-Operativo, the Banco Nacional de Credito Ejidal, the Banco Nacional Agraicola and the Aseguradora Nacional Agricole y Ganadera, and state holding company the Sociedad Mexicana de Credito Industrial.

Six taxation policies have direct impact on investment in Mexico. (1) The dividends tax to be withheld by the paying firm and going directly to the government would be from 15 to 20 percent, without regard to the overall income of the recipient of the dividends. (2) If the proceeds of capital gains are invested within one year in specified areas, then capital gains are tax-exempt, except in real estate and gains accruing from liquidations and mergers. (3) Interest can be taxed at rates from 2 to 10 percent. In the case of interest on foreign loans, the range is between 10 and 42 percent. (4) Distributable profits are taxable only when payed out to shareholders. (5) Should stock dividends be derived from a capitalization of retained earnings on which taxes have not been paid, then such dividends can be taxed. (6) Authored payments for technical services paid outside of Mexico can be included in taxation on the corporation tax scale up to 42 percent.[96]

The 1980 budget (table 2-16) displayed Mexico's determination to keep its development pace of economic activity high. A large part of this effort will depend upon a deficit-finance approach. Overall expenditures, when broken down into principal areas, indicate "a 35 percent increase in new state investment and a 25 percent rise in current outlays. 197 billion pesos go to servicing the public debt. . . . the deficit will be 182 billion pesos, of which 74 percent is to be financed domestically and the balance by loans raised abroad."[97]

By 1981-82, plans for the immediate future had not been finished. However, we can comment to some extent on the tenor of the portions of the plans now completed. First, the incredibly complex system of economic planning that Mexico employs should be noted. In the early 1970s during President Jose Lopez Portillo's term in office, no fewer than eight national plans were prepared to outline and project development in different sectors of the economy. During that same span, four more plans were in the preliminary stages. "Plans have also been published in an attempt to coordinate the activities of various sectors, while each of Mexico's 31 states has released its own plan. So far, together they total 558 volumes."[98] The plan that has received most recent acceptance (as of June 2, 1980) is 1980-1982 Global Plan, "the long-delayed—and third—master blueprint spelling out the future for the whole of Mexico."[99]

Figure 2-4 presents the distribution of oil income to various sectors of the economy. As a general strategy Mexico intends not to finance development out of current oil revenues but to borrow funds to finance development expansion, using the oil in the ground as a type of collateral to back up its debt and using the appreciating flows of future oil revenues to retire debt. A major problem that Mexico shares with all LDCs that are major oil exporters is wariness of too many petrodollars "carrying their consequent threat of economic indigestion."[100] Another immediate problem is that the appreciation of the value of moderate oil sales has not occurred because of the 1981-1982 oil glut. The retirement of debt suddenly depended upon the depreciation of the value of crude petroleum.

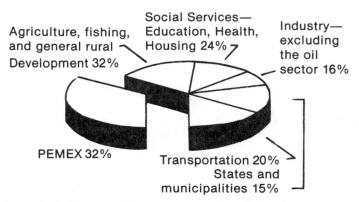

Source: Secretaria de Programación y Presupuesto, *Plan Global de Desarrollo 1980-1982* (Mexico City, 1980).

Figure 2-4. Sharing Pemex's $41 Billion Cake

Political Structure, Social and Cultural Change

Mexican politics since 1946 has been dominated by the Partido Revolucionario Institucional (PRI). It is somewhat of an aberration in the history of democratic political systems. The present ruling party took root in 1929 as the Partido Nacional Revolucionario when, after the assassination of Plutarco Elias Calles' successor-elect, Mexico was again threatened by domestic turmoil. This unity party was formed by the consent of many contending political factions. In 1935 it was renamed Partido de la Revolucion. This party encompassed several broad functional interest groups by admitting peasants, and representatives of labor, the military, and the popular or middle-class sector to the party's executive committee.[101]

In a sense, the political system is very much in a class by itself. It defies efforts to pigeonhole the system as a democracy, dictatorship, or other clear-cut category. This characteristic derives from Mexico's unique method of political succession. The PRI, before the end of the six-year presidential term of office, picks the successor to the incumbent. Since the PRI for the past fifty years has encountered no significant political opposition, this hand-picked candidate has had almost virtual assurance of election. This lack of viable opposition was vividly shown in the election of President Jose Lopez Portillo in 1976, with 94.4 percent of the popular vote, running "against a field of independents, no other party having presented an endorsed candidate."[102]

The present constitution was adopted in 1917. There are several aspects of the constitution that are noteworthy. The constitution is frequently amended but the strength of the presidency over all branches of government remains unaltered. In fact, the Mexican congress has no power to override a presidential veto. Some have called this institution of power "the six-year dictatorship."[103] Provision is made for the "collective ownership of land, waters, seas, natural resoures and sources of power and fuel."[104] The right of *amparo*, analogous to a combination of habeas corpus and the First Amendment, safeguards personal equities and property rights. The first twenty-nine articles of the constitution relate to protecting the right of amparo. Voting is compulsory for all citizens (universal suffrage) over eighteen years of age. This law is seldom enforced.[105]

The turnover in offices at election time is quite large since no one is allowed to hold the same post for more than one term of six consecutive years.[106] Figure 2-5 depicts the organization of the Mexican government. The centrality of the president and his cabinet is clearly shown.

Supreme Court members are appointed for life by the president with the approval of the Senate. The Supreme Court has twenty-one members and four divisions: administrative, civil, labor, and penal. The parliament, the National Congress, is a bicameral legislative body. The Senate (Camara de

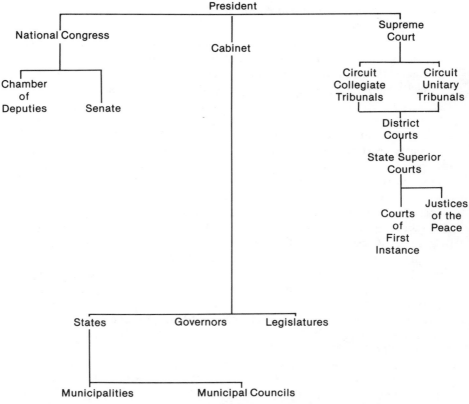

Source: George Kurian ed., "Mexico," *Encyclopedia of the Third World*, p. 989.
Figure 2-5. Organization of the Mexican Government

Senadores) has sixty-four members, two from each state and two from the Federal District. Each member serves a six-year term.

The powers of Congress are abridged by the Executive Branch. The Congress enjoys no provision that would empower it to override a presidential veto. The powers tend to be relegated to a rubber stamping of presidential actions.[107]

The 94.4 percent popular vote for Portillo indicated a strong degree of political solidarity within the country. Furthermore, the dominant party permitted "a token opposition in the Chamber of Deputies, even when opposition parties are unable to obtain seats."[108]

State governments are unicameral. Municipalities are the prevailing system of government on the local level. Members of the city government are elected by direct vote. Municipalities are not allowed to pass tax legislation. There are approximately 2,300 municipalities in Mexico.

The social system is generally stable with some racial problems. Mestizos are the ethnic majority, accounting for over 60 percent of the total population. The largest minority are Indians, comprising 30 percent of the population. The Mexican government provides certain incentives for the Indians to integrate into the Mexican culture. The main determinant of whether one is an Indian or a Mestizo is not so much race but culture system: "language, community type, village government, economic organization, family and kinship, and religion."[109] Indians are exploited but are also the subject of integration attempts. For the most part, the Indians remain outside of the mainstream of Mexican society but the National Indian Institute was established to facilitate the integration of Indians into the national society.[110]

Ninety percent of the Mexican population is Roman Catholic. This is a large proportion despite historical attempts to discourage strong Roman Catholic ties. There were two major anti-church periods: the rule of Benito Juarez (1867-1872) and the Revolution of 1910. The Constitution reflects this influence.

> Ecclesiastical corporations have no legal rights and theoretically cannot acquire property. Religious ceremonies cannot be held in public, and all church buildings are considered national property. The establishment of monastic orders is prohibited. Ministries of religion must have Mexican nationality; they have no political rights and may not criticize the fundamental laws of the country in either public or private meetings.[111]

Many of these prohibitions have not been enforced because in the mid-1970s many clergy had allied themselves with social concerns of the underprivileged.

The legal system derives from Spanish civil law with a heavy influence from the United States. Spanish civil law is very much a derivative of Roman law, which places greater authority in the hands of magistrates. This law is from the top down, whereas, English common law is from the bottom up. Spanish law puts greater power in the hands of the prosecution or state through its juridical decisions.

It is significant that Lopez Portillo and PRI chose a technician such as De la Madrid with a background in economic planning as secretary of the Planning and Budgeting Ministry. That choice has alienated important labor groups who opposed De la Madrid's candidacy and also other important groups within PRI who preferred a politician with closer ties to the party. De la Madrid's major problem will be to reconcile the opposition within his own party while broadening his political base in the country. As a candidate he played down his academic background in the United States and cultivated a more nationalistic populist image.

De la Madrid's domestic economic policies have been more conservative than those of his predecessor. For example, De la Madrid has given private investors the option of buying back the stock in bank-held companies that was taken into the public sector when banks were nationalized in the autumn of 1982. Although this rebuying option has not been well received by the private sector, it does reveal the direction of the new administration's

These new political forces will not change the dominance of PRI in Mexican politics, but they will tend to reduce the concentration of so much power in the presidency. De la Madrid will have to be more sensitive to the opposition voices inside and outside of his party. This is already evident in the attempts in 1982 to slow down the rapid pace of development. Moderation in fiscal and monetary policies and the redirection of resources away from the energy sector toward agriculture and the traditional sectors is in part designed to solve the external and internal disequilibria that have emerged in the Mexican economy. But that policy shift is also a response to the political pressures to expand job opportunities and improve the standards of living of the mass of Mexican workers. With unemployment in the rural sector remaining at 40 percent and with standards of living marginal for much of Mexico's population, there will be increasing pressure to share the new wealth from energy. The problem for De la Madrid is to expand employment opportunities and social-welfare programs without jeopardizing the Global Plan for Rapid Economic Growth. In the long run, success in improving jobs and standards of living is tied to the plans for rapid economic growth. But that goal can be jeopardized in the short run if the government wants to improve the lot of the poor. PRI has lost a great deal of support at the local level, and this is being exploited by opposition political parties. The potential for internal political stability will be very much influenced by the success of De la Madrid's policies to integrate the poorer groups and regions of the country with the process of economic development.

Perhaps the most enigmatic aspect of Mexican politics is foreign policy. De la Madrid has recently stated that his government will continue to support El Salvador's leftist groups. This is consistent with Mexican traditional foreign policy to support organized forces claiming to fight for a social revolution anywhere in Latin America. Most Mexican leaders assert that Mexico's revolutionary tradition requires a foreign policy sympathetic to other revolutionary movements in Latin America. Thus Lopez Portillo has praised Fidel Castro and the Sandinistas. That policy is increasingly in conflict with the foreign policy of the United States and other Latin American countries that oppose the political and military intervention by Castro, the Sandinistas, and other governments in support of guerilla movements in various Latin American countries. The Mexican revolution was very much a nationalist movement in which efforts by communist groups to link the movement with communism in Russia were suppressed, at times by force. The contradiction between Mexico's own revolutionary tradition and their support for communist guerilla movements in Latin America is recognized by some leaders. They see the risks to the Mexican security in communist regimes across their borders that are linked to Cuba and the Soviet Union. However, they pay lip service to guerilla movements in those countries in order to placate the left in Mexican politics and to discourage the growth of Mexican guerilla groups.

Absorptive-Capacity Constraints and Structural Imbalances

A broad definition of absorptive capacity, and thus one accommodating most interpretations of the concept, would define a country's absorptive capacity as the ability of the domestic economy to absorb resources at an acceptable rate of return within a given time period. Variations arise over, first, the nature of the resources to be absorbed and, second, what constitutes an acceptable rate of return. Most definitions equate investment with resources.[112] As for the second issue of an acceptable rate of return, a productivity criterion can be utilized, as well as certain sociopolitical benefits, when the principal investor (as in the case of Mexico) is the government and its agencies. A more refined definition of absorptive capacity thus could be the amount of investment with zero marginal efficiency of social investment. The social rate of return is a subjective concept and one which is determined by policymakers.

Five conventional constraints to the absorptive capacity of Mexico can be identified. Simply stated, Mexico's absorptive capacity could be expanded by: upgrading manpower (specifically skills), removing physical bottlenecks (usually in transportation and storage), utilizing and/or importing technology for greater productivity, removing the sociocultural constraints that keep part of the population from wider participation in the nation's economy, and improving and expanding educational opportunities (social investment that impacts in turn on such areas as technology and manpower).

In addition to the conventional constraints on absorptive capacity, there are other limiting factors in the case of Mexico. The governmental structure leads to a concentration of power in the executive branch and such centralization, coupled with a sizable bureaucracy, can delay project implementation and cause inefficiencies. The population drain from the rural areas to the cities—a plight Mexico shares with many other developing countries—is epitomized in Mexico City. Excessive urbanization can weaken the agricultural sector and, at the same time, severely tax the limited infrastructure in the cities in transportation, communications, water supplies, and sewerage. Although the infrastructure can absorb investment, the magnitude and immediacy of the need can lead to paralysis or stop-gap measures that do not contribute to long-term development. Maldistribution of income is another constraint on absorptive capacity when a large segment of the population exhibits only a very limited demand for goods and services. Among those benefitting from the inflow of oil and general wealth, many show little concern for long-term development and some aggravate the problem of capital flight. There is growing awareness of the adverse impact of pollution in Mexico, with the government seeking to alleviate the worst environmental impact in the capital, which suffers from the urbanization trend. Although antipollution measures could provide investment outlets for industries dealing with environment, the implementation could be slow because of the cost. In the meantime, the level of pollution dissuades some local industries from expanding. Inflation constrains absorptive capacity by distorting decisions made for future investment, as well as by stimulating capital flight and dampening the demand of the portion of the population with fixed incomes. Finally, unemployment and underemployment form a major limitation to absorptive capacity through the reduction of demand for goods and services by the labor force.

Conventional Constraints

Manpower. Unskilled manpower constraints are not a significant problem in Mexico. The reverse appears to be the major problem—labor surplus. Each year the economy is challenged to provide an additional 700,000 jobs just to keep pace with the nature of Mexico's demographic pyramid that assures a continually increasing labor force. However, the quality of labor may be a problem. Will Mexico be in a position to provide the highly skilled employees that an increasingly modern economy will require? This question will be addressed under the educational considerations. The immediate problem for Mexico is a constraint on jobs to provide suitable employment to the large numbers of unskilled workers who are underemployed or unemployed.

Physical Bottlenecks. Mexico does have a problem with physical bottlenecks. Its port facilities are presently insufficient to handle the rapidly increasing volume of international trade. Its railroad system is outdated, falling into disrepair and manned by an aged work force. There has been a delay in the online operation of Mexico's first of two 654-MW light-water nuclear units scheduled to begin operation in 1983. However, because of tremendous sources of other energy, this should not pose a serious bottleneck. Production rates of petroleum have been ahead of schedule and now the pressure may come to deliberately slow exploration and production rates.

The transportation sector appears to be the largest bottleneck in Mexico's infrastructural development. But it has been recognized as a serious problem and the Mexican government plans to allocate $42 billion or 20 percent of its planned expenditure over the three-year period from 1980 to 1982, for modernizing transportation.[113] And second to transportation, though perhaps not technically a bottleneck, the declining performance of agriculture is attracting considerable attention as well. Agriculture, fishing, and rural development was slated to receive 25 percent of total government expenditure during this three-year period.[114]

Technology. Technology does not appear to be a constraint to Mexico's development. When and where there is a deficiency in technology, it can be imported. However, the large external debt situation makes this recourse less and less attractive. Protectionism may worsen Mexico's technological lag since protectionism has historically tended to slow technological transfer and impede efficiency.

Sociocultural Constraints. Integrating the Indian population into the mainstream of Mexican economic life seems to be the most difficult sociocultural constraint. Progress is slow but there is reason for optimism: incentives are in place and an agency has been established whose purpose is to achieve this integration.

Education. It is not apparent that education is a constraint to Mexico's economic development. Clearly, as the population grows expenditures for education will have to increase. Also, as Mexico adopts more sophisticated industrial processes, qualified and skilled workmen will be necessary. The latest education figures available indicate that Mexico's educational sector is expanding faster than the overall rate of population increase. There does remain a serious question regarding the equal access to higher education in Mexico. Some maintain that such restricted access has perpetuated class barriers.[115] However, Mexico has made great strides in the provision of increased access. In 1900,

> . . . about 1.7 percent of the literate adult population had attended a university in 1900; by 1960, four decades after the Revolution, the figure had risen to only 2.7 percent. Mexico's national university system has recently expanded; its 124 campuses now enroll some 470,000 students, about 9 percent of the eligible population. Yet . . . it will be at least a generation before the social effects of expanded higher education are felt.[116]

Sufficient supplies of skilled managers for many of Mexico's development projects are becoming more difficult to find. Education will have to increasingly focus upon filling this gap if any development projects are to be successfully carried out.

New Constraints

Sociopolitical Constraints. Mexico's political system, which invests tremendous power in the executive branch, avoids many of the problems that more fractured political systems encounter. The Mexican president, who is the final arbiter, is less hampered by the need to compromise, since Congress has no power to veto a presidential initiative. However, though action is more likely to be carried out unaltered and things are more likely to get done rather than be suspended in political debate, without appreciable information input policies might be initiated that are inadequate or inappropriate. This situation seems inherent in any large and powerful centralized decision-making body. And it is a problem of which the Mexican government must always be aware.

Also, as wealth or command over resources is increasingly concentrated in the government, problems are to arise. It has already been shown that, compared to LDC economies, Mexico's government comprises a relatively small proportion of total GDP activity. But this proportion is likely to grow as the government enjoys windfall wealth and income from the development of petroleum. Political means are likely to be used to gain largely economic ends, and attention could be diverted from economic activity toward the increasingly profitable political dispensation of the economic windfall.

This had been occurring to a limited extent in the agricultural sector in relation to the politically controlled and nationally owned oil company (Pemex) prior to 1980. Money or effective control over resources has begun to pour into the economy through the petroleum sector. This sector at once is favored relative to other sectors with respect to more purchasing power. A "carrot-and-stick" effect appeared to begin operating upon the agriculture sector. Enticed by the economic "carrot" of rewards flowing into the economy from the petroleum sector and its linkages, farmers left the agricultural sector. Since, in a relatively closed economy, each sector competes with the others for scarce resources, the oil sector effectively outbid the agriculture sector. Farmers who are reliant upon these scarce inputs experienced higher production costs and lower profit margins. These two forces may have acted to lessen farm output. And we can see from the experience of other oil-exporting LDCs—for instance, the member states of OPEC—that such forms may be in operation. Mexico, for instance, began to import cereal, and such imports were expected to leap by 94 percent between 1979 and 1980. Much of the petroleum money flowed into the urban areas with its concentration of markets of various sorts. Thus, many of the rural inhabitants moved to the cities, accounting for the tremendously higher population-growth rates of the urban areas over the rural population-growth rates. The reforms that added emphasis upon agricultural and rural development have recently tended to reverse this process by decreasing the imbalance of financial advantage.

In summary, new purchasing power tended to disproportionately favor Pemex, or the government, and greatly disadvantaged other sectors. The Mexican government has recognized this problem by planning to expand 25 percent of its budgets for the next three years to inject money and resources in agriculture, fishing, and rural development. This is important, but one should also caution about specific ways that this money is allowed to enter the agriculture sector.

Urbanization. The urbanization problem is being attacked primarily in two different ways. First, as mentioned before, 25 percent of Pemex's estimated $41 billion over the next three years will be directed toward agricultural development. This should help to stem the declining output of the agricultural sector and also help to retard the high rate of rural-to-urban migration. Second, the government intends to partially accommodate the large numbers of persons who have already settled in urban areas by allotting 24 percent of the $41 billion Pemex revenues to social services—education, health, and housing.

The new-housing growth rate tends to lag well behind increases in the population, which will double by 130 million by the year 2000. Housing in general is in short supply; Mexico City, the largest city, is a case in point. Rental housing is critically scarce. High real-estate taxes and legislation hampering the eviction of delinquent tenants have made the construction of rental units unattractive. On the other hand, inflated building costs—brought about in part by excessive government demand for materials—have squashed the dreams of many Mexico City residents of ever owning a home. Even small government-subsidized condominiums, without heating and erected in the higher-crime and traditionally working-class areas of the city center, easily fetched $20,000 per unit in 1979. Middle-class apartments started at $40,000; houses at $60,000. Architects and engineers have lowered their professional standards so as not to price their products out of the market. Significantly, many new buildings sustained damage during the earthquakes of late 1978 and early 1979, while older structures suffered hardly a crack.[117] Mexico's urbanization problems are serious. The steadily increasing population is sure to exacerbate the size of the urbanization problem.

Income Distribution. Income distribution in Mexico is another very serious problem. According to the development economist Montek Ahlwalia, though Mexico is classified as a middle-income LDC, it had a very high Gini index in 1968 of .58 (the closer to zero the index is, the more equal income is distributed, but the closer to one the worse the income distribution). The bottom 40 percent of the population, in terms of income, received only 10.2 percent of the total income whereas the top 10 percent income groups received 65.8 percent of the total.[118] Other sources depict this relatively serious income distribution problem in Mexico. Irma Adelman and Cynthia Taft Morris present a table of income distribution in their book, *Society, Politics and Economic Development: A Qualitative Approach*, which shows the following pattern of income distribution in Mexico: the poorest 20 percent receive 3.66 percent of the income; the poorest 60 percent receive 21.75 percent of the income; the middle 40 to 60 percent receive 11.25 percent of the income; the highest 50 percent receive 28.52 percent of the income; and the highest 20 percent receive 58.04 percent of the income.[119]

This poor distribution of income is starkly represented by the difference between a skilled workman in Mexico City and a rural laborer. In the capital, the skilled worker in 1976 earned in excess of $500 per month (including benefits). By contrast, minimum wages for agricultural sector workers were about $5 per day. Moreover, due to underemployment, many farm laborers had an annual income as low as $100.[120]

The 1970 population census (table 2-17) shows the pattern of income going to Mexico's economically active population. Several policies and institutions tend to perpetuate this pattern of very unequal distribution of income among Mexico's citizens. One such influence might be Mexico's trickle-down or bimodalist approach to economic development that concentrates on rapid industrial development, the benefits of which will eventually rebound to other sectors of the economy as linkages are established. The stress has seemed to be upon efficiency, despite the predominantly populist rhetoric of most Mexican leaders. This approach is increasingly viewed with doubt by outsiders who note that:

> So far . . . the effect . . . has been to funnel great wealth to a minority, while, according to the government's own figures, only one-third of Mexico's 67 million people can afford adequate diets and some 40 percent suffer from outright malnutrition.[121]

Second, the style of state capitalism existing in Mexico may neglect the nature of the existence of market knowledge in society. Heavily centralized economic decision making tends to depend on the limited knowledge available to decision makers. Particular circumstances are often ignored and inappropriate development plans are often based upon this inherent blindness.[122] A more decentralized approach to development might help to overcome this disability. Recent emphasis on increased rural allocation has, at least, helped decentralize financial-resource entry.

Third, individuals fortunate enough to be near the particular entryway of new purchasing power tend to be favored. Those nearest the resource entry have much more command over resources than those far away, since

Table 2-17
Mexico: Employed Population by Income Strata, 1969
(*pesos, monthly averages*)

	Economically Active Population		
	Thousands of Inhabitants	*Percentage of Total*	*Percentage of Informants*
Total	12,994.4	100.0	—
Did not declare information	1,340.0	10.3	—
Declared income	11,654.0	89.7	100.0
Up to 199	2,144.0	16.5	18.4
200–499	3,083.2	23.7	26.5
500–999	3,437.5	24.1	26.9
1,000–1,499	1,474.8	11.4	12.7
1,500–2,499	951.6	7.3	8.2
2,500–4,999	555.6	4.3	4.8
5,000–9,999	200.2	1.5	1.7
10,000 +	107.5	0.8	0.8

Source: Secretaria de Industria y Commercio, *IX Censo General de Poblacion 1970* (Mexico City, 1972).

prices have not been affected by the incoming money. Those remotely located from the money source confront an upwardly adjusted array of prices or decreased purchasing power.

Fourth, even though one of the stated goals of the Constitution is to recognize the common nature of land, land still is, in effect though not in fact, owned or controlled disproportionately. Land-ownership or tenure patterns are at fault for a great deal of the poor distribution of income in Mexico. Of the three major agricultural groups (the ejidatarios who are the communal farmers, the proprietors, and the farm laborers), the ejidatarios are poor: on about the same economic level as the lowest-ranking proprietors (for example, the minifundis owners). The small to medium-size landowners comprise something of the agricultural elite. This group holds approximately 84 percent of all privately owned land, and this same group accounts for about 50 percent of the net national agricultural income. Despite land reforms, this elite has maintained its position. The final agricultural grouping is that of landless workers, some 3,500,000 strong, the labor force employed for seeding/sowing and harvest at exceedingly low wages by the landowners and the ejidatarios.[123]

Fifth, the ejido system of land tenure, occupancy, or management is also open to question. Though perhaps equitable, the system tends to keep productivity low and thus the potential surplus that could be equitably distributed is also low. This could well be because of the separation of effort from reward that exists on the ejido.

In many ways, the Mexican government plans to address these problems. First, it is recognized that Mexico has given overwhelming attention to the development of its petroleum potential:

> Over the past three years Pemex has expanded at a remarkable rate, but at a huge cost and at the expense of heavy foreign borrowing. Pemex has swallowed the lion's share of public investment money—money that could have gone toward improving the miserable standard of living of the unemployed and the underemployed.[124]

Less will be spent as a proportion of Pemex resources for further oil development and more spent for agriculture, social services, and infrastructural development. Second, centralization will tend to give way to decentralized industrial development. In addition to expanding the national product, policies will be directed toward improving income distribution:

> The national industrial plan has, as one of its goals, the re-orientation of the industrial plant to the production of goods that are socially necessary. Schemes have been implemented for the establishment of the incentives to encourage industrial decentralization both between economic activities and regions.[125]

Better income distribution is a severe challenge to Mexico's future. The precise way in which the new-found petroleum wealth finds its way into the Mexican economy matters very much. A centralized conduit will likely worsen the condition, while decentralized conduits seem to hold greater promise in improving the poor distribution of income in the Mexican economy.

Pollution. Mexico City suffers from at least two types of pollution: noise pollution and air pollution. It had the dubious distinction in 1979 of being the world's second noisiest and third most polluted city. This situation does not seem likely to change since effective efforts will require sacrifices of economic opportunities in other sectors of the economy that Mexico can ill afford at this juncture in its economic development. Mexico City's high altitude worsens the air-dilution factor, which means less pollution has a more serious impact than the same amount of pollution at lower altitudes. As Mexico's standard of living improves and incomes rise, it is likely that Mexico will become increasingly concerned with pollution. But until then, Mexico's attitude toward pollution might approximate other LDC perspectives: "In their eyes, the Third World's relatively unpolluted environments had become resources in themselves. 'We have plenty to pollute' roared a Latin American delegate at one of the [environmental] conferences 'and we're going to go right on polluting.' "[126]

Inflation. Inflation appears to be an almost intractable problem. Continued influxes of money into the economy, coupled with the external and structural problems, will assure continued high rates of inflation and the subsequent problems that inflation poses to accurate economic calculation.

Inflation is having extraordinary effects on the areas that are close to the developing petroleum areas. Tabasco, a very underdeveloped state in the southeastern part of Mexico, is a case in point. The oil wells newly brought on stream in that region have been the source of a large portion of the $1.6 billion in petroleum revenues earned during 1978. Oil workers, commanding high salaries, have flowed into Tabasco, putting pressure on the limited housing and consumer goods. The result has been rapidly rising prices. In the state's capital of Villahermosa, an apartment renting for 300 pesos per month ($15) in 1976 increased tenfold to 3,000 pesos ($150) per month in 1978. In the same period, food prices doubled. And oil-related activity has lured many unskilled laborers into Tabasco with the hope of employment. A resident of Villahermosa complained that, while he and the other indigenous inhabitants had always been poor, they had never really been desperate: "Now we are surrounded by desperate people from other states."[127]

The inflation situation may diminish many of the expected gains that Mexico had expected and still expects to gain from its program of economic development.

Employment. The unemployment problem is also very serious. As high as 40 percent of Mexico's population is unemployed and underemployed.[128] Some have estimated that as many as 800,000 Mexicans annually cross the United States border illegally to find jobs.[129] The economy requires as many as 700,000 new jobs each year to stand still and not lose ground. Former president Jose Lopez Portillo "claims it will take 20 years to create enough new jobs to defuse the unemployment crises."[130] There seem to be no quick fixes in sight, but if the economy can continue to grow at its present high real rate, the situation is more manageable.

External Absorptive-Capacity Constraints. In view of all of the domestic problems—poverty, unemployment, urbanization—and its development goals, Mexico has no surplus revenues that it cares to invest abroad. In fact, Mexico has borrowed heavily to support its massive development projects.

Summary and Conclusions

Patterns of economic development in Mexico are similar to those in many other LDCs that have begun to exploit their petroleum resources. One of these similarities was the decline in the rates of domestic agricultural production per capita, resulting in the need to import greater quantities of basic foodstuffs. As agriculture declines, urban populations grow. This creates a greater need for resources to be diverted to the urban areas. Another similarity is a high rate of inflation as larger quantities of money enter the economy to finance greater government expenditures. High rates of inflation create disincentives for long-term private investments. The government assumes an increasing role in resource allocation while displacing significant private investment. These patterns were emergent in Mexico.

Mexico had planned to take a slow and carefully planned approach to the development of its oil-production potential. Such a policy is considered desirable in light of the tendency of other oil-exporting LDCs to spend too rapidly and to exceed their absorptive capacities. Imbalances in sectoral growth are consequences Mexico wishes to avoid by this policy. Mexico had planned to produce only those revenues from its oil that it felt that it could easily digest.

Unfortunately, pressures to produce more oil are overcoming the Mexican government's resistance. The pressures to increase spending to deal with domestic problems and concern over foreign indebtedness may prove unbearable. There is some evidence of resistance giving way. Mexico had planned to raise total production of oil in 1980 to 2.3 million barrels per day. It was to hold production at this level until 1982 to give Mexico adequate time to digest its revenue. In January 1980 this annual production limit was raised to 4 million barrels per day by 1982.[131] Considering the size and immediacy of many of Mexico's problems—agricultural decline, continued balance-of-payments deficits, housing shortages—and also considering the ease with which oil can be used to finance attempts to solve these problems, it would seem likely that Mexico will again raise its production level when market conditions allow over the period of the 1980s. Many other LDC oil-exporting nations have shown an incredible ability to use, either efficiently or inefficiently, all the revenues gained from the petroleum sector, particularly those nations having large unemployed or underemployed populations. Mexico fits this pattern well.

Mexico is certainly more likely to exceed its announced oil-production ceilings than to keep below them. It is not inconceivable that Mexico could far exceed the ceiling of 5 million barrels per day by 1985, given revived worldwide petroleum demand. A study by the U.S. Central Intelligence Agency has predicted this likelihood.[132] There is some possibility that Mexico's production by 1990 would reach as high as 10 million barrels per day. It is telling that Pemex has increased its oil-export facilities to a capacity that outstrips its stated export goals of the 1980s.[133] Moreover, in late January 1982 the Mexican Petroleum Institute recommended eliminating export ceilings on crude oil and natural gas to finance its ambitious development plans and to correct many of the plans that have gone awry.[134]

The present (early 1983) world oil situation is negatively impacting Mexico. Surpluses of oil on the market are rapidly forcing prices downward. Structural changes in the United States energy consumption, the world's single largest energy consumer, make it unlikely that the United States will quickly rebound to former energy-use rates. Other oil-dependent economies have also made changes to conserve energy. Mexico will most likely be forced to sell more oil to make up for the cut in price.

Notes

1. Carl J. Migdail and Joseph L. Benham, "Strains on U.S.-Mexican Ties: Oil, Migrants, Castroism," *U.S. News and World Report*, March 9, 1981, p. 37.

2. Ibid.

3. "Mexican Industry: A Vulnerable 'One Crop' Economy," *World Business Weekly* (London), October 5, 1981, p. 39.

4. "Prospectus: United Mexican States," *Financial Times* (London), September 15, 1981, p. 30.

5. Migdail and Benham, op. cit., p. 39.

6. Jorge Castaneda cited in Richard Fagen, "An Inescapable Relationship," *Wilson Quarterly,* summer 1979, p. 145.

7. "Mexico: Dangers of Petrolization," *Energy Detente,* August 20, 1981, p. 2.

8. Peter Montagnon, "Testing Time for Two Years," *Financial Times* (London), December 18, 1981, section III, p. 1.

9. William Chislett, "Mexican Budget Seeks to Slow Growth and Create One Million Jobs," *Financial Times* (London), November 30, 1981, p. 2.

10. International Monetary Fund, *International Financial Statistics* (Washington, D.C.: International Monetary Fund), April 1977, pp. 270-71; March 1981, pp. 266-67.

11. Robert H. McBride, "The United States and Mexico" in *Mexico and the United States* (Englewood Cliffs, N.J.: Prentice-Hall, 1980), p. 6.

12. William Chislett, "Mexico Tightens Credit to Private Sector," *Financial Times* (London), September 27, 1981, p. 2.

13. "Prospectus: United Mexican States," *Financial Times* (London), September 15, 1981, p. 30.

14. Gretchen Heimjsil, "Trade Boom with Mexico Creates Problems and Opportunities," *Foreign Agriculture,* November 1981, p. 5.

15. "Prospectus: United Mexican States," *Financial Times* (London), September 15, 1981, p. 33.

16. The public sector investment program for 1980 had slated about 55 percent of total investment for industry and only 20 percent for agricultural

and rural development combined. See "A Plan That Includes the Means to Carry It Out: Mexico—A Survey," *Euromoney,* March 1981, p. 14.

17. George Getschow, "Trouble at the Mill: Steel Problems Imperil Mexico's Long Dream of Industrial Strength," *Wall Street Journal,* January 27, 1981, p. 12.

18. Ibid.

19. William Chislett, "Foreign Investment Pouring in at Unprecedented Rate," *Financial Times* (London), December 18, 1981, p. IV.

20. William Chislett, "Market Test for Mexico," *Financial Times* (London), February 22, 1982, p. 17.

21. William Chislett, "Foreign Investment Pouring in at Unprecedented Rate," *Financial Times* (London), December 18, 1981, p. IV.

22. Ibid.

23. Ibid.

24. Ibid.

25. "Prospectus: United Mexican States," *Financial Times* (London), September 15, 1981, p. 35.

26. "Mexico: Dangers of Petrolization," *Energy Detente,* August 20, 1981, p. 4; and "The Debt-Bomb Threat," *Time,* January 10, 1983, p. 43.

27. Ibid.

28. Miguel S. Wionczek, "Mexico: Energy Policy," paper presented to the second international area conference of the International Research Center for Energy and Economic Development on "Mexico: Energy Policy and Industrialization," August 27-28, 1981, University of Colorado, Boulder.

29. *Oil and Gas Journal,* December 28, 1981, p. 87.

30. Jaime Corredor, "Oil in Mexico: Summary of Relevant Information and Some Comparisons with Other Oil-Producing Countries," informative appendix prepared for the Oxford Energy Seminar, Oxford University, Oxford, England, September 1980.

31. United Nations, Economic Commission for Latin America, "El Desequilibrio Externo en el Desarrollo Economico Latinoamericano: El Caso de Mexico," 2 vols., 1975 (mimeographed).

32. "Mexico Confirms 34-Billion Barrel Jump in Proved Hydrocarbons," *Platt's Oilgram News,* November 13, 1981, p. 1.

33. It is important to remember that Mexico includes natural gas with its crude petroleum figures. A rule of thumb is to assume that two-thirds of the total figure is crude petroleum and one-third is natural-gas equivalent.

34. David Ronfelat, Richard Nehring, and Arutro Gandara, *Mexico's Petroleum and U.S. Policy Implications for the 1980s* (Santa Monica, Cal.: Rand Corporation, 1980), p. 3.

35. *Middle East Economic Survey,* January 18, 1982, p. 13. (Hereafter *Middle East Economic Survey* will be cited as *MEES.*)

36. Ibid., January 11, 1982, p. 2.

37. Frank E. Niering, Jr., "Mexico: Oil Policy at the Crossroads," *Petroleum Economist,* August 1981, pp. 343-44.

38. *MEES,* January 11, 1982, p. 2.

39. "Mexico Doubles Domestic Petrol Price," *Financial Times* (London), December 23, 1981, p. 4.

40. William Chislett, "Mexico Nears Its Food Goal," *Financial Times* (London), December 30, 1981, p. 17.

41. Ibid.

42. Ibid.

43. Ibid.

44. United States, Foreign Service, "Mexico," *Foreign Economic Trends and Their Implications for the United States,* January 1980, p. 5.

45. Marlise Simons, "The People Next Door," *Wilson Quarterly,* Summer 1979, p. 123.

46. George Kurian, ed., "Mexico," *Encyclopedia of the Third World* (New York: Facts on File, 1978), p. 995.

47. Ibid.

48. Ibid.

49. Ibid.

50. Economist Intelligence Unit, Ltd., *Mexico, Annual Supplement* (London: Economist Intelligence Unit, Ltd., 1979), p. 15.

51. Ibid.

52. Ibid., p. 11.

53. "Prospectus: United Mexican States," *Financial Times* (London), September 15, 1981, p. 33.

54. Ibid.

55. Ibid.

56. Ibid.

57. Ibid.

58. "Mexico," *Encyclopedia Britannica Yearbook* (Chicago: Encyclopedia Britannica, Inc., 1977, 1978, 1979).

59. United States, Foreign Service, "Mexico," *Foreign Economic Trends and Their Implications for the United States,* January 1980, p. 5.

60. Ibid.

61. William Chislett, "Mexico to Restrict Car Production," Financial Times (London), November 11, 1981, p. 21.

62. Ibid.

63. "Expanding the Mexican Steel Sector," *World Business Weekly* (London), January 26, 1981, p. 44.

64. Ibid.

65. "Economic Digest: Mexico," *World Business Weekly* (London), April 7, 1980, p. 27.

66. Kurian, ed., "Mexico," p. 996.

67. Ibid.

68. Ibid., p. 997.

69. "Mexico: A Stumbling Transportation System," *World Business Weekly* (London), June 30, 1980, p. 22.

70. Ibid.

71. Ibid.

72. Ibid.

73. William Chislett, "Mexico May Cancel Nuclear Programme," *Financial Times* (London), April 2, 1982, p. 1.

74. William Chislett, "Massive Programme Attracts World's Nuclear Companies," *Financial Times* (London), December 2, 1981, p. 4.

75. Ibid.

76. Kurian, ed., "Mexico," p. 998.

77. Ibid.

78. Peter H. Smith, "The Wounds of History," *Wilson Quarterly,* Summer 1979, p. 137.

79. Ibid.

80. *The Hammond Almanac, 1980* (Maplewood, N.J.: Hammond Almanac, Inc.), p. 625.

81. Kurian, ed., "Mexico," p. 999.

82. B. Griffiths, *Mexican Monetary Policy and Economic Development* (New York: Praeger, 1972), p. 30.

83. Economist Intelligence Unit, Ltd., *Mexico, Annual Supplement* (London: Economist Intelligence Unit, Ltd., 1979), p. 17.

84. International Monetary Fund, *International Financial Statistics* (Washington, D.C.: International Monetary Fund), various issues, 1982 and 1983.

85. "Mexico: Dangers of Petrolization," *Energy Detente,* August 20, 1981, p. 2.

86. Peter Montagnon, "Testing Time for Two Years," *Financial Times* (London), December 18, 1981, Section 3, p. 1, and William Chislett, "Mexican Budget Seeks to Slow Growth and Create One Million Jobs," *Financial Times,* November 30, 1981, p. 2.

87. International Monetary Fund, *International Financial Statistics* (Washington, D.C.: International Monetary Fund), various issues, 1982 and 1983.

88. "Programa de Energia: Mestas a 1990 y Proyecciones al Ano 2000," *Energeticos,* vol. 4, no. 11 (November 1980), p. 12.

89. International Monetary Fund, *International Financial Statistics* (Washington, D.C.: International Monetary Fund), April 1976 and April 1981.

90. Robert E. Looney, *Mexico's Economy: A Policy with Forecasts to 1990* (Boulder, Colorado: Westview Press, 1978), p. 49.

91. Ibid., p. 44.

92. Ibid., p. 47.

93. "Mexico Tries to Slice Its Cake So That Everyone Gets a Share," *World Business Weekly* (London), June 2, 1980, p. 22.

94. Economist Intelligence Unit, Ltd., *Mexico, Annual Supplement* (London: Economist Intelligence Unit, Ltd., 1979), p. 17.

95. Ibid.

96. Ibid.

97. Economist Intelligence Unit, Ltd., *Quarterly Economic Review of Mexico* (London: Economist Intelligence Unit, Ltd., First Quarter 1980), p. 5.

98. "Mexico Tries to Slice Its Cake So That Everyone Gets a Share," *World Business Weekly* (London), June 2, 1980, p. 22.

99. Ibid.

100. "Mexico: Trying to Use Oil in Place of GATT," *World Business Weekly* (London), July 7, 1980, p. 21.

101. Peter H. Smith, "The Wounds of History," *Wilson Quarterly,* Summer 1979, p. 134.

102. *Political Handbook of the World, 1979* (New York: McGraw-Hill, 1979), p. 300.

103. Kurian, "Mexico," p. 990.

104. Ibid., p. 986.

105. Ibid., p. 990.

106. Ibid.

107. Ibid., p. 992.

108. Ibid., p. 990.

109. Ibid., p. 982.

110. Ibid.

111. Ibid., p. 988.

112. The views of B. Higgins, R.F. Mikesell, J.H. Adler, R. Gulhati, H.B. Chenery, and A.O. Hirschman in support of investment as resources are presented succinctly by W.J. Stevens, *Capital Absorptive Capacity in Developing Countries* (Leiden, Holland: A.W. Sijthoff, 1971), p. 3. A more detailed discussion of the concept of absorptive capacity and its application to an oil-producing country is Ragaei El Mallakh and Jacob Atta, *The Absorptive Capacity of Kuwait* (Lexington, Mass.: Lexington Books, D.C. Heath and Company, 1981).

113. "Mexico Tries to Slice Its Cake So That Everyone Gets a Share," *World Business Weekly* (London), June 2, 1980, p. 22.

114. Ibid.

115. Smith, "The Wounds of History," p. 137.

116. Ibid.

117. Sergio Sarmiento, "Mexico City: A Troubled Giant," *Encyclopedia Britannica Yearbook, 1980,* p. 529.

118. Montek Ahlwalia, "Dimensions of the Problem," in Chenery, Duloy, and Jolly, eds. *Redistribution with Growth: An Approach to Policy* (Washington, D.C.: International Bank for Reconstruction and Development, 1973), (2)4 cited in Michael P. Todaro, *Economic Development in the Third World,* (New York and London: Longman Group Ltd., 1977), p. 106.

119. Cited in Michael P. Todaro, *Economic Development in the Third World* (New York and London: Longman Group Ltd., 1977), p. 106.

120. "A No-Nonsense Mood Takes Hold in Mexico," *U.S. News and World Report,* June 21, 1976, pp. 63-66, cited in Paul R. Ehlrich et al., *Ecoscience* (San Francisco, Cal.: W.H. Freeman & Co., 1977), p. 890.

121. Simons, "The People Next Door," p. 129.

122. For more on this, see F.A. Hayek, "The Use of Knowledge in Society," *American Economic Review*, September 1945, pp. 519-30.

123. Simons, "The People Next Door," p. 129.

124. "Mexico Tries to Slice Its Cake So That Everyone Gets a Share," *World Business Weekly* (London), June 2, 1980, p. 22.

125. Gustavo Romero Kolbick, "The Mexican Economy in the '80s," *Euromoney,* April 1980, p. vii.

126. Benjamin Higgins and Jean Dawns, *Economic Development of a Small Planet* (New York: W.W. Norton, 1979), p. 10.

127. "The Land of Promise That Awaited Carter," *U.S. News and World Report,* February 19, 1979, p. 22.

128. Ibid.

129. "Mexico: Carter Goes A-Wooing," *U.S. News and World Report*, February 19, 1979, p. 21.

130. Ibid.

131. Economist Intelligence Unit, Ltd., *Quarterly Economic Review of Mexico* (London: Economist Intelligence Unit, Ltd., First Quarter 1980), p. 13.

132. "Mexico: Carter Goes A-Wooing," *U.S. News and World Report,* February 19, 1979, p. 21.

133. "It is not clear why investments are still being made to develop the export infrastructure if the limits are accepted. As Pemex officially announced, the present load capacity of 1.2 million barrels a day at Port Pajaritos will almost double which means that this port alone will soon be able to export 2.2 million barrels a day—47 percent more than the energy programme's limit of 1.5 million barrels a day." Norma Giaracca, "Agrarian Crisis," *South* (London), July 1981, p. 47.

134. "MPI Urges Mexico to Abolish Crude Oil, Gas Export Ceilings," *Petroleum Information International,* February 1, 1982, p. 1.

3 The Case of Norway

Overview of the Norwegian Economy

Among the industrial countries, Norway enjoys a unique energy situation; apart from abundant hydroelectricity, there are vast petroleum reserves.[1] For a long time Norway has had the world's highest per-capita consumption of electricity; since the mid-1970s Norway has been a net exporter of oil and natural gas, being perhaps the only industrial country able to retain this position for decades, if not for generations. This favorable energy situation has profound economic implications. Abundant and inexpensive energy historically has been the most important comparative advantage for Norway's industrial development.

Petroleum exports provide foreign exchange, thereby improving freedom of action in macroeconomic policy. The capture of part of the economic rent related to petroleum, defined as the sum of income and profits over and above normal return on capital, means that the petroleum rent makes up a certain proportion of the Norwegian economy, around 11 percent of the gross national product (GNP) since 1980.[2] This can be seen as a transfer of income that Norway, together with other oil-exporting countries, received from the oil-importing nations. Because of this element of petroleum rent, the Norwegian economy differs qualitatively from those of practically all other industrial countries. Petroleum revenues not only represent a quantitative supplement, essentially consisting of an economic rent (a transfer of income), but they also represent a qualitative change of the economic context. Thus, they also present new problems of economic management and policy. For example, the large proportion of economic rent means that the generation of petroleum revenues only to a fairly small extent mobilizes the supply factors in the economy, thus potentially leading to problems of excess liquidity and demand pressure. This highlights the structural effects of the domestic use of petroleum revenues. Proportion is an important part of the problem, as the petroleum sector already accounts for about 15 percent of the total economy and a third of total exports.

Norway essentially is a case of a small country with a large petroleum sector, but where, until the advent of the petroleum industry, the factors of production were already fully utilized and structural change was not very welcome. This has changed in light of the international economic recession in the early 1980s. This recent experience is an indication of how petroleum

77

revenues and industrial income coexist uneasily; as petroleum exports have been building up, industrial output has stagnated, and there has been a fairly consistent loss of market shares. This indicates that the inclusion of a large petroleum sector presents important overall structural problems, creating planning challenges that the current institutional framework may not be too successful in dealing with. Norway's constraint in relation to petroleum revenues, therefore, may be as much of an institutional and political character as of an economic nature, meaning that the critical factors are the management of the economic rent and the kind and pace of structural change that are acceptable.

Background

Norway covers the western part of northern Europe's Scandinavian peninsula. It is bounded on the north by the Arctic Ocean, on the east by Sweden, Finland, and the Soviet Union, on the west by the Atlantic Ocean and the North Sea, and on the south by the Skagerak branch of the North Sea. The area of continental Norway, including the immediately surrounding islands, and the outlying islands of Jan Mayen and the Spitzbergen archipelago is 386, 974 square kilometers. However, in any petroleum-related context, the maritime territory should be included; considering the extension of the economic zone to 200 nautical miles, Norway has a maritime territory of approximately 2,000,000 square kilometers in addition to its continental territory.

Most of continental Norway is covered by mountains; indeed, less than a third of the territory is situated at less than 300 meters (1,000 feet) above sea level. About a quarter of the area is covered by forests, and only 4 percent is arable land. There are some dispersed areas of fertile land along the west coast and in southeastern and central Norway, and there are quite fertile valleys along a number of rivers. Most of continental Norway is made up of Precambrian and Caledonian geological structures without any petroleum potential as far as is known. The adjacent maritime geological structures are of much more recent origin and have proved to have considerable petroleum potential.

As a comparatively modest amount of exploratory drilling has been carried out on the Norwegian continental shelf, especially in the areas north of 62°N, estimates of oil and gas deposits are necessarily conservative. A reasonable guess is that the Norwegian continental shelf has some of the world's largest reserves of oil and natural gas, but at varying depths under the sea and with varying accessibility. So far, the oil found is light, approximately 37-41° API, with an extremely low sulfur content;[3] correspondingly, the natural gas found also has a low sulfur content. Most of the natural gas is associated with oil, but there are some fields of natural gas only. In recent years, the ratio between oil and gas in new discoveries has been shifting toward natural gas.

By January 1, 1981, total discoveries were about 1,105 million standard cubic meters of oil and NGL (natural gas liquids) and 1,380 billion standard cubic meters of natural gas.[4] As already indicated, these figures should be seen as very conservative; new discoveries currently under evaluation are likely to raise these proved reserves substantially. As of 1982, government estimates of both oil and natural gas were 4.7 billion standard cubic meters of oil equivalent for both proved and expected total reserves in the southern portion of the continental shelf. Of this total, 2.7 billion cubic meters of oil equivalent were considered proved reserves.[5] Furthermore, there is evidently a geological potential for large new discoveries. Against this background, any reserve estimate, on the basis of geological indications and not based on exploration, is purely speculative, but total reserve figures of 10,000 to 12,000 million tons of oil equivalent could be a reasonable guess, perhaps on the moderate side, and with an oil-to-gas ratio of 40:60. Besides petroleum, the Norwegian continental shelf is believed to have a wealth of other minerals, some in the form of nodules, others in the form of mineral deposits. The North Sea covers extensive coal deposits.

Continental Norway has a number of minerals, usually in fairly low-grade ores, including iron, copper, nickel, manganese, titanium, zinc, sulfur, gold, and silver. Coal is found in Spitzbergen. Continental Norway is very well endowed with energy resources. There is a hydroelectric potential of perhaps 130 TWh, (terawatt-hours), corresponding to 22 million tons of oil equivalent of which only about 75 TWh have been developed so far.[6] However, future development is likely to clash with environmental interests. There are also deposits of uranium and thorium in continental Norway.

Practically all of the country has an ample supply of free-flowing fresh water. Artificial irrigation is only used in a few valleys located in the rain-shadow of mountains. Norway's climate is dominated by the Gulf Stream and the accompanying southwesterly winds. The western parts of Norway, (essentially the areas along the Atlantic coast) have a moderate and rainy climate, with mild winters and cool summers. The eastern parts of the country, especially the southeastern region, have a more continental climate with cold winters with fairly heavy snowfalls and comparatively warm summers, considering the latitude. Consequently, conditions for agriculture vary; the growing of grains predominates in eastern Norway and livestock farming is more important in western Norway. Since the Middle Ages Norway has been a net importer of grains; dependence upon foreign food supplies has been a major problem in times of crisis. However, Norway's fisheries have some of the world's most important catches, and the country is Europe's largest exporter of fish and fish products.

The Norwegian population is one of the most homogeneous in Europe. Estimated mean population for 1980 was 4,086,000, plus less than 100,000 foreigners, most of whom were other Scandinavians, British, and Americans. Apart from Iceland, Norway has Europe's lowest population density, about thirteen inhabitants per square kilometer. The degree of urbanization is less than in many other European countries; according to the 1970 census, only 66 percent of the population was living in densely populated areas, and only 57 percent in areas with at least 2,000 inhabitants. In recent years the trend toward urbanization has slowed, and there has been an absolute population decline in the capital city, Oslo, and its surroundings. Only three cities, Oslo, Bergen, and Trondheim, have populations higher than 100,000; three more, Drammen, Kristiansand and Stavanger, have between 50,000 and 100,000 inhabitants. In recent years, population growth has declined; between 1970 and 1980 average annual population growth was 0.52 percent, including net immigration.

The low rate of demographic growth and the fairly moderate level of domestic migration mean that the Norwegian population only to a small extent suffers from problems that usually accompany rapid structural change, such as housing shortages, congestion, and pressures on social infrastructures. The housing situation is certainly one of the world's best, with an acute excess demand only in some specific areas influenced by the rapidly growing petroleum industry. Public services such as education, medical care, hospitalization, and old-age pensions and care, are provided free or at a modest fee, even if they are not always sufficiently developed in the more remote parts of the country. In any case, in terms of hospital beds and doctors in relation to population, infant mortality, and full-time school enrollment, Norway ranks among the best in Western Europe and the world. The standard of living, measured in terms of GNP per capita as well as by indexes of consumption, is also one of the highest in the world.

Low demographic growth rates mean that the Norwegian population is getting relatively older. By the end of 1979, persons under 15 years of age made up 22.4 percent of the total population, and persons 65 years or older constituted 14.4 percent. Unless there is a sudden change in demographic dynamics, the proportion of aged persons will increase, and there will be a relative decline both in the number of young persons and in the number of persons of working age. This development will influence the employment situation and the labor market.

In 1979 the total average employment was 1,872,000, representing 46.0 percent of the total population. There were 762,000 women and 1,110,000 men in the labor force. The total level of employment, compared to total population, is lower in Norway than in neighboring Denmark and Sweden. The relative coefficient of employment, measured as the number of persons who are employed or who are looking for employment as a percentage of

total population aged 15-74 years, in 1979 in Norway was 66.2, compared
with 70.1 percent in Denmark and 71.0 percent in Sweden. This difference
can essentially be explained by the lower female coefficient of employment in
Norway, 54.2 percent, against 60.9 percent in Denmark, and 63.5 percent in
Sweden.[7] However, during the 1970s the overall coefficient of employment in
Norway has risen steadily, especially as regards women, meaning that more
employment opportunities have been created for married women. Much of
the female employment is part-time, particularly among married women.

The Norwegian employment structure historically has been characterized by a fairly high proportion in primary activities, such as agriculture,
forestries, and fishing; currently it is characterized by the predominance of
the service sector. Employment in manufacturing has never had the importance in Norway which has been the case in the heavily industrialized
Western European countries such as the United Kingdom, West Germany,
and Belgium. Today, employment in primary activities is considerably
higher than in neighboring Sweden, and practically at the same level as in
Denmark. Table 3-1 shows employment by economic activity.

Thus, by the composition of its economy, Norway is one of the least industrialized countries of Western Europe; only in Denmark is the relative
share of industrial employment lower. Industrialization came late to Norway, only in the beginning of this century, based largely upon the exploita-
tion of natural resources, essentially abundant hydroelectric power. Tradi-

Table 3-1
Norway: Employment by Economic Sectors, 1980
(*1,000 persons/percent*)

Sector of Economic Activity	Norway		Denmark*		Finland		Sweden	
Agriculture, forestry, fishing	161	8.4	207	8.2	253	11.5	237	5.6
Mining and manufacturing	401	21.0	531	21.0	579	26.3	1,040	24.6
Construction and power supply	166	8.7	218	8.6	174	7.9	323	7.6
Trade	327	17.1	336	13.3	315	14.3	582	13.8
Transportation and communication	171	8.9	171	6.8	169	7.7	295	7.0
Other services	684	35.8	1,040	41.1	692	31.4	1,755	41.5
Total	1,913		2,529		2,203		4,232	

Source: *Yearbook of Nordic Statistics 1981* (Stockholm: Nordic Council, 1982), pp. 76-77.
*figures are for 1979

tionally, Norway has imported far more industrial goods than she has exported, paying for the industrial import surplus by exports of raw materials such as ores, wood, fish, and more recently petroleum, or services, mainly in shipping.

Norwegian industrial exports have to a large extent consisted of semifinished products, to serve as input factors in manufacturing industries of other countries.[8] This situation created a serious structural problem for Norwegian industry, since it is operating in fields with a low degree of finishing and generally with a low value added. In this way Norway's economic relations with the industrial core of Europe are to some extent those of a developing country; as an exporter of raw materials and an importer of finished goods. This is further exacerbated by Norway's emergence as an exporter of petroleum. The impression of structural underdevelopment is also underlined by Norway's traditional role as a net importer of capital; over time the country has not managed to finance her own development.

Other indicators that Norway does not have a very highly developed economy are the low level of female employment outside the household (until recently one of the lowest in Western Europe) and the low degree of urbanization. With petroleum, Norway is in many ways an economic paradox, being one of the richest countries as measured by gross product per capita (in 1980 third in the OECD (Organisation for Economic Cooperation and Development) after Switzerland and Sweden and well ahead of Canada and the United States), but structurally the economy does not seem to be very highly developed. This situation presents serious structural economic problems.

The Norwegian political system is a combination of constitutional monarchy and parliamentary democracy. Pariliamentary government was introduced in 1884. Since then the monarch has had no real political power. Since 1945 there has been a shift of power away from Parliament to the civil service, partly because of the predominance of majority or one-party governments, partly because of the increasingly complex task of practical government, requiring detailed insight, and partly because of the growth and influence of the large special-interest organizations, which maintain a close consultative relationship with the parts of government dealing with their sectoral interests.

Norway is characterized by exceptionally strong economic-interest organizations. The level of unionization approaches 80 percent among salaried employees and wage earners, the majority of whom are organized in the Trade Union Confederation. Furthermore, employers and industrial, agricultural, and fishing interests are also well organized, and the Norwegian political economy is dominated by a small number of extremely powerful interest organizations. The close consultative relationship between these interest organizations and the different branches of government seems to compromise the cohesion of government, in the sense that the different parts of government appear to more easily cooperate with their respective client organizations than with each other.[9]

Typically, sectoral planning, to a large extent on the premises of the interests concerned, is fairly well developed, whereas overall economic planning is poorly developed and fairly powerless. Because of the weight of the interest organizations, the Norwegian political system is often characterized as "corporate pluralism."[10] Political decision making, at least in important economic matters, is less the affair of Parliament than the subject of bargaining between the various interest groups and their allies within government. Consequently, the Norwegian economic system is fairly far removed from the neoclassical ideal of the market. Instead, it has been described as a *bargaining economy*, meaning that it consists of a number of interests, formally or informally organized, crossing the borderline between the private and public sectors, whose resources are both of economic and political character, including organizational reserves as well as financial ones.[11]

The relative bargaining power of these different interests is decisive for the outcome of a number of key economic factors, such as relative prices of industrial and agricultural products, wage development, interest rates, investment priorities, and so on. The active participation of the various branches of the state is of critical importance to this process, and typically the state has in recent times been particularly involved in wage bargaining between employers and trade unions. Thus, in the Norwegian political economy, the division between the private and the public sectors is of more formal than real significance, as is the separation of economics and politics. The Norwegian market is to a large extent politically determined, but economic matters are also to a predominant extent the lifeblood of politics, given a large consensus on foreign policy and an increasing political marginalization of issues such as religion, temperance, and language, which formerly were of at least great regional importance.

This so-called economization of Norwegian politics is reflected in an increased bipolarization, with the Conservative party taking an increasing share of the nonsocialist vote, at the expense of intermediaries such as the ex-agrarian Centrist party, the Christian People's Party, and the now-marginal Liberal Party. Labor and the Conservatives are in the early 1980s the two predominant political parties, and it is symptomatic that in the autumn of 1981 a single-party minority Conservative government was established for the first time since 1928. In the 1970s electoral patterns have changed, and there is now much more mobility of votes than used to be the case.[12] This may indicate that ideological and organization ties are becoming less important to voters, and economic issues correspondingly more so.

Norway is probably one of the most homogeneous and stable societies in Europe. Homogeneity is not only ethnic, it is institutionally linked to the predominance of a centralized state, culturally to a unitary church, to a unitary educational system, and to a fairly unitary and centralized media structure.[13]

Economically, homogeneity is linked to a comparatively high degree of income equalization and less marked social inequalities than in most other capitalist countries. Stability is manifest through a remarkable degree of institutional and political continuity.[14] It is also manifest in a low level of tension and conflict, visible in low crime rates and low figures for labor disputes.[15] Furthermore, stability expresses itself in a comparatively low mobility, probably less socially than occupationally and regionally. There is a great reluctance among most Norwegians to change occupations and areas of residence, and there are signs that this has been accentuated in recent years. This can be interpreted as a sign that many if not most Norwegians emphasize the welfare effect of occupational and residential continuity, and that mobility is seen as accompanied by serious inconveniences that to a large extent offset potential economic gains. Thus, there appear to be fairly clear politically determined limits to the rate and extent of structural change and adaptation of patterns of employment and residence that are acceptable to the Norwegian public. This is especially important in relation to absorbing petroleum revenues.

The Norwegian political economy may appear both cumbersome and fragile, to the extent that economic decision making requires a consensus of several well-organized interests (which objectively are divergent). This may be slow to work out, and some may say that the system contains the seeds of its own destruction, in the sense that well-organized corporate cooperation may be replaced by well-organized corporate confrontation. The system still has to prove its viability during a prolonged economic recession. The Swedish general strike of 1980 may be a sign that the corporate pluralism essentially generates large-scale conflict, as small-scale conflict is prevented by internal corporate control. However, Norway, like Sweden, has managed the transition from an agrarian, rural society to an industrialized urban one within a fairly short span of time, and with probably less social cost and less social tension than elsewhere in Europe.[16] This may indicate a capacity for self-tranformation, provided consensus is maintained, and in this perspective the clumsiness of the corporate pluralism may turn out to be an asset, as it generates compromise and assures the participation of different social forces.

For Norway the key question is how this model of political economy reacts to the sudden emergence of a large petroleum sector, whose productivity of capital is far above that of the other sectors. Evidently, the petroleum sector to a large extent was seen as an alien element, even by Norwegian capitalism, in spite of the obvious potential for quick profits. The reason is essentially that the petroleum sector has requirements of capital, technology, and skilled management that Norwegian capitalism cannot provide alone, and that petroleum revenues, if integrated in the Norwegian economic circuit without any specific safeguards, could easily wipe out a large part of Norwegian industry exposed to foreign competition.

In this perspective, there has been a widespread acceptance that the state should play a key role in petroleum development and in the control of the use of revenues. Also in this perspective, the high degree of nationalization of the Norwegian petroleum industry can be seen as a shield for the bulk of Norwegian capitalism against market forces with which it could hardly cope. For example, it is remarkable that Norwegian shipowners, who traditionally have made up the hard core of Norwegian capitalism, have been virtually excluded from the petroleum industry, except in providing drilling services, and this has been met with a significant degree of consensus.

In general, all the organized economic and political forces profess a certain hostility to structural change in the wake of petroleum revenues, but show less hostility to incremental income on this basis. Hostility to structural change is the most pronounced in the agricultural and industrial organizations.[17] Apparently, an alliance is in the making between industrial interests exposed to foreign competition, banking interests that want to handle large-scale capital exports, and certain intellectuals opposed to rapid change, claiming that petroleum revenues should be essentially exported, and possibly that petroleum development should be kept at a fairly low pace.

A counteralliance could also be in the making between directly petroleum-related industry, trade unions, industry sheltered from foreign competition, the service sector, and certain intellectuals less fearful of change, claiming that petroleum revenues essentially should be used domestically in order to improve living standards and public services, and that eventually the pace of development should be raised. This may be indicative of a significant shift in Norwegian petroleum politics. Initially, enthusiasm for petroleum was declining from right to left; currently, in the early 1980s, the forces of the right are becoming increasingly critical of the overall effects of petroleum development and its revenues upon Norwegian society, whereas the forces of the left show an increasing interest in the public revenues from the petroleum sector and the resulting potential for social transformation, especially in a period of prolonged international recession.

This is partly linked to the effect of the petroleum industry and petroleum revenues upon Norway's political economy. Even if, as argued earlier, the distinction between the private and the public sector is largely of a formal nature, it is evident that petroleum development, through the high degree of nationalization and through state control of a large part of the petroleum rent, does strengthen the public sector in relation to the private one. Access to petroleum revenues means that the public sector can finance itself to a larger extent, with the bargaining power of the private sector correspondingly reduced. Thus, within the current institutional framework, the petrolization of the Norwegian economy is also largely its socialization. This is one of the most intriguing aspects of the Norwegian petroleum experience. Marx and Lenin never thought of the possibility that the capitalist class could largely be pushed out by the market forces when the state appropriates the economic rent from an important natural resource. That alone could explain the ongoing shift in petroleum politics in Norway.

Recent Economic Performance

Norwegian economic performance during the 1970s can be divided into three distinct periods: (1) the industrial expansion from 1970 to 1973, before the advent of petroleum revenues; (2) the continued expansion from 1974 to 1977, stimulated by the countercyclical economic policy, financed by foreign borrowing, and thereby mortgaging anticipated petroleum revenues; and (3) voluntary contraction since 1978, aiming at restoring industrial competitiveness and at keeping petroleum revenues largely outside the Norwegian economy, by repaying the foreign debt at a fast pace.

Each of these periods is marked by distinct performances of key economic indicators that have important structural effects. The shifts in economic policy in 1974 and in 1978 were the results of conscious policy choices, given apparent macroeconomic possibilities and constraints, and of apparent power relationships among the key bargaining partners in the Norwegian political economy. The shifts in economic policy during the 1970s have the character of discontinuities, contrasting with earlier experience and indicating turbulence, internationally as well as nationally. In a wider perspective, the Norwegian economic performance of the 1970s is characterized by the inclusion of petroleum revenues and by the effects of the change in the international economic environment in 1973-1974. The concurrence of these two factors has accentuated the structural effects, and the fight against them. Exactly when petroleum revenues entered the Norwegian economy on a large scale is a matter of definition; strictly speaking it happened around 1977-1978, but through borrowing it had been happening since 1974.

Before Petroleum Revenues—1970 to 1973. In the early 1970s, the growth of the Norwegian economy was stimulated by an expansionary international economic environment, and the emerging petroleum industry was seen as adding marginally to what was already a healthy growth rate. Thus, the *Long-Term Program*, published in the spring of 1973, anticipated a steady 4.5-percent growth rate of the nonpetroleum portion of the economy, with petroleum adding another 1.0 pecent, giving an anticipated average overall growth rate of 5.5 percent a year until 1977.[18] At this time there was a trade surplus corresponding to about 2 percent of the gross national product, and priority was given to maintaining the trade surplus and boosting industrial investment rather than to private and public consumption. This program proved to be of little significance, as the basic economic and political premises were short-lived. At the elections of September 1973 the outgoing Liberal-Centrist coaltion government was replaced by a Labor government, with a strong left-socialist opposition in Parliament. The oil price rise and the change in the international economic environment meant that the relative proportions of the petroleum and the nonpetroleum sectors would change markedly.

Continued Expansion—1974 to 1977. The new Labor government in the winter of 1974 presented a subsequent petroleum plan, which also was thought of as an alternative overall economic program.[19] The risk of overheating the economy because of the rapid growth of petroleum revenues was now seen as the key problem. Consequently, a moderate pace of development of the petroleum sector was recommended together with a moderate domestic use of petroleum revenues.

This time, a high priority was given to the growth of private and public consumption. The underlying assumption was that no significant change would occur in the growth pattern of the nonpetroleum part of the Norwegian economy. Almost immediately after presenting the new plan, the government embarked upon a very different policy. As it became evident that there would be an international recession affecting demand for Norwegian goods and services, it was decided to implement a counter-cyclical policy to neutralize the effects of the international economic recession, so that a high level of employment could be maintained. As a substantial financial surplus was forecast to occur as soon as 1977, the counter-cyclical policy was seen as taking part of a fairly near future surplus to bridge an immediate gap; this was approved unanimously by Parliament.

At the same time a large-scale rescue operation was initiated for Norwegian shipowners, who had overinvested in the wake of the first oil crisis. As the international recession continued, the countercyclical policy developed into a massive subsidization of the manufacturing industry, as well as of shipping. By the beginning of 1978 about a quarter of the jobs in manufacturing depended upon direct government subsidies, and in some cases the subsidies were higher than the wage bill. Political pressure for increasing real wages had built up as a result of modest wage settlements in the years 1971 to 1973, giving stagnant or declining real wages in contrast with a significant rise in profits and related income. Furthermore, the countercyclical policy created a very tight labor market as some firms were paid to hoard labor while others were crying out for it. Not surprisingly, labor found itself in a strong bargaining position. Real wages rose by about 25 percent from 1974 to 1977, the bulk of which was caused by wage drift, coming in addition to the wage increases negotiated between the Trade Union Confederation and the Employers' Federation in 1976 and 1977 with active state participation in order to moderate nominal wage increases.

At the same time, Norwegian policy was to link their currency to the European snake and thus to the West German mark, which in these years was appreciating. This currency arrangement, widely termed a "snake," embodied cooperation among several Western European central banks to control excessive fluctuations of the various currencies involved by setting upper and lower limits. A multitude of factors led to poor performance of Norwegian traditional exports and a persistent loss of market shares. Finally, petroleum development, as it moved into deeper waters and more hostile weather conditions, proved much more costly and time consuming than originally anticipated, and the expected petroleum revenues did not materialize. Thus, by 1977, instead of having a comfortable financial surplus as anticipated three years earlier, Norway found herself deep in debt; by the spring of 1978 the foreign debt amounted to about $20 billion, corresponding to half the gross national product; this was the highest debt ratio ever attained by an OECD country. Even if Norway's foreign debt was backed by large petroleum reserves, the situation was worrisome.

Voluntary Contraction—Since 1978. In early 1978 economic policy was completely reversed. After a devaluation, the Norwegian currency was taken out of the European "snake." In the early fall of 1978 a mandatory wage and price freeze was introduced, to last until the end of 1979, aimed at restoring industrial competitiveness and exports. In petroleum policy licensing was drastically stepped up; at the same time, access to acreage was linked to industrial deals, aimed at using petroleum as leverage to increase industrial employment. The wage and price freeze was a short-lived success; after bringing down the rate of inflation in 1979, a substantial inflationary pressure was built up, leading to high rates of inflation in 1980 and 1981. There has been so far no lasting restoration of industrial competitiveness and the loss of market shares has continued. In hindsight, it was the second oil price rise of 1979-1980 that saved the situation, raising substantially the level of petroleum revenues; simultaneously output expanded. This also underlines the dependence of the Norwegian economy upon the petroleum sector, a situation that economic policy a few years earlier explicitly sought to avoid.

At this point reference should be made to the 1974 plan, mentioned earlier, as it so far constitutes the only economic strategy ever worked out in Norway in relation to petroleum. Even if its basic premises changed substantially and its recommendations were not followed up, the exercise merits considerable attention.

The key assumption of this plan was that the pre-1973 growth rates of the international economy essentially would continue; in this perspective the risk of overheating the economy naturally emerged as the chief concern. Particular attention was given to the effects of the oil industry and of the petroleum revenues on the domestic economy, especially on the labor market. The transition of labor between industries and regions was of key concern, and the plan was based on detailed calculations and projections about the position of industries exposed to foreign competition and those sheltered from it. The direct labor demand of the petroleum industry was seen as a minor problem, but the demand for labor resulting from the domestic use of oil revenues was seen as a major problem, justifying the recommendation that only half the petroleum revenues be used domestically. Furthermore, the priority given to the growth of private consumption was justified by calculations on the employment effects of different uses of incremental revenues.

Thus, increasing public consumption clearly appeared as the most labor-intensive way of spending petroleum revenues, whereas increasing private consumption and investing in equipment and machinery were the least labor intensive, as shown in table 3-2. The lower figures for 1980 compared with 1974 are due to an expected productivity increase of about 2 percent a year, so that a constant use of oil revenues would have a gradually diminishing effect upon the labor market (see table 3-3).

Table 3-2
Norway: Estimated Increase in Labor in the Sector Sheltered from Foreign Competition with Increased Deliveries to Different End Uses
(*1 billion NOK, 1974 prices*)

	Required labor increase	
End use	1974	1980
Private consumption	5,000	4,000
Public consumption	18,000	16,000
Gross investment in:		
Construction	8,500	7,600
Plant and machinery	4,300	3,800

Source: Government of Norway, Ministry of Finance, *Petroleumsvirksomheten I Det Norske Samfunn*, St.meld.nr. 25 (1973-1974) (Oslo, 1974).

Note: NOK 1 billion in 1974 prices corresponds to approximately U.S. $200 million.

Table 3-3
Norway: Anticipated Growth of Employment, 1974-1980

	Numbers
Increased employment in petroleum industry	10,000
Increased employment in industries sheltered from foreign competition	85,000–100,000
Without use of petroleum revenues	75,000– 85,000
Increase due to reduced working hours	10,000– 15,000
Sum	95,000–110,000
Minus increase in employment	(75,000)
Anticipated decrease in employment in other industries without use of petroleum revenues	20,000– 35,000
Increase by using NOK 6 billion	40,000– 50,000
Anticipated decrease in other industries	60,000– 85,000

Source: Government of Norway, Ministry of Finance, *Petroleumsvirksomheten I Det Norske Samfunn*, St.meld.nr. 25 (1973-1974) (Oslo, 1974).

In 1974 total employment was 1,593,000, measured by man-years.[20] In the 1960s and early 1970s employment growth had been about 0.6 percent a year, and through special measures it was thought that employment growth could be increased to an annual 0.8 percent. No policy of stimulating immigration was considered. Thus, the bottom line of the calculation was that even with an accelerated employment growth and the domestic use of 6 billion Norwegian krones (NOK) of petroleum reserves (which was considered moderate), the net effect would be an employment decline in other industries in the order of 40,000 to 50,000 persons over the period 1974-1980 (see table 3-4).

This indicates that the Norwegian government, when deciding upon an economic strategy in relation to petroleum, had more than a rudimentary insight into alternatives and that the policy choice was both conscious and rational, according to information available. It is also evident that the capacity to absorb petroleum revenues was seen as a political issue, linked to the amount of structural change that was deemed acceptable.

Public revenues from the petroleum sector were roughly estimated to be NOK 8 to 12 billion (in 1974 prices) in 1978 and NOK 10 to 15 billion (in 1974 prices) in 1981-1982. The estimate was based on a projected level of petroleum extraction of 60 million tons of oil equivalent (toe) in 1978 and 90 million toe in 1981-1982. Spending all the petroleum revenues domestically, illustrated by the figure of NOK 12 billion by 1980, was considered unacceptable because of the pressure on the labor market and the structural effects, giving a decline of employment in industries exposed to foreign competition

Table 3-4

**Rough Calculation of Employment Decline in Norwegian Industries
Exposed to Foreign Competition 1974-1980 at Different Uses of
Petroleum Revenues in the Domestic Economy**
(*1974 prices; man-years; including effect of reduced working hours
corresponding to 10,000-15,000 additional man-years required*)

Employment	Domestic Use 1980 in Billion NOK			
	None	3 bn.	6 bn.	9 bn.
Total increase in employment	75,000	75,000	75,000	75,000
Increased employment in petroleum sector	10,000	10,000	10,000	10,000
Increased employment in sheltered industries	95,000	115,000	135,000	165,000
Required employment decline in other industries exposed to foreign competition	30,000	50,000	70,000	100,000

Source: Government of Norway, Ministry of Finance, *Petroleumsvirksomheten I Det Norske
Samfunn*, St.meld.nr. 25 (1973-1974) (Oslo, 1974).

of about 100,000 persons between 1974 and 1980 (see table 3-4). Instead, it
was decided to spend domestically half the projected petroleum revenues,
NOK 6 billion (in 1974 prices) by 1980, which according to calculations
should give an employment decline of about 70,000 persons in industries
exposed to foreign competition between 1974 and 1980. Even this more
moderate use of petroleum revenues was met with heavy criticism, as structural effects were seen as too strong. This again underlines the political
character of the notion of absorptive capacity of oil revenues, at least in the
Norwegian context.

First, the gross rate of economic growth has been somewhat lower than
projected, the annual average being 4.5 percent instead of 5.5 percent (see
table 3-5 and 3-6). However, during the 1970s Norway has had a remarkably high rate of economic growth; average annual volume growth in the
OECD area from 1974 to 1979 was second only to that of Japan, which per-
formed at an annual average rate of 5.0 percent, and Greece and Turkey,
countries at different levels of development.

The growth performance outside the petroleum sector, an annual
average of 2.5 percent, is fairly comparable to the rest of Northwest
Europe, but this was, as already mentioned, much less than anticipated.
This was partly made up by the growth of the oil sector at a faster pace than
projected. Total exports rose at a considerably slower rate than anticipated,
and for nonpetroleum exports there is a fairly dramatic difference between

Table 3-5

Anticipated Performance of the Norwegian Economy, 1972-1980

(million NOK in constant 1972 prices)

	1972			1977			1980		
	Total	Norway without Petroleum	Petroleum Sector*	Total	Norway without Petroleum	Petroleum Sector*	Total	Norway without Petroleum	Petroleum Sector*
Gross national product	96,666	96,552	114	128,800	121,500	7,300	147,800	138,300	9,500
Export surplus	275	889	-614	3,600	-2,200	5,800	4,300	-3,800	8,100
Exports	39,609	39,401	208	63,200	56,000	7,200	77,600	68,500	9,100
Imports	39,334	38,512	822	59,600	58,200	1,400	73,300	72,300	1,000
Net deliveries to Petroleum sector	—	200	-200	—	400	-400	—	100	-100
Deliveries to petroleum sector	—	230	-230	—	900	-900	—	1,000	-1,000
Deliveries from petroleum sector	—	-30	30	—	-500	500	—	-900	900
Supply of goods and services	96,391	95,463	928	125,200	123,300	1,900	143,500	142,000	1,500
Gross Investment	27,533	26,605	928	40,100	38,200	1,900	45,400	43,900	1,500
Petroleum sector	928	—	928	1,900	—	1,900	1,500	—	1,500
Remainder	26,605	26,605	—	38,200	38,200	—	43,900	—	—
Private consumption	52,955	52,955	—	65,400	65,400	—	75,800	—	—
Public consumption	15,903	15,903	—	19,700	19,700	—	22,300	22,300	—
Use of Goods and Services	96,391	95,463	928	125,200	123,300	1,900	143,500	142,000	1,500

Source: Government of Norway, Ministry of Finance, *Petroleumsvirksomheten I Det Norske Samfunn*, St.meld.nr. 25 (1973-74) (Oslo, 1974).

*Petroleum sector includes extraction of oil and natural gas, transportation of oil and natural gas by pipelines.

Table 3-6
Actual Performance of the Norwegian Economy, 1972-1980
(million NOK in constant 1972 prices)[a]

	1972			1977			1980		
	Total	Norway without Petroleum	Petroleum Sector[b]	Total	Norway without Petroleum	Petroleum Sector[b]	Total[c]	Norway without Petroleum	Petroleum Sector[b]
Gross national product	96,666	96,552	114	121,996	116,994	5,002	137,841	117,165	20,676
Export surplus	275	889	-614	-13,060	-11,823	-1,237	2,133	-13,069	15,202
Exports	39,609	39,401	209	48,576	43,134	5,442	62,393	45,262	17,131
Imports	39,334	38,512	822	61,636	54,957	6,679	60,260	58,331	1,929
Net deliveries to petroleum sector	—	—	—	633	—	—	3,039	—	—
Supply of goods and services	96,941	97,441	-500	109,569	105,171	3,765	143,013	104,096	35,878
Gross Investment	27,533	26,605	928	44,266	35,628	8,608	37,646	33,424	4,222
Petroleum sector	928	—	928	8,608	—	8,608	4,222	—	4,222
Rest	26,605	26,605	—	35,658	35,658	—	33,424	33,424	—
Private consumption	52,955	52,955	—	66,188	66,188	—	65,829	65,829	—
Public consumption	15,903	15,903	—	24,602	24,602	—	27,411	27,411	—
Use of Goods and Services	96,391	95,463	928	135,056	126,448	8,608	130,886	126,664	4,222

Source: Government of Norway, Ministry of Finance, *National Budgets 1979* and *1980* (Oslo, 1978 and 1979).

[a]Figures in 1972 prices are derived from actual figures for 1977 in 1977 prices and for 1980 in 1979 prices through a general deflating factor, based on the overall rate of inflation. The table is meant as an illustration of development trends only. As at the time of writing figures for 1980 were provisional, in 1979 prices, the price rises on oil from 1979 to 1980 were not captured; consequently figures underestimate importance of petroleum sector.

[b]Petroleum sector includes extraction of oil and natural gas, and transportation of oil and natural gas.

[c]General price deflator used to adjust 1977 figures to 1972 prices is 1.57; the one used to adjust 1980 figures, originally given in 1979 prices, to 1972 prices, is 1.77.

projection and performance, an annual average of 1.8 percent as opposed to the anticipated 7.2 percent, indicating the change in the international business climate and the loss of market shares, both of which were unexpected. Again, this was partly compensated for by petroleum exports growing in value at a faster pace than projected, essentially because of the second oil price jump of 1979-1980, which also was unexpected.

Gross investment grew less than projected, especially outside the petroleum sector. In the petroleum sector gross investment grew at a rate more than three times what had been forecast, reflecting the unexpected cost escalation of North Sea petroleum development. Finally, private consumption grew less than anticipated, whereas public consumption grew much more, indicating that the intentions concerning the balance between private and public consumption had not been respected.

Actual performance has differed remarkably from what was projected (see table 3-7). This is essentially related to the poorer performance of the nonpetroleum portion of the economy compared to expectations. The oil sector has grown more than anticipated in terms of value, as unexpected price increases have more than offset the lower development in volume. Consequently, by 1980 the petroleum sector had a more predominant role in the Norwegian economy than that anticipated in 1974.

To sum up, the overall economic growth from 1973 to 1980 was not much less than what had been projected, measured in aggregate quantitative

Table 3-7
Comparison of Projected and Actual Performance of Norwegian Economic Indicators, 1974-1980
(*percentages*)

Indicator	Average Annual Growth Rates	
	Projection	Performance
Gross national product (GNP)	5.5	4.5
GNP without petroleum sector	4.6	2.5
Petroleum sector	73.8	91.6
Exports	8.8	5.8
Exports without petroleum	7.2	1.8
Petroleum exports	60.4	73.6
Imports	8.1	5.8
Gross investment	6.5	4.0
Gross investment without petroleum	6.5	2.9
Gross investment petroleum sector	6.2	20.9
Private consumption	4.6	2.8
Public consumption	4.3	7.0
Petroleum sector/GNP status 1980	6.4	15.0
Petroleum sector/gross investment 1980	3.3	11.2
Petroleum sector/exports 1980	11.7	27.5

Source: Tables 3-5 and 3-6.

terms, but qualitatively, measured by its composition, the performance was quite different from projections (table 3-8). Petroleum and public consumption grew much more than anticipated, at the expense of manufacturing, private consumption, and investment outside the petroleum sector (table 3-9). Thus, the kind of structural change that had been feared in 1973-1974 and was seen as undesirable had been realized.

One of the more unexpected developments was the much faster growth of total unemployment compared with projections. (In mid-1983 unemployment was close to 4 percent.) As pointed out earlier, total employment in Norway until the early 1970s had grown at an average annual rate of 0.6 percent, which was considered raised to 0.8 percent through special measures.[21] By comparison, the average annual rate of increase of employment measured by man-years from 1973 to 1980 was 1.3 percent, or more than twice the historical average and considerably higher than what had been considered possible even with special measures added. The number of persons employed, which also includes part-time work, rose even more quickly, at an average annual rate of 2.1 percent a year from 1973 to 1980 (table 3-10). The total rise in employment was primarily the result of more women entering the labor market; the discrepancy between the rise in the number of persons employed and the increase in man-years worked indicates the expansion of part-time work,

Table 3-8
The Generation of the Norwegian Gross National Product
(million NOK at current prices)

	1973		1977		1980	
	Amount	*Percentage*	*Amount*	*Percentage*	*Amount*	*Percentage*
Agriculture, forestry, fishing	6,169	5.6	11,075	5.8	12,623	4.5
Mining			949	0.5	1,328	0.5
Petroleum extraction	1,009	0.9	7,156	3.8	39,894	14.1
Industry, construction, power	35,747	32.6	56,301	29.7	74,649	26.4
Trade and transportation*	38,942	35.6	48,459	25.5	67,887	24.0
Services	27,632	25.2	58,386	30.8	86,739	30.6
Total	109,499		189,709		283,120	
Sheltered from foreign competition			143,548	75.7	190,430	67.2
Exposed in foreign markets			13,853	7.3	21,714	7.7
Exposed in home markets			24,753	13.1	29,127	10.3
Petroleum extraction and transportation			7,565	4.0	41,849	14.8

Source: Compiled from Government of Norway, Central Bureau of Statistics, *Economic Survey 1973* and *1980* (Oslo, 1974 and 1980).

*Includes oil and gas pipeline transportation.

Table 3-9
The Use of the Norwegian Gross National Product
(*million NOK at current prices*)

Uses	1973 Amount	1973 Percentage	1977 Amount	1977 Percentage	1980 Amount	1980 Percentage
Private consumption	58,332	53.3	103,915	54.2	133,299	47.1
Public consumption total	17,746	16.2	38,625	20.2	53,653	19.0
Civilian	14,320	13.1	32,884	17.2	45,520	16.1
Military	3,426	3.1	5,741	3.0	8,133	2.9
Gross investment total	33,771	30.8	69,498	36.3	79,668	28.1
Petroleum	2,820	2.6	13,515	7.1	6,898	2.4
Shipping	5,154	4.7	7,428	3.9	3,724	1.3
Other	27,457	22.6	50,131	29.1	60,937	21.5
Stock changes	1,044	0.9	−1,576	−0.8	8,109	2.9
Export surplus	−350	−0.3	−20,504	−10.7	16,500	5.8
Exports	48,700	44.5	76,264	39.8	134,800	47.6
Imports	49,050	44.8	96,768	50.5	118,300	41.8

Sources: Compiled from Government of Norway, Central Bureau of Statistics, *Economic Survey 1973* and *1980* (Oslo, 1974 and 1981).

essentially by married women. This rapid rise in employment largely resulted from the countercyclical policy and the growth of public consumption.

These figures indicate that the potential growth of employment could have been even higher, 1.3 percent as the yearly average, if registered unemployed are counted as potentially working a full man-year. Measured in man-years, the growth of employment from 1974 to 1980 was 124,000, or 65 percent higher than the projected figure of 75,000. The additional ap-

Table 3-10
Norway: The Development of Employment, 1973-1977
(*1000s*)

Total employment	1973 Numbers	1973 Percentage	1977 Numbers	1977 Percentage	1980 Numbers	1980 Percentage
Agriculture, forestry, fishing	189	11.4	165	9.1	161	8.4
Mining, manufacturing, power	413	25.0	434	23.8	421	22.0
Building and construction	142	8.6	156	8.6	146	7.6
Trade and transportation	397	24.0	480	26.6	498	26.0
Services	525	31.2	586	32.1	684	35.8
Total persons employed	1,653		1,824		1,913	
Man-years worked	1,571		1,657		1,717	
Jobs vacant yearly average		8.2		8.8		8.0
Registered unemployed		12.8		16.1		22.0

Source: Government of Norway, Central Bureau of Statistics, *Statistical Yearbook 1981* (Oslo, 1981), p. 51, and *Organization for Economic Cooperation and Development (OECD), Norway: OECD Economic Survey* (Paris: OECD, 1981), p. 59.

proximate 50,000 man-years available in the iabor market meant that with a given amount of domestic use of petroleum revenues, there was a correspondingly smaller requirement for reducing employment in the industries exposed to foreign competition, assumptions about productivity development being unchanged. From 1975 to 1979 the number of man-years in manufacturing and mining exposed to foreign competition declined from 274,000 to 255,000, at an average yearly rate of 1.8 percent, giving a total decline of 19,000 man-years. Even if exact figures for the period 1973-1980 are not yet available, it is evident that the decline of employment in the industries exposed to foreign competition has been much less than the projected 70,000 man-years.

Capital formation and investment have fluctuated considerably during the period 1973-1980, partly because of a changing pattern of petroleum investment, which has taken up an increasing share of total investment. This development was evident already in the early 1970s; gross investment had a volume increase of 15.4 percent from 1972 to 1973 and of 10.4 percent from 1973 to 1974. By 1974 gross investment represented 32 percent of the gross national product. Gross investment continued to increase at a fast pace until 1977, after which there has been a decline in total investment, stabilizing in 1979 and 1980 at a level somewhat lower than that of 1975, measured in constant prices (see table 3-11).

The decline in investment since 1977 is essentially related to the termination of some large petroleum projects and to the shipping crisis. Investment in other items, such as machinery and equipment, houses and buildings, construction projects, and the like has kept fairly constant, measured in real prices, since 1977. Over the period 1974 to 1980 total gross investment in fixed capital was (in million NOK in 1975 prices) 359,695, of which petroleum investment was NOK million 51,801 or 14.4 percent.

The size of the petroleum investment in relation to the Norwegian economy, together with its fluctuations over the years, made it rational both to finance petroleum investment largely from foreign sources and to import a

Table 3-11
Norway: Gross Investment in Fixed Capital by Items, 1974-1980
(constant 1975 prices, million NOK)

Item	1974	1975	1976	1977	1978	1979	1980
Petroleum	6,318	7,542	10,072	11,267	7,408	4,882	4,312
Ships	5,571	6,831	7,716	4,427	1,273	1,731	2,159
Other	33,247	36,418	38,145	42,247	42,790	42,038	43,274
Total	45,136	50,791	55,933	57,968	51,471	48,651	49,745

Source: Government of Norway, Central Bureau of Statistics, *Economic Survey 1978* (Oslo, 1979), p. 97, and *Economic Survey 1980* (Oslo, 1981), p. 95.

considerable part of the equipment required. This had important repercussions both for the trade balance and for Norway's international financial position.

By 1973 Norway had a small trade deficit, corresponding to 0.5 percent of the GNP. The trade deficit increased rapidly from 1974 to 1977, when it represented 10.8 percent of the GNP. The reversed economic policy quickly restored a positive trade balance: the trade deficit in 1978 was only 0.9 percent of the GNP; by 1980 there was a trade surplus corresponding to 5.8 percent of the GNP. However, petroleum was also an essential factor in restoring the trade balance. Whereas the oil sector had a negative trade balance until 1976 (and a small positive balance in 1977), by 1978 it had a positive balance corresponding to 4.8 percent of the GNP; by 1980 this figure represented 14.6 percent of the GNP.[22] The surge in petroleum exports was essential as the shipping sector showed a stagnation of net foreign earnings (in real terms; by 1980 not reaching the level of 1973) and as the exports of other commodities also had a poor performance, with a fairly persistent loss of market shares on the average at a pace of 4 percent a year.

In 1970 Norway had no net foreign debt, except related to shipping. Between 1970 and 1973 the shipping debt was somewhat reduced, whereas there was net foreign borrowing both for the petroleum activities and for mainland Norway. After 1974 foreign borrowing accelerated, first to finance petroleum investment, second to finance the shipping rescue operation, and third to finance the countercyclical policy relating to the level of mainland economic activity (see table 3-12).

Until the end of 1976, the petroleum sector represented almost half the foreign borrowing, so that this part of the foreign debt was matched by investment in the oil sector, which was essentially export oriented. About a third of the foreign borrowing by this time had been earmarked for the shipping sector, essentially to prevent Norwegian ships from being sold at low prices abroad. Finally, borrowing to finance the countercyclical policy represented about a quarter of the foreign debt at this moment. In 1977 the expansionary countercyclical policy was continued, and this item then accounted for the bulk of foreign borrowing, meaning that the level of activity of the Norwegian economy outside shipping and petroleum largely was financed by borrowing abroad.

In 1981 the current balance deficit corresponded to 14.0 percent of the GNP, and the petroleum sector showed a slight positive balance. The reversal of economic policy, together with the increase of petroleum exports, soon led to an improved current balance, which by 1980 showed a surplus corresponding to 1.7 percent of the GNP. Estimates in 1980/81 were that the foreign debt would be paid by 1985-1986, unless there is new borrowing to finance an accelerated petroleum development. This, in light of the 1982 world oil-market conditions, may prove too optimistic on the retirement of Norway's foreign-debt burden.

Table 3-12

Norway: Current Balances and Credits to the Economy, 1974-1981

(million NOK)

Balances/Credits	1974	1975	1976	1977	1978	1979	1980	1981
Balance of payments								
Current balance	-6,164	-12,692	-20,370	-26,802	-11,005	-5,278	5,495	12,100
Official	8	4,659	4,771	6,377	10,000	4,693	-1,743	—
Financial institutions	-2	415	930	3,427	4,812	4,941	2,128	—
Shipping companies	1,316	1,350	1,815	1,938	-1,179	187	-274	—
Direct investment	1,105	211	977	3,435	2,232	1,804	-963	—
Other	3,564	6,961	8,857	7,592	3,172	-40	-3,242	—
Long-term capital net	5,985	13,480	17,090	22,889	16,842	11,535	-4,094	—
Credits to the economy								
Domestic credit	—	—	137,665	161,005	183,399	207,357	230,525	—
Security market (bond issues, domestic and foreign currency)	8,193	17,491	15,870	22,400	24,485	24,735	24,480	—
Gold and foreign exchange holdings	1,861	2,207	1,743	1,820	2,628	3,642	4,632	—

Source: Compiled from Government of Norway, Central Bureau of Statistics, *Economic Survey 1974 to 1981* (Oslo, 1975 to 1982).

It is now evident that some critical assumptions behind the choice of economic and petroleum policies in 1973-1974 proved wrong.

1. The petroleum development, as it moved further north in the North Sea, ran into unexpected cost and delay problems, meaning that for the Norwegian government petroleum revenues were both reduced and delayed compared with projections.
2. The change in the international economic environment had serious implications for the demand for Norwegian goods and services other than petroleum, in part because Norwegian exports to a large extent consist of semifinished products that are sensitive to changes in the business cycle and of goods with a low-income elasticity and little potential of expanding markets. This is a structural problem.
3. The application of the countercyclical policy, with subsidies being handed out fairly uncritically mainly in order to conserve employment, reinforced this structural problem in the sense that it discouraged change instead of stimulating it; it also created cost and productivity problems in the sense that it financed a rapid increase in labor costs without stimulating productivity.
4. The currency policy, tying the Norwegian krone to the European currency snake, had a negative effect upon competitiveness.
5. The calculations on the employment balance were wrong, seriously underestimating the potential for increasing labor supply, and thus overestimating the structural constraints on absorptive capacity.

If planners and politicians had shown better judgment in 1973-1974, it is possible if not probable that Norway would have embarked upon a fairly different economic and oil strategy, aimed at both accelerated petroleum development and improvement of the manufacturing industry's competitiveness. In practical terms, this could have led to more aggressive petroleum licensing in the years 1974-1977, also emphasizing acreage in the southern part of the North Sea (where costs and lead times were less), so that petroleum revenues could be maximized at an earlier time. This could have been accompanied by a different countercyclical policy, stressing industrial investment instead of expanding public consumption in order to stimulate productivity improvement and structural change.

The currency policy could have been quite different by untying the Norwegian currency since 1973 from any link with the currencies of countries following a contrary economic policy. Such a stance could have led to even higher foreign borrowing for petroleum development, but with much less subsequent foreign borrowing for the countercyclical policy and for maintaining the level of economic activity in mainland Norway. This policy would probably have given a less drastic rise in real wages during the years

1974-1977 yet compensated by improved freedom of action in economic policy in subsequent years as the debt burden and structural adjustment then would have been less serious problems.

The experience of the 1970s thus shows that Norway's absorptive capacity for petroleum revenues had been seriously underestimated, especially if absorptive capacity is seen as the ability to spend such revenues, not as the ability to invest them with a reasonable rate of return. The key factors are the greater supply of labor, as compared to projections, and the change in the international economic climate meaning that petroleum revenues were welcomed as a substitute for other revenues. To a large extent, petroleum revenues, at first anticipated by borrowing abroad, offset the slack in demand for the rest of Norway's export industries. As already shown, the impact upon the employment balance, and thus the structural impact of using petroleum revenues domestically, has been much less than projected, and domestic expenditure has been much more than projected. It should also be noted that to some extent the economic system has changed as petroleum revenues have been used largely to support other activities. This use of petroleum revenues was not anticipated when absorptive capacity was considered in 1973-1974.

Whereas the plan in 1974 was to spend approximately NOK 6 billion annually of petroleum revenues domestically, it is possible that the amount of money spent domestically, financed by foreign borrowing (which is functionally equivalent to petroleum revenues), has been close to twice that amount on the average during the years 1974-1977. By 1980, as already pointed out, petroleum revenues made up a substantial part of the Norwegian economy and, even if some is used to service the foreign debt, there is a fairly considerable net transfer of income from the petroleum sector to the economy of mainland Norway essentially through petroleum taxation and the public budget.

Transferring income from an external sector to mainland Norway is nothing new; this was the case with shipping until the crisis of 1973-1974. However, the transfer from shipping was of smaller magnitude, and it went more directly to the private sector than to the government. In 1982, about NOK 29-30 billion (corresponding to about 8 percent of the GNP) are transferred from the petroleum sector to the government, an amount that would have been the budget deficit without petroleum taxes. This can be seen as a problem or as an advantage, depending upon the political perspective. It is a problem if expanding the public sector, even within limits that are financially reasonable, is seen as negative, compromising the competitiveness of the private sector. It is an advantage if expanding the public sector is seen as positive and as a means to improve living standards and social conditions.

A debate is currently building in Norway over the use of petroleum revenues. This is related to a dispute over the nature of the structural problem and the cause of declining industrial competitiveness. There are essentially two schools of thought: one conservative, one radical. The conservative school of thought sees the domestic use of petroleum revenues as the main cause of Norway's lagging industrial competitiveness because using petroleum revenues domestically leads to rising labor costs and declining competitiveness.[23] It recommends paying off the foreign debt as soon as possible, and subsequently to invest petroleum revenues on a large scale abroad. This school of thought explicitly wants to preserve the place of the manufacturing industry in the economy. It also wants to reduce the current transfer of income from the petroleum sector to mainland Norway, seeing this as a condition for raising industrial competitiveness. This approach largely represents a coalition of manufacturing industries exposed to foreign competition who fear the impact of petroleum revenues, and banking, which wants to handle large-scale capital investment abroad, plus some more marginal forces such as agricultural interests that also fear structural change.

The radical school of thought sees Norway's industrial problem as structural, linked to an outdated pattern of production and an inability to follow the change in export markets caused by a managerial problem rather than a cost problem. For example, several studies indicate that labor costs do not make up the essential factor behind lagging industrial competitiveness. There is evidence that only a third of the loss of market shares in the 1970s was due to the labor cost problem, the rest traceable to a structural and managerial problem in the sense that the composition of exports did not catch up with the changing foreign markets.[24] There is also evidence that the current policy and productivity problems arising from both the countercyclical policy and managerial performance could explain much of the loss of competitiveness.[25]

This school of thought recommends the domestic use of petroleum revenues so that they can be of benefit to the Norwegian population.[26] It finds that the problems of adaptation have often been exaggerated, that the kind of structural change which is needed, industrially and managerially, would be discouraged by keeping the petroleum revenues outside mainland Norway, and that consequently the process of industrial and managerial change will be stimulated by the domestic, selective use of petroleum revenues.[27] This approach even sees the transfer of income to mainland Norway as a way of increasing means available for investment in plant and equipment and in education as well as in social services. It considers the preservation of the current industrial pattern irrelevant and counterproductive, given the longevity of Norway's petroleum reserves.[28] This school of thought represents a coalition of trade unions, public-sector employees, and petroleum and petroleum-related industry that sees benefits in a tight labor market and accelerated structural change. So far, this discussion has concerned mainly the use of petroleum revenues, but it also implicitly concerns the level of extraction, substantiating the shift in Norwegian petroleum politics referred to earlier.

In this perspective, the question of absorptive capacity is essentially a question of political economy, referring not only to the pace of structural economic change that is seen as tolerable but also referring to the power relations between labor and capital (as well as between the different parts of capital) and not the least to the balance between the private and the public sector. When Norway's foreign debt eventually will have been repaid (optimistically by 1985), more money will be available for domestic use and consequently these issues will become even more acute.

Structural Analysis

Petroleum. In a global perspective, Norway is a marginal exporter of oil and gas, both in the sense of small volumes and in the sense of high costs. The volume, about 55 million tons of oil equivalent extracted in 1981, represents some 2 percent of total OECD petroleum consumption. However, within the natural market areas (Northwest Europe and the eastern part of North America for oil and Western Europe for gas), the position is somewhat stronger, especially if considering the market for light crude in this area. Also, the market share for natural gas in Western Europe is not negligible; in the United Kingdom Norwegian gas accounts for about 20 percent of the market, while in the combined area of West Germany, France, Belgium, and The Netherlands the figure is about 12 percent.

As indicated earlier, the reserve estimates are uncertain and highly conservative, given the fairly limited amount of exploratory drilling carried out to date. Reserves in the Norwegian portion of the North Sea, that is, south of 62°N, are estimated now to be about 4,000 to 5,000 million tons of oil equivalent; this figure excludes some major recent discoveries which are under evaluation. The area south of 62°N represents about 15 percent of the total Norwegian continental shelf. A cautious guess is that the area north of 62°N contains twice the reserves of the southern zone; thus the total of estimates adds up to approximately 12,000 million tons of oil equivalent. However, this figure is hypothetical and could possibly underestimate the total reserves. In this perspective, it is quite probable that Norway will be able to sustain oil and gas extraction for a considerable time, possibly far into the next century. The figure of 90 million tons of oil equivalent, which has been presented as an indication of a moderate level of activity, could possibly be sustained for well over 100 years.

Such an output level yet has to be reached (table 3-13), and so far development on the Norwegian continental shelf has proved to be more difficult, more costly, and more time consuming than expected. In the North Sea development takes place at water depths of 100 to 250 meters, in extremely heavy weather conditions. Further north, water depths are somewhat greater, and weather conditions roughly comparable. With the cost escalation that has taken place, the cost of extracting petroleum on the Norwegian continental shelf varies from about $3 to $20 a barrel. The Norwegian oil extraction takes place on a technological frontier, which requires a high degree of innovation. In this sense, Norwegian petroleum development is comparable to that of offshore Eastern Canada and of Alaska.

Norway's petroleum history commenced in 1962 when the government was first approached by foreign oil companies. In 1965 a concessionary framework was ready, and exploratory drilling could commence. The first commercial discoveries were made in 1969, and oil extraction began in 1971, with gas extraction starting in 1977; by 1975 Norway was self-sufficient in oil.

The institutional framework, the concessionary regime designed in 1965, has basically been retained with some adjustments. The principle of state participation was introduced in 1969 on a carried-interest basis. In 1972 a national oil company, Statoil, was established to take care of the government's commercial interests in the petroleum sector. Also in 1972 a separate Petroleum Directorate was established to take care of coordination and regulation of activities. In 1978 a separate ministry for oil and energy matters was established as the petroleum activities then had reached a level of great national importance. Since 1974 there has been a minimum state participatiou of 50 percent in all new concessions, potentially sliding up to 85 percent, depending upon the size of the field.

Table 3-13
Norway's Extraction of Oil and Gas, 1971-1980

Year	Oil (million tons)	Gas (1,000 million cubic meters)
1971	0.3	—
1972	1.6	—
1973	1.6	—
1974	1.7	—
1975	9.2	—
1976	13.6	—
1977	13.4	2.6
1978	17.2	13.4
1979	19.0	20.8
1980	24.2	25.8

Source: Government of Norway, Ministry of Petroleum and Energy, *Fact Sheet: Norwegian Continental Shelf* 1981:1 (Oslo, 1981).

At the outset, the petroleum activities were subject to normal company taxation only. The oil price rises of 1973-1974 and of 1979-1980 yielded large windfall profits, and consequently a need for special petroleum taxation. In 1975 a special petroleum-tax regime was introduced, including an extraordinary tax on petroleum profits after the company tax had been applied, but also incorporating a provision that capital costs could be written off two-and-a-half times as a safeguard against unexpected cost increases. The purpose was to capture a large part of the additional petroleum rent arising from the oil price increase for the government. The result was a very progressive tax: that also meant the major burden of cost increases would be carried by the government as lost tax receipts, especially given the capital-cost write-off provision. Thus, the tax system did not significantly stimulate cost consciousness. In 1980 the rate of the special tax was increased from 25 to 35 percent, and the capital-cost deduction was reduced from 250 to 200 percent. After 1975, the purpose was to catch about 70 percent of net profits as tax; after 1980 the ambition was to take around 85 percent, but it is doubtful whether this ambition will be fulfilled given the deduction facilities, including financial costs. Deduction facilities are more generous in the Norwegian petroleum-tax regime than in the British one, and the total government take is probably somewhat lower in Norway than on comparable fields in the United Kingdom.

Against this background, there is some criticism in Norway of both the petroleum tax system and of the concessionary regime. Currently, modifications of the concessionary system are being reviewed by the Norwegian administration, and the possibility of substituting concessions by entrepreneurial contracts is also being studied. For a long time it has been an important political priority to use an increasing share both of Norwegian goods and services and of personnel and to give Norwegian companies a preferential position. This policy of Norwegianization is running into some difficulties because of limited industrial capacity and limited human resources in particular, so that the petroleum sector to some extent takes qualified personnel away from other industries, adding to their problems. This is but one of several reasons why Norway would find it difficult to do without foreign oil companies, especially if petroleum development is to be stepped up.

The immediate prospects may appear modest in relation to the resource base, but consideration should be given to technical complexity and lead times of around ten years in many cases. Total output of oil and natural gas is likely to rise to 60 million tons of oil equivalent by 1985 and to 75 million toe by 1990, essentially on the basis of fields that presently are operating and a few other fields that will be developed in the early 1980s (see table 3-14). After 1990 output will decline unless more fields are brought on stream, but output could also rise considerably if new large fields are

Table 3-14
**Estimated Output of Petroleum, Price and Gross Production Value,
1980-1990**

Year	Petroleum Output (million tons of oil equivalent)	Price (US $/bl., 1980 prices)	Price (US $/bl., current prices)	Gross Value (1,000 million NOK, 1980 prices)	Gross Value 1,000 million NOK, current prices)
1980	50	34.00	34.00	49.8	49.8
1981	52	35.02	37.40	53.3	56.6
1982	54	36.07	41.10	57.0	64.3
1983	56	37.15	45.20	61.0	73.1
1984	59	38.27	49.80	65.3	83.1
1985	62	39.42	54.80	69.9	94.5
1986	65	40.60	60.20	74.8	107.4
1987	67	41.82	66.30	80.0	122.1
1988	70	43.07	72.90	85.6	138.8
1989	73	44.36	80.20	91.6	157.8
1990	75	45.69	88.20	98.0	179.3
Annual growth rates	4.0	3.0	10.0	7.0	14.0

Source: Olav Bjerkholt, Lorents Lorentsen, and Steinar Strøm, "Norge i 1980-Årene: Ol-jepenger og Omstillinger," in *Bergen Banks Kvartalsskrift,* no.1/1981, p. 207.

developed. As discoveries recently have had a gas to oil ratio of about 60:40, this composition is likely to be reflected in future output.

Future petroleum revenues are highly uncertain, depending not only upon volumes of oil and gas extracted, but also upon prices and exchange rates. Recently, this uncertainty has been shown by a wide variance of estimates. In the national budget for 1982, presented in the autumn of 1981, estimated public petroleum revenues over the years 1982 to 1985 were put at NOK 170 billion. In the revised national budget, presented in the spring of 1982, this estimate was reduced by two-thirds to NOK 60 billion. However, later in 1982 the estimate of public petroleum revenues for 1982-1985 was revised yet again, this time upwards because of higher oil output than expected and a more favorable exchange rate in relation to the U.S. dollar. This has several practical implications, apart from making government and Parliament more careful about spending programs. The foreign public debt could possibly be repaid by 1985. Should this materialize, there would be funds available for investment abroad or domestic consumption. By early 1983 Norway was running a substantial foreign trade surplus. This trade balance, combined with the more recent 1982 projections, indicate that reduction in estimated public petroleum revenues was an overreaction, and that petroleum revenues for the period mentioned again could be closer to the figure considered initially. The new estimate (late 1982) is linked to an expectation of a lower exchange rate of the krone in relation to the U.S. dollar. In this case, the foreign debt could be repaid more quickly and disposable income increase more than anticipated in the spring of 1982. However, these changing estimates indicate the complexities that economic planning and economic policy confront in a petroleum economy.

Moreover, the foreign trade surplus of early 1983 presents Norway with a dilemma: domestic spending could fuel inflation and decrease the competitiveness of domestic industries; yet, if not spent domestically, growing foreign financial reserves and pressure on the krone could also negatively affect Norway's industrial competitiveness.

Agriculture, Forestry, and Fisheries. The primary sector, including agriculture, forestry, and fisheries, in 1980 generated 4.5 percent of the gross national product (table 3-8), with an employment representing 8.4 percent of the labor force (table 3-10). The expansion of all three is affected by problems related to the resource base.

Norwegian agriculture has natural obstacles related to climate and topography. Only a few areas have soil conditions and climate that are favorable to the large-scale growing of grain, and Norway's grain deficiency has been a recurrent problem since the Middle Ages, surfacing most recently during World War II. The mountainous character of the country means that most parts are unfit for farming, and areas fit for farming are often steep hillsides or scattered fields.

This is probably the key reason why Norway developed a property structure in agriculture quite different from most other European countries. There have only been a few large agricultural properties, and there have always been a large number of small farms. Indeed, together with Greece and Portugal, Norway is among the European countries having a large proportion of small-scale farming. Furthermore, Norwegian peasants were never serfs, and until recent times there has been new land to develop. Most Norwegian farms have an agricultural area of less than 5 decares, with the cultivated area making up 2.2 percent of total territory.

Crops grown include wheat, rye, barley, and oats, with barley being predominant and with a deficiency particularly in wheat. Livestock in 1980 comprised about 2 million sheep, 1 million cattle, and about 665,000 swine. There is also an extensive stock of blue fox and mink as well as tame reindeer. Norwegian agriculture is heavily mechanized, possibly with the world's highest ratio of agricultural mechanization. There is also an extensive use of artificial fertilizer, making Norwegian agriculture technologically very advanced by international standards.

Institutionally, Norwegian agriculture is fairly unique in the sense that it is protected and regulated, essentially under the auspices of the agricultural organizations. Marketing of agricultural products is, for practical purposes, a monopoly of cooperatives, protected by law. Pricing is differentiated in order to assist producers in more difficult areas, and there are strict regulations on large-scale industrial production of livestock. Through a specialized bank, owned by the state, farmers are assisted by preferential loans. Furthermore, Norwegian farmers have paid vacations, with the state paying for help, and a guaranteed escalation of real income similar to that of industrial workers.

Finally, there is considerable price subsidization of agricultural products. The total cost of support for agriculture was in 1981 around NOK 7 billion, or about 2.5 percent of the gross national product. It should be added that Norwegian farmers are exceptionally well organized politically and are a political force whose influence is larger than indicated by their number. Typically, they were a fairly decisive force in the struggle over membership in the European Economic Community, a membership that would have terminated their current protected situation.

Expansion of agricultural production can take place through improving yields, but more so through more efficient use of equipment, which requires larger holdings, and is thus a fairly slow process.

A relatively large part of Norway's territory, about 22.4 percent, is covered by forest, of which almost four-fifths are productive. Historically, Norway has been an important exporter of wood and wood products, and the forests have provided the resource base for a fairly substantial wood-processing industry. Most of the productive forests belong to individual farmers. Concerns for forest regeneration mean that the volume cut cannot be increased sizably without attention to the future resource base.

Employment in fisheries has declined drastically over the past twenty years, from about 45,000 in 1960 to 14,000 in 1980, measured by persons who are engaged in fishing as their sole or main occupation. Norwegian fisheries essentially consist of two different trades: mechanized fishing by large, modern trawlers, and fishing in small open boats. In recent years there has been a decline in volumes caught, because the resource base has been eroded due to serious overfishing in the maritime areas adjacent to Norway. Any expansion that is not to compromise the future resource base will have to be deferred until larger stocks have been regenerated. However, the rearing of fish is becoming a new industry along Norway's coast. Norway has Europe's largest catches, apart from the Soviet Union, and is Europe's leading exporter of fish, making the country a net exporter of proteins.

Industry. The Norwegian economy prior to petroleum development can be described as moderately industrialized, with the manufacturing sector being less important in terms of employment and share of gross national product than in countries such as Sweden, West Germany, or the United Kingdom.

The share of raw materials in exports was high, and semifinished products and standard goods as opposed to branded goods made up a higher proportion of industrial exports than in most other Northern European nations. Consequently, a large part of Norwegian industrial production was destined as inputs for production processes abroad. This meant that the value added was fairly modest as all the finishing did not take place in Norway, plus demand was sensitive to changes in the level of industrial activity abroad. As opposed to this, there was a smaller sector producing and exporting highly finished goods such as electronics and chemicals.

The capital structure in the Norwegian manufacturing industry is marked by a duality to some extent resembling the situation of the fisheries. On one hand there are a number of highly capital-intensive enterprises, essentially related to energy, in which the state has an important stake; on the other hand there are a large number of small firms, often owned by individuals or families. In general the technological level is high and equipment modern because of historically high rates of investment and reinvestment. Thus, the technical aspect of production is quite satisfactory. However, the managerial aspect is much less so, especially with regard to marketing and planning, and there is an acute shortage of skilled management.

In 1980 manufacturing accounted for about 16 percent of the gross national product. Even without using petroleum revenues domestically, industry's share of employment and the gross national product is likely to decline moderately through the 1980s; using petroleum revenues domestically will speed up this process.[29] If forecast petroleum revenues are used wholly in the domestic economy, the cost pressure could lead to stagnation of overall industrial production in terms of the gross value of production. The sectors exposed to foreign competition, such as textiles and clothing, paper and pulp, the chemical industry except for petrochemicals, metal production, and the mechanical industry (see table 3-15), would be the most affected.

Some managerial underdevelopment is revealed at several levels.

1. There is comparatively little research and development in the Norwegian manufacturing industry, in relative terms much less than in countries with a similar level of economic output, such as Sweden, The Netherlands, and the United States; a high proportion of expenditure on research and development takes place in the four or five largest firms, meaning that the vast majority of Norwegian enterprises have little or no expenditure on this item.
2. As a result, there is little independent product development, meaning that the product range of many firms is outdated and increasingly has to compete with countries with much lower costs.
3. Marketing, especially international marketing, is poorly developed in most Norwegian manufacturing firms. The prevailing philosophy is often

Table 3-15
Norwegian Manufacturing Industry by Sectors, 1979
(millions NOK)

Sector	Number of Enterprises	Employment	Gross Value of Production	Value Added	Wages and Salaries
Food	1,837	55,877	28,256	3,583	4,210
Textile, clothing	625	21,865	4,238	1,605	1,372
Wood	1,245	32,249	9,977	3,354	2,481
Paper, pulp	948	51,905	14,638	5,164	4,001
Chemicals	467	29,944	25,342	7,111	2,869
Minerals	436	12,525	4,125	1,674	1,102
Metals	107	26,103	14,273	4,918	2,589
Mechanical	2,325	124,625	36,072	14,048	11,741
Other	134	3,402	739	291	261
Total	8,124	358,495	137,661	41,748	30,627

Source: Compiled from Government of Norway, Central Bureau of Statistics, *Industrial Statistics, 1979* (Oslo, 1980).

   that good products will sell themselves; market planning usually comes after production planning in priority and in sequence, revealing a high degree of inward orientation.

4. Consequently most Norwegian manufacturing firms have little ability to innovate and to respond quickly to basic changes in their external environment through specialization of production and new market orientation; this essentially applies more to product development than to the introduction of new production technology.

5. In most cases there is a prevailing organizational climate that is not very conducive to innovation; new ideas are often seen as a threat to stability and the established order, as they threaten personal positions and established goals, functions, and work routines. This organizational climate is linked to personal or family ownership of many firms, with the owner in an active managerial position.

6. Business strategy in most cases can be described as passive, traditional, and imitative; most manufacturing firms have few ambitions of being technological leaders; innovation is based on the purchase of licenses and know-how; product development essentially takes place according to consumer demand and consumer specification; and what little research and development there is focuses on improving existing production processes.

   This divergence between the technical and managerial aspects of production means that traditional Norwegian manufacturing could operate fairly well in a stable and expanding economic environment, with labor costs well below those of neighboring Sweden. It also means that most products were well established in the market, with high or increasing international competition, many of which were standardized bulk products or products to be used as input factors in more advanced manufacturing abroad.

Contrary to neighboring Sweden, which until the 1970s had higher labor costs, Norwegian industry has had a fairly modest development of special brands of manufactured goods for international marketing; instead, the proportion of standardized bulk manufactures has been relatively high. This kind of manufacturing yields less added value (see table 3-16), usually less profits, and is generally more sensitive to changes in demand and labor costs than is the case with special brands that have established international markets. The fairly heavy proportion of bulk manufactures reflects Norway's backwardness in product development as well as in marketing and in management in general. Thus, in output structure and managerial structure, the Norwegian manufacturing industry has been in an especially unfavorable position to encounter the combination of rising labor costs, rising currency exchange rates, and the slack in international demand that occurred in the 1970s.

The industrial picture discussed here has its roots in Norwegian culture and society. It can be seen as an expression of a highly homogenous society with a traditionally high degree of social and economic equalization, little occupational and regional mobility, and fairly strong social controls to enforce traditional norms and values and maintain social patterns. Thus, conformity and loyalty to established institutions and values to a large extent

Table 3-16
Value Added in Scandinavian Industries, 1979
(millions of local currency units)

	Norway	Denmark	Finland	Sweden
All manufacturing				
Gross output	137,661	135,956	124,861	275,732
Raw materials	65,304	77,782	65,907	132,460
Value added	41,748	58,174	45,859	122,114
Value added/gross output	0.30	0.43	0.37	0.44
Value added/raw materials	0.64	0.75	0.70	0.92
Mechanical industry				
Gross output	36,072	35,059	24,366	103,123
Raw materials	12,563	15,801	10,142	44,384
Value added	14,048	19,258	12,175	53,514
Value added/gross output	0.39	0.55	0.50	0.52
Value added/raw materials	1.12	1.22	1.20	1.25

Source: *Yearbook of Nordic Statistics 1981* (Stockholm: Nordic Council, 1982), pp. 104-111.

have been encouraged more than performance, ingenuity, and inventiveness. Typically, in the 1970s the system of government subsidies to manufacturing industry stimulated continuity of managerial structure and output more than innovation.

The survival of this particular model of manufacturing depended upon a continued expansion of demand and some important comparative advantages, such as a moderate wage level in relation to productivity. Such firms are highly sensitive to changes in demand and in cost level. Because products are essentially made according to customer needs, the result is short series and high costs, a combination that is dangerous in either a situation of depressed demand or with comparatively rising costs. Thus, the traditional Norwegian manufacturing firm, especially in sectors such as electronics, electrical and mechanical engineering, and shipbuilding, but also in textiles and clothing, was the product of specific historical conditions: a sustained expansion of the Western European economies and a well-educated labor force with a moderate wage level. When these conditions changed, traditional Norwegian manufacturing entered into a crisis.

In the mid-1970s the Norwegian manufacturing industry received a double shock: the international business environment suddenly deteriorated and simultaneously Norwegian labor costs jumped. Within a few years, there was an entirely new historical situation, and the major comparative advantage, the moderate wage level in relation to productivity disappeared amid a deteriorating international business environment. The government's immediate response, with wide support from business leaders, was to embark upon a countercyclical policy to bridge what was assumed to be a short but sharp international recession. The policy had two aspects: to directly subsidize business firms that were threatened by the recession in order to maintain employment, and to stimulate domestic demand.

From 1974 to 1977 there was an exceptionally expansionist economic policy, with the government intervening in wage bargaining. The result was that by 1977 about a third of employment in manufacturing was directly subsidized by the government, and real wages increased by 25 percent during the same period. The countercyclical policy sheltered Norwegian industry from the signals of the market, thus permitting the traditional model to survive in a recession and with a suddenly high wage-cost level, but also distorting the information base for managerial decisions and the adaptation to new historical conditions. This was particularly harmful for a small country with an open economy.

The policy also had a distorting effect on the labor market as some firms were paid to hoard labor while others were unable to get the labor they needed. This in turn reduced mobility in the labor market, further upsetting the process of industrial change. Pressure in the labor market also laid the ground for a substantial wages drift, which explains much of the real wage increase from 1974 to 1977. By 1977 it became evident that the countercyclical policy had been based on false premises, that 1973-1974 signified a turning point in the international economy, and that low economic growth rates would probably prevail in the OECD area for a long time. By 1978 the countercyclical policy was abandoned, accompanied by a currency devaluation, and Norway exited from the currency cooperation in Western Europe that had tied the local currency to the West German mark. However, the countercyclical policy left two results—one lasting, that Norway had become a high wage-cost country, and the other that the process of industrial adaptation had been distorted and productivity compromised. Both government and employers in Norway argue that the cost of wages is the major economic problem in Norway today. However, there are reasons to think that the wage-cost level is only part of the problem. First, the wage-cost level in Norway is currently about the same as in Sweden, and both are very high by international standards. Second, the wage-cost development in Norway in the mid-1970s has been particularly rapid by international comparisons, so that Norway within a few years changed from a medium-cost to a high-cost country. Thus, it is less the wage-cost level itself than the rapidity of change that was the problem. Industry had no time to adapt. Seen over a longer period of time, from the early 1960s to the early 1970s, the wages development in Norway was not extraordinary by international standards. There was another aspect of the cost problem, that is, the policy of tying the Norwegian currency to the West German mark, a currency of a much larger country that pursued an entirely different economic policy. The result was an appreciation of the Norwegian currency, together with a modest revaluation in the fall of 1973, that made the Norwegian currency rise by close to 20 percent in relation to a weighted average of the trade-partner currencies from 1972 to 1976. This meant, of course, that Norwegian labor costs rose even more strongly by international standards. Differential inflation rates with fixed rates of exchange can also explain the harmful effects of membership in the West European currency "snake." Thus, currency policy must take a good deal of responsibility for the cost problem. However, the currency revaluations of the 1970s may constitute a first taste of what could happen to the Norwegian currency and comparative cost levels with potential future financial surpluses from petroleum revenues.

The cost problem can only be seen in relation to that of productivity. Wage increases constitute a pressure for higher productivity, and to rationalize, invest, and innovate in production as in marketing. A high-wage-cost level does not necessarily give poor competitiveness; specialized products with a high technological level are usually produced with a profit in countries with high labor costs as pressure to innovate here is the strongest and because with this kind of product prices may be raised to cover costs. Also, a high wage level does not necessarily give a high overall cost level, if those wages are compensated for by high productivity or if other input factors are inexpensive. Thus, the cost level should not be focused upon alone, but should be seen in a wider perspective, including capital equipment, cost of other input factors, and quality of management, among other things.

Norwegian productivity in manufacturing, measured as value added in relation to input of hours worked, has been poor in the 1970s. Until 1974 productivity growth was close to that of Sweden and West Germany and lower, for example, than that of Japan, Belgium, or Denmark, but higher than that of the United States or the United Kingdom. In 1974 and 1975 productivity actually declined, and the 1974 level was only reached again in 1978. For the 1970s as a whole, Norwegian productivity growth has been among the weakest of the OECD area, higher than that of the United States, Canada, or the United Kingdom, but lower than that of practically all other Western European countries, not to mention Japan.

Part of the productivity decline is of a statistical character. As enterprises were subsidized they were less compelled to lay off workers when sales and output declined, concealing a potential for a quick recovery of productivity in case sales and output improved, as happened in 1978 and 1979. But the countercyclical policy undeniably also had a real negative impact on productivity. As management had easy access to government subsidies, it was less compelled to improve internal productivity. Moreover, the general atmosphere of economic euphoria could also have had a negative impact upon work morale, as there was the widespread impression that a better life could be had for less effort. Finally, there has been a strong political pressure in the direction of full employment.

Lagging productivity meant that relative labor costs measured according to output increased more quickly than the nominal costs. However, it seems that the most critical factor for cost development was the revaluation of the currency; the second most important factor was lagging productivity; and the rising labor costs only third.

Not surprisingly, Norwegian industry lost market shares at home and abroad. Only by 1983 did exports of traditional goods reach the level of 1973; meanwhile, demand in the markets for these exports had grown by about 30 percent, implying a loss of about a quarter of the market shares, on the average 4 percent a year.

As pointed out earlier in discussion of table 3-14, in constant prices the gross value of Norwegian petroleum extraction could double from 1980 to 1990. In current prices, the gross value of the petroleum sector should increase between three and four times, assuming an average rate of inflation of 7 percent. For reasons of simplicity, two ways of using these funds will be analyzed: alternative 1, using all the petroleum revenues for foreign investment; and alternative 2, using the petroleum revenues so that the foreign debt is repaid by 1985 and that by 1990 Norway has accumulated foreign reserves of a value of NOK 100 billion (U.S. $40 billion), with the remainder being used at home for consumption and investment (table 3-17 and 3-18).

The first alternative has been proposed by traditional Norwegian industry, arguing that this use of money avoids drastic changes in the social fabric. The second alternative expresses the point of view that the petroleum revenues should be used at home if they are to benefit the people. This alternative implies different forms of investment: at home in real capital and in education; abroad in real capital and in portfolio; and in oil in the ground. The return on the different forms of investment is attempted to be equalized. Calculations assume that employment growth is 0.7 percent a year, that return on real investment in Norway will decline slightly in the 1980s, that the general international rate of inflation will be 0.7 percent a year, that the real return on foreign investment abroad will be 3 percent a year, and finally that imports and exports by different sectors will develop according to information available today (1983).

The main difference between the two alternatives is that by using petroleum revenues domestically (alternative 2) the gross national product increases somewhat faster, private consumption grows at twice as high a rate, and public consumption increases at a significantly faster pace. Furthermore, gross investment increases much faster by using petroleum revenues at home, and correspondingly imports grow at twice as high a rate,

Table 3-17
Main Indicators of the Norwegian Economy, 1980-1990, According to Alternatives for Petroleum Revenues
(billion NOK, in 1978 prices)

		1990	
Category	*1980*	*Alternative 1*	*Alternative 2*
Gross national product	232.4	271.4	282.7
Imports	100.3	120.0	142.5
Exports	102.7	131.9	119.1
Private consumption	120.0	140.2	166.6
Public consumption	46.3	53.0	58.7
Investment	64.8	66.1	80.8
Stock changes	−1.1	0.2	0.0
Current prices			
Exports surplus	18.3	123.8	35.2
Financial surplus	−12.6	62.6	−0.5
Current surplus	5.7	186.4	34.7
Accumulated financial surplus	−96.7	711.2	84.5

Note: 1 billion NOK = U.S. $200 million.

Source: Olav Bjerkholt, Lorents Lorentsen, and Steinar Strøm, "Norge i 1980-Årene: Oljepenger og Omstillinger," in *Bergen Banks Kvartalsskrift*, no. 1/1981, p. 213.

Table 3-18
Main Indicators: Average Annual Rates of Change, 1980-1990
(percentages)

Category	Alternative 1	Alternative 2
Gross national product	1.6	2.0
Imports	1.8	3.6
Exports	2.5	1.5
Private consumption	1.6	3.3
Public consumption	1.4	2.4
Investment	0.2	2.2

Source: Olav Bjerkholt, Lorents Lorentsen, and Steinar Strøm, "Norge i 1980-Årene: Oljepenger og Omstillinger," in *Bergen Banks Kvartalsskrift,* no. 1/1981, p. 213.

but exports grow at a much slower rate and the accumulated financial surplus is significantly less. When petroleum revenues are used domestically, gross investment picks up, and this explains why the gross national product grows more quickly.

However, the domestic use of petroleum revenues also has a significant impact upon the structure of the Norwegian economy. The domestic use of petroleum revenues first of all leads to a decline in the economic importance of manufacturing (table 3-19). The domestic use of petroleum revenues also stimulates the growth of construction and especially of public services. Table 3-20 shows the impact upon the different sectors of manufacturing, in terms of value of output and in terms of employment, of the domestic use of petroleum revenues.

The domestic use of petroleum revenues essentially threatens the manufacturing sector which, if petroleum revenues were not channeled to the domestic economy, would grow at an average annual rate of 1.5 percent, but when exposed to petroleum revenues has a negative annual growth rate of − 0.3 percent. The sectors of manufacturing that are the most directly threatened are the textile and clothing industry, the pulp and paper industry, the secondary chemical industry, the mechanical industry (including electronics), and shipbuilding. These are the sectors that are the most sensitive to increases in the cost of labor, as they are the most labor-intensive branches (table 3-21) with the most precarious competitiveness. Calculations indicate that total employment in manufacturing will decrease by about 22 percent as a result of the domestic use of petroleum revenues, whereas otherwise it will increase by about 4 percent. Correspondingly, the domestic use of petroleum revenues will stimulate employment growth in construction and commerce as well as in private and public services.

The basic philosophy behind these calculations is that the Norwegian economy is divided between one sector that is exposed to foreign competi-

Table 3-19
Parts of Norwegian Gross National Product by Industry, Current Prices
(Percentages)

Industry	1980	1990 (1)	1990 (2)
Agriculture, fishing	4.5	3.2	3.0
Mining	0.4	0.3	0.3
Manufacturing	16.0	14.2	11.1
Electricity	4.4	7.7	7.7
Construction	7.2	5.1	6.9
Petroleum	15.9	24.8	23.1
International shipping	3.6	5.2	4.9
Other transport	6.1	5.4	5.5
Private services	28.1	21.3	23.6
Public services	13.8	12.8	14.1
Total	100.0	100.0	100.0

Source: Olav Bjerkholt, Lorents Lorentsen, and Steinar Strøm, "Norge i 1980-Årene: Ol-jepenger og Omstillinger," in *Bergen Banks Kvartalsskrift*, no. 1/1981, p. 214.

tion and another that is sheltered from it. The sector exposed to foreign competition, whether in the home market or in foreign markets, cannot raise its prices without losing competitiveness, whereas the sheltered sector does not have to worry about its own cost level—it can raise the prices of its goods and services as costs increase. Calculations also indicate that a rising standard of living is increasingly oriented toward goods and services from the sheltered sector, and this sector therefore has to draw manpower from the exposed sector. In this way, the increase in living standards and in private consumption resulting from the domestic use of petroleum revenues is a menace to the cost level, the competitiveness, the employment, and the output of the exposed sector. In this respect, the calculations presented here do not differ from those used in the preparation of the 1974 plan.

Each of these two scenarios indicates a considerably different impact upon investment prospects in various branches of industry, both in terms of return and in terms of types of projects that are viable.

In the first alternative (channeling petroleum revenues largely outside the Norwegian economy), there will be a fairly modest expansion of manufacturing, requiring a gradual renewal of business ideas, plants, and leading personnel, but to a large extent keeping the current organizational structure. This means that investment projects in areas such as pulp and paper, chemical feedstock, petroleum refining, chemicals, metals, engineering, and shipbuilding could give a moderate return on investment, perhaps up to 10 to 15 percent in the best cases, and that projects will not have to be strikingly original in relation to the present industrial structure in Norway.

Table 3-20
Gross Value of Output by Sector of Industry, Two Alternative Scenarios[a]

	Billion NOK in 1978 Prices			Average Annual Growth	
Industry	1980	1990 (1)	1990 (2)	Alt. 1 %	Alt. 2 %
Agriculture	15.8	18.1	18.1	1.4	1.4
Forestry	2.4	2.7	2.7	1.2	1.2
Fisheries	3.6	4.3	4.3	1.8	1.8
Mining	2.1	2.5	2.5	1.7	1.7
Food processing	28.7	31.7	31.1	1.0	0.9
Beverages, tobacco	4.1	4.6	4.7	1.4	1.4
Textiles, clothing	4.9	5.6	2.6	1.3	−6.1
Wood	11.9	12.3	13.6	0.3	1.4
Pulp and paper	8.6	10.1	7.9	1.6	−0.8
Chemical feedstock	5.1	6.6	5.1	2.6	0
Petroleum refining	7.4	9.6	10.5	2.6	3.6
Chemicals	13.7	15.6	10.3	1.3	−2.8
Metals	12.9	16.9	13.2	2.7	0.2
Engineering	19.9	22.2	15.1	1.1	−2.7
Shipbuilding	23.5	27.2	19.5	1.5	−1.9
Graphic	8.4	10.3	10.7	2.1	2.5
Manufacturing total	149.1	172.7	144.3	1.5	−0.3
Electricity production	8.0	9.2	9.6	1.4	1.9
Electricity distribution	6.7	8.1	9.4	1.9	3.4
Construction	51.2	45.6	61.5	−1.2	1.9
Petroleum extraction	26.9	41.9	41.9	4.5	4.5
Shipping	20.2	22.3	22.3	1.0	1.0
Transport	25.9	31.7	32.0	2.1	2.2
Other private services	60.1	79.0	83.9	2.2	3.4
Public services	3.3	4.5	4.9	3.2	4.1
Grand total	431.7	504.7	511.2	1.6	1.7

Source: Olav Bjerkholt, Lorents Lorentsen, and Steinar Strøm, "Norge i 1980-Årene: Olje-penger og Omstillinger," in *Bergen Banks Kvartalsskrift*, no. 1/1981, p. 215.
[a]Figures indicate volume size by value.

In the second alternative of using petroleum revenues largely inside the Norwegian economy, there will be stagnation of manufacturing, imposing a higher degree of differentiation and selectivity of projects. This will require a more drastic change in business ideas, plants, and leading personnel, as well as modifying the current organizational framework for these industries. This means that investment projects in areas such as pulp and paper, chemical feedstock, petroleum refining, chemicals, metals, engineering, and shipbuilding will not be very attractive, unless projects are really innovative, and based upon rising labor costs, in which case fairly high returns could be expected in the best cases.

Table 3-21
Employment by Sectors, 1980-1990, Two Alternative Scenarios

Industry	Million man-hours			Percentage Parts		
	1980	1990 (1)	1990 (2)	1980	1990 (1)	1990 (2)
Agriculture	191.1	179.0	157.1	6.5	5.6	4.9
Forestry	20.0	17.4	14.7	0.7	0.6	0.5
Fisheries	40.1	46.7	43.8	1.4	1.5	1.4
Mining	15.2	16.2	14.8	0.5	0.5	0.5
Food processing	86.7	77.4	70.4	2.9	2.5	2.2
Beverages, tobacco	10.7	11.4	11.4	0.4	0.4	0.4
Textiles, clothing	38.8	39.2	17.0	1.3	1.2	0.5
Wood	53.8	45.4	46.2	1.8	1.4	1.5
Pulp and paper	32.9	35.1	25.6	1.1	1.1	0.8
Chemical feedstock	17.0	21.9	16.5	0.6	0.7	0.5
Petroleum refining	1.3	1.7	1.9	0.0	0.1	0.1
Chemicals	70.2	75.6	47.9	2.4	2.4	1.5
Metals	58.5	69.3	53.8	2.0	2.2	1.7
Engineering	124.1	125.6	85.1	4.2	4.0	2.7
Shipbuilding	97.2	99.6	64.2	3.3	3.1	2.0
Graphic	47.5	59.7	− 60.7	− 1.6	1.9	1.9
Manufacturing total	638.7	661.9	500.7	21.6	20.8	15.8
Electricity production	0	0	0	0	0	0
Electricity distribution	38.1	46.1	53.8	1.3	1.5	1.7
Construction	265.6	212.9	273.0	9.0	6.7	8.6
Trade	394.3	445.9	478.0	13.3	14.0	13.0
Petroleum extraction	13.0	19.7	19.7	0.4	0.6	0.6
Shipping	67.0	67.0	67.0	2.3	2.1	2.1
Transportation	264.1	313.9	312.7	8.9	9.9	9.8
Private services	428.8	514.3	546.6	14.5	16.2	17.2
Public services	587.7	637.1	695.9	19.8	20.1	21.9
Total	2,963.8	3,178.0	3,178.0	100	100	100

Source: Olav Bjerkholt, Lorents Lorentsen, and Steinar Strøm, "Norge i 1980-Årene: Olje-penger og Omstillinger," in *Bergen Banks Kvartalsskrift*, no. 1/1981, p. 217.

The two alternatives presented correspond to two different images of what the future Norway should be. This is relevant as well for petroleum policy. The options may be described as the industrial economy and the service economy.

The service economy may be described as the result of a policy that has consciously lost the inhibitions concerning the domestic use of petroleum revenues that were relevant at an earlier stage. This means giving a high priority to raising living standards, to both private and public consumption. It is politically much easier to opt for an annual growth rate of private consumption of 3.3 percent and of public consumption of 2.4 percent as indicated by the second alternative of using petroleum revenues domestically, than keeping both at growth rates around 1.5 percent a year. In a competitive democracy with a strong and unified trade-union organization, it will be difficult not to choose this option.

The result will be an even higher cost environment, with fairly lavish public services and very high standards of living enjoyed by practically all members of society. However, this result will also entail a considerable change in the social fabric, with a decline in manufacturing and strong growth in the service sector, leading to a centralization of settlement around bigger urban centers. Another result will be that imports of industrial goods will increasingly substitute for domestic production. The social cost will be high, as measured by the personal inconveniences of those who will have to change employment and residence as entire parts of the country will be threatened by depopulation. The arguments in favor of this option are that the benefit to the population of using petroleum revenues domestically is higher than the social cost, that much of Norway's industrial base is obsolete anyway, that it is irrational to worry about the industrial profile in the latter half of the next century, and that in any case improvements in technology and productivity will give future generations an even higher standard of living. However, in this school of thought there are worries about the extent and pace of structural change.

The proponents of this option are generally against subsidizing agriculture and fisheries and sheltering these sectors institutionally against foreign competition as is the case today. Instead, a structural rationalization is required here. They are, of course, also against a continued subsidization of manufacturing, but this is being reduced in any case. Still, the argument continues that it may not be entirely wise to pursue a protectionist petroleum policy—to Norwegianize the petroleum activities—as this will contribute to pressure and as the presence of foreign oil companies may be beneficial in terms of competition as well as in terms of learning. The proponents of this policy further question the wisdom of linking access to petroleum to industrial projects and investment. This may imply hidden and uncontrolled subsidies to private foreign firms and lead to industrial ventures without a viability of their own, as has been demonstrated in several cases. However, there should be a stronger emphasis on the transfer of technology, managerial know-how, and research and development, essentially through cooperative ventures between foreign oil companies and Norwegian firms.

This policy is explicitly aiming at a high-cost environment, with the argument that changes in the social fabric should be more readily accepted; industrial employment would have to decline, but there would probably be new industries thriving in a high-cost environment. Finally, the high cost of labor should at least partly be compensated for by a massive educational effort at all levels, so that Norway's labor would not only be the most expensive in the OECD area, but also the best educated. Industrially, the aim should be to create firms that survive in a tight labor market with a high-cost level and, nevertheless, operate at a profit without subsidies. In light of this attitude toward the domestic use of petroleum revenues, the ceiling of output should be reviewed, and output should be increased if there is a reasonable need for revenues. This philosophy logically would lead to a radically changed Norway.

Politically, the state, through its control of petroleum revenues, would be in an even more commanding position. Economically, Norway's interaction with the rest of the world would increasingly be characterized by a system in which the export of petroleum would pay for the imports of well-off consumers. Socially, Norway would be a fairly well-educated postindustrial society.

The counterpiece to the vision of the service economy is that of an industrial economy, in which petroleum revenues add to the wealth of the country without excessive harm to the established industries and the social fabric, essentially by investing the petroleum revenues abroad. This means giving a high priority to maintaining industrial employment, production, and continuity, even if it means consciously opting for a lower growth in private and public consumption.

In Norway there is a strong attachment to traditional values and to the present social fabric, and this attachment is strong among capitalists and workers as well as among the middle class and intellectuals. The argument for an industrial economy is that it is both unwise and wrong to opt for a service economy that is highly dependent upon petroleum revenues, and that the social cost of excessive disruptions in the social fabric is too high in relation to the possible benefits in terms of private and public consumption. In particular, given the present high living standards, it is no great sacrifice to forsake one or two additional percent of income increase a year for the benefit of maintaining patterns of production, employment, and settlement.

It is also pointed out that petroleum revenues are uncertain, that even if Norway may have reserves for 100 years of oil and gas output at a high level, there is no guarantee that future prices will remain high, especially in the next century. Therefore, care should be taken not to disrupt the industrial continuity and know-how that is the result of generations of work. It is also argued that industrial income is qualitatively better than petroleum revenues, as it is not a free gift of nature, but the fruit of human effort, implying a constant industrial learning process, whereas living off petroleum-rent income implies a negative industrial learning process.

There is a further strong argument that people have a natural right to continue performing the work they do and living where they are, and that labor and residential mobility are harmful both because of the social cost and because of the inconvenience to the individual. This kind of argumentation appeals to a protestant and fairly puritan country, where the inhabitants of the geographical periphery have a long and fairly successful record of fighting centralizing trends caused by market forces and public policies.

Thus, the argument of the proponents of the industrial economy is that Norway would essentially be a poorer country if it should divest itself of its manufacturing industry, even if, perhaps for a short time, it might be financially richer by developing a petroleum economy. The argument is that a balanced manufacturing industry gives productive skills that permit a high degree of flexibility in the pattern of production, which again permits adjustment to changing circumstances and less vulnerability to changing terms of trade in the world oil market.

The proponents of the industrial economy logically warn against an excessive buildup of petroleum extraction, even if few so far have argued in favor of a negative supply curve, that is, to adjust the output ceiling downward as the price of petroleum increases. Instead, petroleum revenues should, if they rise as a result of price increases, be channeled abroad to a greater extent. In the future, there could be a stronger argument in favor of a negative supply curve, but most seem to find the current level of about 1.1 million barrels per day moderate, thinking that it could be raised to 1.5 million barrels per day without damaging the economy, provided revenues are not used at home.

In general, proponents of the industrial economy are in favor of an increasing degree of Norwegianization of petroleum activities, as this benefits Norwegian manufacturing. Usually they are also in favor of linking industrial projects to access to petroleum; this is seen as a way of strengthening the manufacturing industry, even if shortcomings and failures of current deals are readily recognized. Such a philosophy leads to preserving the Norway that exists today, attempting even a strengthening of the role of the manufacturing industry. Politically, this would mean maintaining more or less the status quo between the private and the public sectors. Economically, it would be a balanced economy, exporting both petroleum and industrial goods (apart from other raw materials, fish, and so on), maintaining a diversified manufacturing sector, and still enjoying a high standard of living. Socially, it would be a country that would preserve a decentralized and diversified pattern of production, employment, and settlement.

The two alternatives in economic policy outlined and two sets of argumentation are both fairly extreme, but they nevertheless indicate realistic options and oppositions of principle. The assumptions behind the economic calculations used in estimating the impact of the domestic use of petroleum revenues lend themselves to much criticism. This will be commented upon later, and alternative scenarios will be presented. Politically, this means that the opposition between the two schools of thought may not be insurmountable. The question is whether it is possible to design a third way out, to use a large part of the petroleum revenues domestically and at the same time strengthen manufacturing industry and develop a diversified economy. This may require interventions in the economic matrix and changes of an institutional and organizational character that are politically delicate. Nevertheless, the question merits study. Such a third way out may require solutions of a wider, international scope, as the small size of Norway's economy offers important obstacles.[30] In any case, the freedom of choice in economic policy may be greater than anticipated.

The Service Sector. In 1980 the service sector, including trade and transportation, made up about 55 percent of the gross national product, accounting for about 62 percent of total employment. Paradoxically, since 1973 the share of the service sector in the gross national product has declined because of the rising importance of the petroleum sector, but in terms of employment there has been a persistent increase. The dominance of the service sector is essentially related to three factors: first, at a high level of income, an increasing part of private demand is directed toward services of different kinds; second, the priority given to the development of social services, especially in health and education, has contributed to the expansion of the service sector; third, there is in Norway a tradition of export-oriented service trade in shipping which is now likely to be supplemented by international banking. Thus, the Norwegian service sector gives a mixed picture; it is public as well as private, oriented toward exports as well as toward the home market.

In terms of employment, the major items in the service sector are education, health, and related welfare services, which are predominantly but not exclusively public. Employment in 1980 was 383,000, representing a rapid increase during the 1970s. Employment in trade, which includes restaurants and hotels, was 327,000 in 1980, showing a much smaller rate of growth. Employment in transportation, storage, post, and telecommunications was 171,000, practically stagnant over the past few years.[31]

By contrast, employment in banking, financing, real estate, insurance, and business services (110,000 in 1980) shows a fairly rapid increase. In general, this service sector is likely to expand by employment, and this expansion will be accelerated by the domestic use of petroleum revenues. Rising living standards resulting from the domestic use of petroleum revenues will lead to rising demand for health and education services as well as for different kinds of private services. Additionally, there is likely to be a rising demand for trade services, meaning that employment in the trading sector will have to increase.

This pressure resulting from the domestic use of petroleum revenue and requiring an increasing part of total employment in the service sector to the detriment of manufacturing industry, abstracts from institutional and managerial changes. For example, it has been proposed by some observers to charge for public services, even if the net effect upon demand is unknown, which would probably lead to a slower rise in demand for such services. Another possibility is to divert some of the demand for services abroad, for example, by sending long-term patients to foreign hospitals or by letting foreign companies participate in the part of the service sector that is now sheltered from foreign competition, such as allowing foreign airlines to operate domestic routes in Norway. This raises the question of improving productivity in the service sector in general and especially in the public services—questions both managerially complex and politically touchy—but the issue is likely to become more acute.

Labor and Human Capital. Annual average employment in 1980 was about 1,913,000. The employment coefficient, especially among women, is still lower than in neighboring Denmark and Sweden, and taking the high employment growth during the 1970s into account, total employment could continue to expand at a fairly high pace well into the 1980s. At the pace of the 1970s, the total employment coefficient will reach the 1979 level of Sweden by 1984-1985.

There is presently a ten-year compulsory education in Norway, and the average length of education among the adult population is also about ten years. This figure is lower than that for the United States, Canada, or Japan, but higher than that for most Western European countries. In 1977 full-time school enrollment of children aged 15-19 years was 63.6 percent, less than in the United States or Japan but, apart from Switzerland, the highest in Western Europe. In 1978 the percentage of students leaving high school qualifying for university of the given age group, was 35.4 for women and 29.2 for men. Among the total population in 1975, approximately 8.7 percent had a university or college education, about 27.5 percent had completed secondary education qualifying for university, and 63.8 percent had primary or rudimentary secondary education only. During the academic year of 1980/81 total enrollment at universities and colleges was some 72,000 or about 1.8 percent of the total population. Enrollment at upper secondary schools was about 179,000.[32]

In general, there has been insufficient capacity both in the upper secondary schools, preparing for university, and in the vocational schools. Also, there is a clearly insufficient capacity in most institutions of higher learning, especially in technical and managerial studies. These problems are being exacerbated by the development of the petroleum industry. The pace of Norwegianization has had to be slowed down because of a lack of sufficient Norwegian personnel. This reflects either a lack of concern and insight into the educational requirements generated by the petroleum development, or a conscious lack of willingness to give educational matters a higher priority.

In 1980 education and research represented about 3.5 percent of the gross national product, a percentage much lower than in many other countries. Even if the general Norwegian level of education is high by international and European standards, it is clearly not high enough in relation to the pressures and requirements generated by the petroleum development. Moreover, it is doubtful whether the educational effort has been sufficiently specific and tailored to these requirements, given the acute shortages of capacity in such fields as technology and business. This coincides with the problems of the Norwegian industrial culture, with too little emphasis on research and development and insufficient managerial competence.

It is a political priority to expand education and in recent years there has been a special effort in vocational training. Pedagogical training is also expanding, and the total number of teachers is likely to increase from 35,000 in 1980 to about 50,000 by 1990. However, it seems that an overall educational and research strategy tailored to the needs generated by petroleum development is lacking. One problem is the weight of regional interests, leading to the dispersal of the effort, with minor colleges being established around the country instead of concentrating the effort. For example, by 1981 Norway still had only one fully developed technical university and one fully developed business school, which in both cases is clearly below requirements. It could be argued that for the Norwegian economy, which is becoming increasingly dominated by the petroleum sector and thus cannot avoid increasing labor costs, it would be strategically reasonable to compensate the rising labor costs by an increase in knowledge and competence. This reasoning should also be applied to management. In this perspective, improving education, research, and development will be one of the most pressing tasks in the years ahead.

Public Policy

Economic Policy. Economic policy in Norway is essentially macroeconomic, focusing on demand management and the trade balance; there is much less sectoral intervention, and sectoral policies often clash with each other and with macroeconomic policy. Since 1945 there has been a continuous tradition of active government macroeconomic management, essentially along Keynesian lines. This has been fairly successful in the sense that intervention has managed to reduce the amplitude of the oscillations of the international business cycle. There has been a much more even economic development and even capacity utilization in Norway than in most other Western European countries.

However, until the 1970s economic growth rates in Norway were not particularly high; in the 1950s they were low by Western European standards.

A persistent problem until the advent of the petroleum era has been the fairly modest return on capital invested. Norwegian economic growth therefore has been exceptionally expensive, which can explain the high rates of investment and reinvestment. In part this is due to the costly development of an economic infrastructure in a sparsely populated country, but the managerial problems discussed earlier are probably a factor in this picture as well. Traditionally Norway has been an importer of capital in order to develop natural resources and basic industries. A fairly persistent trade deficit has been offset by capital imports, also meaning that capital traditionally has been relatively inexpensive.

In the 1970s, especially since 1973, Norway's macroeconomic policy has been less successful, partly because of erroneous judgment of a turbulent international environment, and partly because the performance potential of the domestic economy was misjudged. This can be seen as related to a lack of specific sectoral insight and to insufficient communication among the various institutions with macroeconomic and sectoral responsibilities.

There is no specific tradition of monetary policy as such in Norway, and the monetarist school is not held in high esteem. However, the control of money supply and of credit has been an important tool in macroeconomic policy. Institutionally, legislation gives the government and the central bank tight control of credit, and public representatives on the boards of commercial banks further strengthen government control of banking. There are also a number of state banks that give credit for specific purposes.

Fiscal policy is dictated both by revenue concerns and by social concerns such as a fairly equal distribution of income after tax. Traditionally the value-added tax of 20 percent has been the main source of revenue, and is still the case, but petroleum taxation will soon replace the tax in this role. Even if income taxes are considererd high, especially as they also include social and medical security contributions, the personal income tax only accounts for about 11 percent of central-government revenue, but for more than half of local-government revenue. Whereas local-government income tax is at a flat rate, central-government income tax is steeply progressive. Company taxation is generally at a rate of 50.8 percent.

Industrial Policy. Industrial policy in Norway has developed quite unevenly, and periods of active state intervention have alternated with periods of nonintervention. Additionally, the interventionist policies have always been limited to specific sectors; there has never been an attempt at a comprehensive industrial policy. After 1945 there was an active state intervention to establish the iron and steel industry, the aluminum industry, and to expand hydroelectric generation. Again, in the early 1970s there was active state intervention, partly to secure state majority ownership of some key firms, and partly to establish new state-owned companies in the petroleum sector, of which Statoil is the most prominent example. The rest of the manufacturing industry has not been the subject of state intervention, except during the countercyclical policy in the 1970s, when many firms received direct government subsidies.

Since 1977 there has been an attempt to draw industrial benefits from the petroleum development by linking industrial ventures by foreign oil companies to their access to acreage. Increasingly, this is taking the form of cooperation between foreign oil companies and Norwegian industrial firms in the fields of research, product development, and joint marketing. Thus, access to petroleum is used as leverage to overcome some of the basic weaknesses of Norwegian industry. So far, the policy has been to let industry itself work out deals, and there is no clear concept in the government about what kind of joint projects are the most required. This essentially reflects an absence of industrial planning.

Absorptive-Capacity Constraints

Traditional Constraints on Absorptive Capacity

Traditionally, the notion of absorptive capacity has referred to the level of interest and the marginal efficiency of an investment. For public projects, where external concerns might be involved, an equivalent condition exists in which social benefits just equal social costs using an appropriate discount rate. If investment is carried beyond this point, resources are being allocated ineffectively since social rates of return are not equal throughout the economy. This discussion relates to the key question of the appropriate discount rate in an oil-exporting country with a comfortable foreign exchange balance, where the alternatives are to invest abroad or to leave oil in the ground.

In the analysis of Norway, conventional economic wisdom suggests that the marginal-efficiency criterion has been violated quite frequently, especially after the impact of petroleum revenues was first felt in 1973. It is an open question whether this is still a relevant allocative criterion in the Norwegian context. Despite the difficulties inherent in evaluating such investment, it could be argued that social and infrastructural investment (in health services, in roads, in communications, and in housing) in many cases has proceeded far beyond the equilibrium point between benefits and costs. However, this investment has been made in order to provide benefits to a marginal part of the population, and explicitly or implicitly to fulfill political demands in order to satisfy powerful pressure groups. Examples are investment in health services, roads and communications, in higher educational facilities, and the like, in order to provide remote and sparsely populated areas of the country with services of a quality more comparable to that of the central, more densely populated areas. This argument could be applied more strongly to investment in agriculture, forestries, and fisheries, facilitated by credit at low interest rates through state banks, which to some extent apparently has led to overmechanization and low utilization of equipment. Also, as noted earlier, agricultural production in Norway is heavily subsidized.

In the case of manufacturing, a certain part of investment has traditionally been financed by credit from state institutions at low interest rates. Apparently the marginal-efficiency criterion has not been respected in all cases, for example, in the decision to establish an iron and steel industry in northern Norway after World War II. More recently, under the impact of the oil wealth, a number of investment decisions have been made where the marginal-efficiency criterion has not been respected, unless initial calculations were based on exceedingly wrong assumptions. The most important examples are the petrochemical industries at Bamble in southern Norway.

Furthermore, the large-scale subsidization of manufacturing industries exposed to foreign competition since 1974 and the rescue operation of the shipping industry during the 1970s were not based on the marginal-efficiency criterion, nor evidently upon any economic calculation, but rather on political judgment. Thus, experience indicates that in Norway the discretionary use of money by the government is based less upon economic criteria of marginal efficiency than upon political criteria such as expediency and short-term benefit. Not surprisingly, this trend has been reinforced since 1973 under the impact of easy money.

A careful analysis of the situation might indicate that the government's options were limited, that in the Norwegian political context it is difficult not to give regional development a priority beyond economic justification, that given the political position of the agricultural constituency it is difficult not to protect and subsidize agriculture, and finally, that given the power of the trade-union movement, it is difficult not to use subsidies in order to prevent unemployment, especially when the trade unions demanding this operate together with local interests and industrialists. However, it could also be argued that the policy of subsidization did not have to reach the same magnitude and take the same form. Selective support measures could have been used in a more economical way, especially to improve productivity and competitiveness instead of conserving the existing industrial structure. It should also be noted that Norway after 1973 has been living with the impression that money is easy, given the prospect of large petroleum revenues, and this has led to a general relaxation of discipline in criteria for allocating money. It is not only the volume of domestic spending therefore that lends itself to criticism, but also the spending mix and the criteria for allocating money.

The rapid growth in domestic spending was quite contrary to explicit intentions, and as pointed out earlier in this study, from 1974 to 1980 public consumption grew at an average annual rate of 7.0 percent, as opposed to the projected 4.3 percent. The corollary was that the labor supply grew at a much higher rate than expected. Thus, the absorptive capacity of Norway was evidently underestimated by planners and politicians in 1973, especially in light of the turn in the international business cycle that seriously affected the part of Norwegian industry exposed to foreign competition.

Investment Criteria. The usual investment criterion is that capital should be allocated to different projects so that the marginal efficiency is equal for all projects. With public projects, both internal and external benefits and costs must be considered and an appropriate discount rate has to be determined; this does not necessarily have to coincide with the current market rate of interest. Such is especially true in the case of nonrenewable resources. The economic evaluation of projects is therefore much more complicated than might be suggested by the usual present-value formulas that are used in elementary discussions of the subject. The issues become even more complex when adding the constraints on mobility and the social cost of high internal migration. The regional-development and industrial-support policies serve as a case in point.

The rapid increase in real wages in the mid-1970s affected profits in industries exposed to foreign competition, especially in those competing in the world market. According to some estimates, their profits were reduced by two-thirds from 1974 to 1977.[33] According to the Central Bureau of Statistics, the total profitability of Norwegian industry was 3.3 percent in 1975 as return on investment; but it has been claimed that profitability was negative if inflation is taken into account.[34] Not surprisingly, investment declined in several industries in 1978, continuing in 1979, but the trend was reversed in 1980. Measured in constant prices, overall investment outside the petroleum sector has grown very moderately from 1976 to 1980, yet has declined as a percentage of the gross national product. It should also be mentioned that investment in petrochemical industries is subsidized by access to cheap feedstock, especially in the form of LPG (liquid petroleum gas). This apparently is needed to compensate for high construction costs in Norway and to overcome the currently slack market for petrochemical products in Western Europe.

Because of the large petroleum reserves, the development of the petroleum sector is likely to absorb investment funds of such a magnitude that considerations for the Norwegian capital market indicate part of the financing be done internationally. The petroleum development also provides investment opportunities in related businesses, such as pipeline transportation of oil and gas, different kinds of equipment, concrete, steel parts, and so on. In other sectors not related to petroleum, the degree of application of the marginal-efficiency criterion is likely to depend upon the availability of money, which again will depend upon petroleum revenues and petroleum investment. Both of these factors are uncertain; petroleum revenues could decline in the early 1980s because of output problems and declining real oil prices, and then increase at a fairly fast rate in the late 1980s as output expands and prices rise.

In the meantime, petroleum expansion could require considerable investment. Thus, there is a certain likelihood of a fairly tight financial situation for some years during the early 1980s. This will impose a more extensive use of marginal-efficiency criteria on investment, possibly together with higher interest rates, which could lead to a decline in nonpetroleum investment. The crucial question is whether, when an easier financial situation is restored, this will lead to a relaxation on the criteria for allocating money, eventually under heavy political pressure, or whether some financial rigidity can be maintained. Experience indicates that the Norwegian economy can absorb unexpectedly large resources as subsidized investment or as subsidies to current operations.

In April 1982 the OECD recommended that Norway take prompt action to improve the performance of the nonoil sectors of its economy.[35] This recommendation underscores the seriousness of the imbalancing effects of oil on the nonoil sectors.

Import Capacity and Other Physical Constraints. Norway has traditionally maintained a fairly liberal trade policy, with low tariffs and few restrictions on most kinds of imports. Norway is a member of the European Free Trade Association (EFTA), and has a trade treaty with the European Economic Community, thus enjoying free trade in almost all industrial goods with a considerable number of European countries. The policy of Norwegianization, that is, of increased utilization of domestic goods and services as inputs to the petroleum industry, constitutes a kind of protectionism and preferentialism, selectively applied to petroleum. Given the importance of the petroleum sector in the Norwegian economy, this policy constitutes a certain breach with traditional trade liberalism.

Contrary to most other oil-exporting countries, especially those in the Middle East, Norway has had few problems of import capacity or other physical constraints to spending. Norway enjoys a well-developed transportation system that includes a large number of ports, airports, and rail links with the outside world, as well as a well-developed distribution system. Thus, demand can be quickly translated into imports without bottlenecks in practically all cases. The problem of physical capacity in Norway and abroad to deliver input factors for petroleum development is another matter.

Manpower Constraints. The employment situation has been discussed at length earlier in this book, concluding that the supply of labor since 1974 has grown at a much faster rate than historical rates or those anticipated by planners, essentially because of rising female participation in working life. If the supply of labor continues to grow at recent rates, the Swedish level of participation in employment will be reached by 1984-1985. Subsequently, the rate of growth of labor supply can be expected to level off, and a very probable reduction in working hours means that the supply of labor measured in man-hours is likely to increase more modestly during the 1980s, especially after 1985. A more liberal immigration policy might offset this, but that would be politically extremely touchy. The leveling off of the growth of labor in the late 1980s, possibly together with a surge in petroleum revenues, could then cause a fairly tight labor market. However, there is a free movement of labor within the Nordic area.

In any case, the gross supply of labor is likely to be less of a problem than the availability of certain special skills. An accelerated petroleum development with an increasing emphasis on Norwegian personnel, plus an increasing domestic use of petroleum revenues with a negative effect on the competitiveness of Norwegian industry and a resulting need for technical and managerial improvement, is likely to lead to a fairly tight labor market for technical and managerial expertise. It is doubtful whether requirements for this kind of personnel can be met by domestic resources, unless there is a major educational effort in these fields.

New Internal Constraints on Absorptive Capacity

In addition to traditional constraints, a number of additional domestic considerations may reduce Norway's flexibility in dealing with a large influx of petroleum revenues. These considerations are essentially: (1) the impact of petroleum revenues upon the domestic distribution of income; (2) the impact of the domestic use of petroleum revenues upon occupational and regional migration; and (3) inflationary pressures resulting from the domestic use of petroleum revenues. These considerations were important in 1973-1974 when the initial policy response to petroleum was designed, but they have not always been equally relevant to the elaboration of actual economic policy.

Distribution of Income. Norway has one of the most equal distributions of income in Western Europe and in the Western world, socially as well as regionally. This relatively equal income distribution is nothing new in Norway; historically, the absence of large agricultural and industrial properties, together with a unified and powerful trade-union movement, have provided the basis for an income distribution more equal than in most other European countries. For a period of about twenty years after World War II, the income distribution was gradually made even more equal through distributive policies and a highly progressive income taxation. After 1965 there was some reversal of this trend, especially in the early 1970s, as profits increased markedly but real wages stagnated or even declined. Even so, by the early 1970s industrial wages in Norway were among the highest in Western Europe, whereas managerial salaries were among the lowest; consumption patterns were less unequal than in most other countries, with a fairly obvious absence of conspicuous consumption. The small income differences limit mobility and the ability of the marketplace to allocate labor to industries and areas in expansion. Furthermore, one industry cannot raise wages without massive spillover and subsequent social and political tensions. Thus, not only is the market at work, but there is a political and cultural context as well.

The rapid growth of a domestic petroleum industry, with high profits and a potential for paying higher wages and salaries than the rest of Norwegian industry, evidently represented a risk that income distribution would become more unequal, and that there would be more conspicuous inequalities in consumption patterns. These concerns were perhaps relevant to the decisions in the early 1970s to limit the number of Norwegian companies operating on the continental shelf and to have firm state control of the petroleum industry. An uncontrolled expansion of the petroleum industry and a dispersal of its revenues could not only lead to a more unequal general income distribution; it could also create a dichotomy between petroleum and petroleum-related sectors and the rest of the economy, in which inflationary pressures would benefit capital and labor engaged in petroleum, but act as a detriment to the rest of the economy. In this perspective it is fairly rational that a very large part of Norwegian capitalism has seemed to favor a high degree of state control of the petroleum industry, not out of sympathy with state control, but out of fear of the petroleum industry.

In the 1970s, though accurate data are not yet available, it appears that petroleum revenues contributed to a more equal distribution of income, as they were used to subsidize industry and raise real wages. For example, the proportion of wage costs, measured as wages and salaries plus employers' contributions to the national insurance as a proportion of total factor income, increased from 71.6 percent in 1970 to 81.5 percent in 1977, but subsequently declined to 67.1 percent in 1980 as a result of the reversal of economic policy. Correspondingly, the share of capital and other labor, excluding that of the self-employed, decreased from 17.8 percent in 1970 to 6.4 percent in 1977, rising again to 21.8 percent in 1980, but this figure hides large petroleum profits.[36]

Occupational and Regional Mobility. Practically all petroleum-exporting countries have experienced rapid social change as a result of the domestic use of petroleum revenues. This has been manifest in drastic changes in the occupational structure and in regional migration, generally leading to accelerated urbanization. The corollary of petroleum development appears thus to be a rapid pace of change in the patterns of production, employment, and settlement. Such changes take place in all societies that are not stagnant, and they often lead to considerable inconveniences for the individuals concerned, but they are difficult to avoid if the advantages of economic growth are to be enjoyed. The pace of change can be substantially accelerated by a rapid petroleum development or by a large-scale domestic use of petroleum revenues, which at a certain point can lead to inconveniences and social costs outweighing the benefits of economic growth.

In this context the benefits of economic growth have to be weighed against the social problems it creates.

In Norway, which is one of the few petroleum-exporting countries with a representative democracy involving extensive political participation, social problems developing from the use of petroleum revenues are likely to cause political backlashes, in spite of the benefits experienced from economic growth. Therefore, social problems related to petroleum development and the domestic use of petroleum revenues have to be taken more seriously in Norway perhaps than in some other petroleum-exporting nations.

This was recognized by planners and politicians in the early 1970s, and perhaps the major point of the 1974 oil plan was that a balance should be found between petroleum development and the domestic use of petroleum revenues on one hand, and the emerging social problems on the other hand. This led to the recommendation that the pace of social change should not be too fast, and that petroleum development and especially the domestic use of petroleum revenues should proceed at a moderate pace.

The basic premises concerning the fear of overheating the economy were changed between 1973 and 1977 because of the international economic recession. This does not mean that the caution expressed was unfounded; on the contrary, according to the premises defined, caution was certainly justified. Subsequent experience has shown that as the basic premises concerning the international economy changed, the ability of the Norwegian economy to absorb petroleum revenues also changed, and so did the structural repercussions of the domestic use of petroleum revenues. Furthermore, the use of petroleum revenues to subsidize manufacturing had not been envisaged at the outset, and this particular use of oil revenues changes the whole problem of absorptive capacity and structural change. The policy maintained for several years can be described as *structural subsidization*, that is, petroleum revenues were used to avoid change instead of to promote it. It could be argued that Norway has entered a vicious circle, as petroleum revenues at first are used to increase public and private consumption, then are employed to offset the structural effects of their initial use. In this perspective, the ability of the Norwegian economy to absorb petroleum revenues without excessive structural change appears practically unlimited, especially since this use of petroleum revenues has a negative effect upon the generation of productive income so that an increasing amount of petroleum revenues will be needed just to substitute for other income.

Inflationary Pressures. Inflationary pressures have been a problem in the Norwegian economy for a long time; this has been accentuated by the domestic use of petroleum revenues. The average annual consumer price increase was 8.1 percent from 1970 to 1979, which was slightly less than the OECD average or the weighted average of Norway's trading partners.[37] However, annual rates of inflation on the average have been higher than in West Germany or the United States. In recent years, inflationary pressures have intensified. In 1980 the consumer price increase was 10.9 percent, still less than the OECD average or the weighted average of trading partners, but the seasonally corrected rate for the first six months of 1981 was estimated to be 16.1 percent, that is, one of the highest rates of inflation in the OECD area, and thus higher than both the OECD average and the weighted average of trading partners. This trend was already evident in the second half of 1980 and persisted throughout 1981 and 1982.

The political importance of the inflationary problem has been manifest through the price and wage freeze from September 1978 throughout 1979 and the price freeze in the latter part of 1981. The first wage and price freeze brought inflation down to 4.8 percent in 1979, but this was only a temporary relief, as it was not followed up by an active price and income policy, so that inflation in 1980 was the highest since 1975. Correspondingly, the effect of the price freeze in the autumn of 1981 also appears to have been but a temporary relief.

In the years 1982-1983 petroleum revenues did not decline because the stronger U.S. dollar more than offset the decline in dollar oil prices. By 1983 the foreign debt has largely been paid down so that the amount of petroleum revenue is much higher than expected. In the short term this leads to large current account surpluses, but the Conservative government is trying to bring inflation down by a tight budgetary policy. In theory, the reduced availability of money should help dampen inflation as expenditure would be down from the recent historical rates. However, a tighter economic situation could also have the opposite effect: by intensifying the struggle for more limited resources, prices are driven up as more resources are sought for than are available.[38]

In such a perspective, Norway is in the paradoxical situation that inflation can be fed both by using petroleum revenues domestically and by not using them. The problem is that expectations appear to be irreversible and that the sum of political powers, especially in the context of the Norwegian bargaining economy, may exceed the sum of economic resources available. Therefore a temporary decline in resources available, through the vagaries of petroleum output and petroleum prices, may trigger an intensified struggle for the partition of what is left, in turn triggering even higher inflation.

The remedy could be one of the following: (1) an authoritarian price and wage policy, curbing, for example, the right of trade unions to freely bargain wages and salaries; (2) a strict monetarist policy, curbing the supply of money even further and cutting public expenditure, stimulating a high level of unemployment that supposedly would weaken the bargaining position of trade unions; or (3) an income and price policy based on the participation of all parties involved, eventually combined with a much stronger element of economic planning.

The point in all three cases is to adjust the sum of bargaining powers to the sum of resources available. It is doubtful whether the first way out, an authoritarian price and wage policy, is politically possible in the longer run in Norway. The second remedy is currently being experimented with in the United Kingdom, so far with little obvious success, and it is doubtful whether this would be politically possible in Norway without provoking fairly intensified conflict among strongly organized participants in its bargaining economy. The third way out would require a high degree of institutional innovation and perhaps could not be attempted before either of the two other solutions had failed. However, the outcome of this discussion is that the absence of petroleum revenues can be as inflationary as their influx, at least in a short-term perspective, and that consequently there is likely to be a strong political pressure in favor of increasing petroleum revenues.

This again raises the question not only of the volume of petroleum revenues available but also of their specific end uses in the domestic economy. As pointed out earlier, different uses of petroleum revenues give quite different effects as to labor requirements, and there is more flexibility in the use of petroleum revenues than was generally anticipated. The question is less whether or not to use petroleum revenues domestically, but rather how to use them. Because of the different impacts upon labor requirements, there are more- and less-inflationary uses of petroleum revenues in the domestic economy.

During the 1970s petroleum revenues to a large extent have been used to expand public consumption, that is, in the most inflationary way. However, it is also possible to use petroleum revenues to expand private consumption, which is less inflationary, given the high import content, and which to some extent, can satisfy labor's demands. Furthermore, petroleum revenues can be used for infrastructural and productive investment, in which the import content can be fairly easily regulated and consequently the domestic inflationary impact also controlled, and to some extent satisfy the demands of private capital. In this perspective, inflation as a constraint on absorptive capacity has more of an institutional and political character than an economic nature. A practical solution could be to overhaul the budgetary procedure and to differentiate allocations quite distinctly between investment and consumption purposes, between end uses with a high import content and those with a high domestic-labor content, and to regionalize the budget, since the level of economic activity varies quite considerably among regions.

Finally, methods could be envisaged to channel some of the growing demand for goods and services from the sector that is now protected from foreign competition to outside Norway. This would also require institutional changes and new ways of organizing the supply of these goods and services.

To sum up, inflationary problems represent a constraint on absorptive capacity essentially only to the extent that there is no institutional and organizational innovation in the Norwegian economy. However, this reasoning primarily concerns absorbing petroleum revenues for the purpose of current expenditure; the absorption of petroleum revenues for the purpose of investment is quite a different issue. Investment in infrastructure and in education could be stepped up considerably without causing inflationary problems, especially to the extent that the demand effect can be channeled abroad. Investment in manufacturing and services competing in the home market or in foreign markets will depend not only on the Norwegian cost level, but also on managerial improvement, and last but not least, on the development of the international economy.

New External Constraints on Absorptive Capacity

In theory the optimal rate of extraction of a natural resource should be determined by the maximization of the value of the assets over the time period considered.[39] Thus, the return on capital invested, either in the domestic economy or abroad, compared with the expected development of the unit price of the resource extracted, should decide the rate of extraction.

In practice, the depletion policy for petroleum is determined by a number of complex economic, political, and social considerations for the government in charge of a national oil industry. Return on investment is but one of several factors, others being current income requirements, market considerations, political considerations, and the like. Even if all petroleum-exporting countries are confronted with the question of whether to extract oil and gas or leave the resources in the ground, there is hardly a case where this issue is decided according to economic theory. Petroleum is seldom extracted for the conscious purpose of foreign investment; instead, the surplus available for foreign investment appears as a residual, after current income and domestic-investment requirements have been deducted from the gross revenues. Consequently, financial surpluses of the petroleum-exporting nations fluctuate considerably over time. They tend to be large after each oil-price rise, and then to diminish as the real price of oil erodes, as the output is adjusted to the market, and as the recipient learns how to spend the incremental revenues.

In the case of Norway, a current-account surplus resulting from petroleum revenues was at first forecast for 1977 by the 1974 oil plan. That year turned out to have the largest deficit ever experienced by Norway, and instead of starting as a capital exporter, Norway entrenched its position as a large-scale capital importer. With the repayment of the foreign debt, an increase in the petroleum output, and rising petroleum revenues, Norway has a substantial current-account surplus in 1983 so that funds are available for capital exports. In the event of another oil-price shock, it would be rational for Norway to export a large part of its sudden financial surplus in order to shelter the domestic economy from an unplanned inflow of easy money and to diversify sources of income. As a traditional net importer of capital, Norway has limited experience in exporting capital and in investing abroad; the Norwegian banking system is more used to operating in international markets as borrower than as lender. This raises some important economic and political questions.

Economically, the question is how an eventual net financial surplus should be invested abroad. Total Norwegian investment abroad rose to more than NOK 1 billion ($168 million) in 1981.[40] The current outlook is that it will first be the subject of portfolio investment, and only later, after the appropriate expertise has been acquired, will it be the subject of large-scale financial investment. In any case, there should be an economic basis for a new export industry (banking), with a large supply of the raw material (money), and possibly capital exports could reach an annual average of NOK 50 to 60 billion or about U.S. $10 billion during the 1980s.[41] This figure is speculative but gives an indication of the potential. However, the potential for capital exports prepares the ground for some important political problems.

Norway, like many other Western European countries, currently has control of capital movements, and even if the control system is far from perfect, it does limit the international mobility of capital in relation to Norway. Practically, it is hardly possible for the Norwegian private sector to export or import capital at a large scale without the consent of the government.[42] Given the anticipated financial surplus (even though estimates of oil revenues have been revised downward), it is sometimes argued that the control of capital movements should be lifted. However, the purpose of this control is to regulate domestic liquidity and to avoid large short-term movements of capital that could give an unstable exchange rate.

The transition of Norway from the role of capital importer to that of capital exporter does not make these concerns less important. Given the buildup

138 Petroleum and Economic Development

of petroleum exports and the prospects for a fairly large financial surplus, the Norwegian currency is likely to become an interesting international object of investment, which, without controls on capital movement, could lead to an upward pressure on the Norwegian currency, eventually combined with an unstable exchange rate and an unwarranted increase in domestic liquidity.

Notes

1. Organisation for Economic Cooperation and Development (OECD), *Energy Policies and Programmes of IEA Countries, 1980 Review* (Paris: OECD, 1981), p. 223.

2. Government of Norway, Central Bureau of Statistics, *Økonomisk utsyn for Året 1980 (Economic Survey 1980)* (Oslo, 1981), pp. 127-128.

3. The API designation is the specific gravity of crude oils as defined by the American Petroleum Institute.

4. Government of Norway, Ministry of Petroleum and Energy, *Fact Sheet: Norwegian Continental Shelf* 1981:1 (Oslo, 1981).

5. Government of Norway, Ministry of Petroleum and Energy, *On the Perspectives of the Petroleum Activities in the Near Future,* Parliamentary report no. 40, 1982/1983 (Oslo, 1982), p. 27.

6. Terawatt-hours are equivalent to billions of kilowatt-hours.

7. Organisation for Economic Cooperation and Development (OECD), *Norway: OECD Economic Survey* (Paris: OECD, 1983), p. 59.

8. Jørgen Randers, "Norges Næringsstruktur i Fremtiden," in *Bergen Bank Kvartalsskrift,* 1/1981, pp. 29-52.

9. Morten Egeberg, Johan P. Olsen, and Harald Sætren, "Organisasjonssamfunnet og den Segmenterte Stat," in *Politisk Organisering,* ed. Johan P. Olsen (Oslo: Universitetsforlaget, 1980), pp. 115-142.

10. Stein Rokkan, "Norway: Numerical Democracy and Corporate Pluralism," in *Political Oppositions in Western Democracies,* ed. Robert A. Dahl (New Haven: Yale University Press, 1968), pp. 70-115.

11. Ole Berrefjord and Gudmund Hernes, "Markedsforvitring og Statsbygging," in *Forhandlingsøkonomi og Blandingsadministrasjo,* ed. Gudmund Hernes (Oslo: Universitetsforlaget, 1978), pp. 81-112.

12. Henry Valen, *Valg og Politikk* (Oslo: NKS-Forlaget, 1981), p. 11 ff.

13. Johan Galtung and Nils Petter Gleditsch, "Norge i Verdenssamfunnet," in *Det Norske Samfunn,* vol. 2, eds. Natalie Rogoff Ramsøy and Mariken Vaa (Oslo, 1975), pp. 742-808.

14. Harry Eckstein, *Division and Cohesion in Democracy* (Princeton, N.J.: Princeton University Press, 1966), p. 68 ff.

15. Bernard Delplanque and Fredrik Werring, *L'archipel Démocratique ou l'Antihierarchisme Norvégien* (Paris: Editions Entente, 1978), p. 119 ff.

16. Lennart Jörberg and Olle Krantz, "Scandinavia 1914-1970," in *The Fontana Economic History of Europe*, ed. Carlo Cipolla (London: Collins/ Fontana Books, 1976), vol. 6, no. 2, pp. 377-449.

17. *Full Sysselsetting og Økonomisk Vekst Uten Inflasjon* (Oslo: Oslo-gruppen 1981).

18. Government of Norway, Ministry of Finance, *Langtidsprogrammet 1974-1977*, St. meld. nr. 71 (1972-73), (Oslo, 1973), p. 327.

19. Government of Norway, Ministry of Finance, *Petroleumsvirksom-heten I Det Norske Samfunn*, St. meld. nr. 25 (1973-74) & Oslo, 1974).

20. Organisation for Economic Cooperation and Development (OECD), *Norway: OECD Economic Survey* (Paris: OECD, 1983), p. 59.

21. Ibid.

22. Ibid., pp. 60-61.

23. *Full Sysselsetting og Økonomisk Vesk uten Inflasjon*, p. 78 ff.

24. Geir Bergvoll, "Norsk Eksports Markedsandeler," in *Penger og Kreditt*, no. 4/1980, pp. 293-299.

25. Jan-Evert Nilsson and Kjell Kalgraf, *Vårt Dyre Fedreland* (Oslo: Cappelen, 1979), p. 19 ff.

26. Olav Bjerkholt, Lorents Lorentsen, and Steinar Strøm, "Norge i 1980-Årene: Oljepenger og Omstillinger," in *Bergen Banks Kvartalsskrift*, no. 4/1980, pp. 202-221.

27. Jørgen Randers, "Norges Næringsstruktur i Fremtiden," in *Bergen Banks Kvartalsskrift*, no. 1/1981, pp. 29-52.

28. Adne Cappelen and Anton Hellesøy, "Strukturelle Endringer i Norsk Økonomi Etter Krigen," in *Vardøger*, no. 11/81, pp. 144-177.

29. Olav Bjerkholt, Lorents Lorentsen, and Steinar Strøm, "Norge i 1980-Årene: Oljepenger og Omstillinger," p. 214 ff.

30. A foreign-investment fund could help to regulate the flow of money into the Norwegian economy. A first step in this direction was a recommendation of a royal commission in 1983 that a foreign-investment fund be established to utilize a part of the petroleum revenues. Such a fund could follow in the lines of similar agencies set up by other major oil-exporting countries, specifically Kuwait.

31. Government of Norway, Central Bureau of Statistics, *Economic Survey 1980* (Oslo, 1981), pp. 43 ff.

32. Organisation for Economic Cooperation and Development (OECD), *Norway: OECD Economic Survey* (Paris: OECD, 1983), appendix table on basic statistics and international comparisons.

33. Government of Norway, Ministry of Finance, *Revidert Nasjonal-budsjett 1978*, St. meld. nr. 82 (1977-1978) (Oslo, 1978), p. 46.

34. Trygve Thu, "Klar Katastrofealarm for Norsk Industri," in *Teknisk Ukeblad*, August 17, 1978, pp. 12-13.

35. "Norway Should Bolster Its Non-Oil Industries, OECD Says in Report," *Wall Street Journal*, April 15, 1982, p. 32.

36. Government of Norway, Central Bureau of Statistics, *Economic Survey 1980* (Oslo, 1981), pp. 63 ff.

37. Government of Norway, Ministry of Finance, *National Budget 1981* (Oslo, 1980), p. 7.

38. Charles S. Maier, "The Politics of Inflation in the Twentieth Century," in *The Political Economy of Inflation,* eds. Fred Hirsch and John H. Goldthorpe (Cambridge, Mass.: Harvard University Press, 1978), pp. 37-72.

39. Anwar Jabarti, "The Oil Crisis: A Producer's Dilemma," in Ragaei El Mallakh and Carl McGuire, eds., *U.S. and World Energy Resources: Prospects and Priorities* (Boulder, Colorado: International Research Center for Energy and Economic Development, 1977), pp. 130-131.

40. Fay Gerster, "Norwegian Overseas Investment Up 56%," *Financial Times,* March 9, 1982, p. 19.

41. Vegard Rian, "Bankene Blir Norges nye 'Ejsportindustri'," *Økonomisk-Teknisk Utsyn,* no. 3/1981, pp. 10-11.

42. Arne J. Isachsen, "Norsk Valutapolitikk og Fremtidig Kapitaleksport," *Bergen Bank Kvartalsskrift,* no. 3/1980, pp. 101-111.

Appendix A:
Econometric Model
for Mexico

Econometric studies of the Mexican economy generally assume that the level of oil output and exports are determined exogenously as a result of government policy. The usual approach is to assume some desired target for petroleum production and exports and then to examine the impact of the resulting oil revenues and foreign-exchange earnings on other sectors of the economy.

We have chosen an alternative approach that assumes the level of oil production and of exports is endogenous to our model of the Mexican economy. Since this approach is unique in the literature on economic models of the Mexican economy, and also at odds with the stated goal of the Mexican government to limit the amount of oil production and exports, we should present some defense of this approach. First, it is important to emphasize the difference between Mexico and other energy-producing countries, especially the OPEC members. The rediscovery of petroleum in Mexico in the mid-1970s occurred in the context of rapid economic growth. Mexico was much further along the path of industrialization than, say, the Arabian Gulf nations in that period. Rapid industrialization and economic growth were accompanied by rapid population growth, placing Mexico clearly in the group of high-absorber countries.

The potential growth of the oil sector appeared to be a panacea for the ills afflicting the Mexican economy in the 1970s. The government projected that a relatively low level of oil production would be sufficient to satisfy domestic energy needs, and that modest levels of oil exports would generate sufficient foreign exchange to eliminate any balance-of-payments problems. Foreign banks were quite willing to lend Mexico the funds required for development programs and these loans could be repaid out of foreign-exchange earnings from oil exports. While initial development of energy resources required substantial investment of government funds, the expectation was that in the long run oil exports would finance new developments in the energy sector as well as pay off loans for the initial years of development. The Mexican government anticipated revenues from oil exports sufficient to carry out ambitious welfare and developmental programs in addition to financing the energy program.

In short, energy development appeared to be a cure-all for the economic problems confronting Mexico. Probably the best evidence of this optimistic view was a decision by the Mexican government to reject the recommendations of the World Bank to limit government spending and monetary expansion as a step to reducing both the rate of inflation and the deficit in the balance of payments. The government of Lopez Portillo pursued even more expansionary policies than that of his predecessor Echeverria.

Clearly, energy development is not the panacea for all the economic and social ills that afflict the Mexican economy. The modest levels of hydrocarbon production and export projected in Mexico's Global Energy Plan are not consistent with the ambitious goals set by the Mexican government for industrialization, welfare programs, and economic development. In contrast with the recent past, the energy sector will be less autonomous and energy development will increasingly be coordinated into the broader set of government programs. Thus, it will be the absorptive capacity of the Mexican economy that will determine the rate of energy development in Mexico rather than the other way around. As a high-absorber country, Mexico will require a rapid development of hydrocarbon production and exports in order to meet the needs for domestic consumption and to generate the export earnings required in other sectors of the economy. It is for this reason that we view energy development as an endogenous variable in a model of the absorptive capacity of the Mexican economy.

We have developed a macroeconomic model of the absorptive capacity of the Mexican economy. The model is based upon the Keynesian theory of aggregate demand, supply, and income determination. Using national income statistics for the period 1961-1977, a set of structural equations is estimated and combined with economic identities to constitute a simultaneous system. Then different scenarios are used to project the endogenous variables over the forecast period 1978-1990. These scenarios were based upon different assumptions regarding exogenous variables as they affect absorptive capacity in the forecast period.

Data

Macroeconomic modeling of developing countries is constrained by the paucity and unreliability of data sources, and Mexico is no exception in this regard. Three major data problems are encountered in attempting to model the energy sector for Mexico and relate that sector to other sectors in the economy. The first is the aggregation of data for petroleum and natural-gas production into aggregates of hydrocarbon output. We were forced to rely upon independent sources such as the *Petroleum Economist* and the *Oil and Gas Journal* to estimate a breakdown of the components of hydrocarbon production.

The second data problem that we encountered was the lack of evidence for labor force and employment. The official statistics for labor force and employment are especially weak, making any analyses based on this data suspect. Therefore, we chose to model the nonoil supply sectors of the

Mexican economy in terms of a Leontief/Harrod-Domar production function, expressing output as a function of the capital stock. This does not mean that we accept the capital-stock estimates for Mexico without reservation. We were forced to generate a capital-stock series based upon rather unreliable historical time series for capital formation. The resulting capital-stock series is obviously subject to a wider range of error but is probably more reliable than any labor-force or employment series that we could generate. In a labor-surplus economy such as Mexico's this specification of the production function is probably not unrealistic because capital rather than labor is the major constraint on expanded output in most sectors of the economy.

The third problem we encountered was inconsistency in the data published by different public and private sources in Mexico. Even the official government statistics of aggregate economic activity are not consistent over time and are subject to large changes in estimates from one year to the next. For this reason we relied primarily on the data from *World Tables* published by the World Bank, and supplemented this with data from official Mexican publications. The latter included annual series from *Anuario Estadistico*, published by the Direccion General de Estadistica, and *Informe Anual*, published by Banco de Mexico. Other sources of data included the International Monetary Fund's *International Financial Statistics* and the United Nations *Statistical Yearbook*.

A major problem in this study, as in other macroeconomic models for developing countries, is the small sample size. Reliable data are available only for the period since 1961; therefore seventeen years (1961-1977) was the largest sample period that could be constructed. Over that span of time the Mexican economy experienced significant structural changes. One of the most important shocks to the economy occurred in 1976 with the devaluation of the peso after several decades of stable exchange rates. To adjust for this shock, a dummy variable for 1976 was introduced into several equations including gross domestic investment, net foreign assets of the Central Bank, and money. Another sizable shock to the Mexican economy was the sharp jump in oil prices in 1973-1974; a dummy variable for this shock was introduced into the equation for oil output.

As in other macroeconomic modeling studies utilizing time-series data, we encountered autocorrelation in estimating several of the equations. The Cochran-Orcutt iterative procedure was used to correct for autocorrelation.

Several equations have large residuals for the more recent years. This heteroscedasticity problem is acknowledged but we were not able to eliminate the problem, because of data limitations. Heteroscedasticity may introduce some inefficiency in the regression estimates, but it does not bias the regression coefficients in the model. We were able to obtain useful simulation results despite this problem.

Equations

Absorptive Capacity

The domestic absorptive capacity of Mexico is defined as the utilization of the flow of goods and services in the economy for the purpose of domestic consumption and investment.[1] Gross domestic absorptive capacity (GDA) is equal to the sum of private consumption (CP), government consumption (CG), and gross domestic investment (GDI).

$$GDA = CP + CG + GDI \qquad (A.1)$$

Private consumption (CP) is a function of gross national product minus government revenue ($GNP - GR$), real-money balances which is a proxy for disposable income ($MONY/P$), and the expected rate of inflation ($RINF_{-1}$).[2]

$$CP = a_0 + a_1(GNP - GR) + a_2(MONY/P) + a_3(RINF_{-1}) \quad (A.2)$$

Government consumption (CG) is assumed to depend on government revenue (GR), the expected rate of inflation lagged one period ($RINF_{-1}$), and lagged government consumption (CG_{-1}).

$$CG = b_0 + b_1(GR) + b_2(RINF_{-1}) + b_3(CG_{-1}) \qquad (A.3)$$

Private investment depends on last year's gross domestic product (GDP) and last year's private investment. Gross domestic investment is a function of gross domestic product lagged one period (GDP_{-1}), gross domestic investment lagged one period (GDI_{-1}), and a dummy variable ($D76$) to capture the effect of the 1976 devaluation.

$$GDI = c_0 + c_1(GDP_{-1}) - c_2(GDI_{-1}) + c_3(D76) \qquad (A.4)$$

The Foreign Sector

The quanity of oil exported ($OIQX$) is the quantity of oil produced ($OILQ$) minus the quantity used domestically ($OILD$).

$$OIQX = OILQ - OILD \qquad (A.5)$$

The real value of exported oil ($OILX$) is determined by the simple identity

$$OILX = \frac{(OILP \cdot OIQX)}{P} \qquad (A.6)$$

where *OILP* is the price of oil in pesos, *OIQX* is the quantity of oil exported, and *P* is the general price level.

Real nonoil exports (*OLX*) are assumed to depend on real nonoil gross domestic product (*GDPN*), and the exchange rate (*EXCR*).

$$OLX = d_0 + d_1(GDPN) + d_2(EXCR) \qquad (A.7)$$

The variable total exports (*X*) is simply the sum of oil exports (*OILX*) and nonoil exports (*OLX*).

$$X = OILX + OLX \qquad (A.8)$$

Total real imports (*M*) depends upon gross domestic absorption (*GDA*) and also upon relative import prices, as well as upon the domestic price multiplied by the exchange rate, (*PIM/P*)(*EXCR*).

$$M = e_0 + e_1(GDA) + e_2[(PIM/P)(EXCR)] \qquad (A.9)$$

The balance of trade (*NBOP*) is the difference between nominal exports (*X · PEX*) and nominal imports (*M · PIM*), plus the difference between net transfers and net factor services (*NTR − NFS*).

$$NBOP = (X \cdot PEX) - (M \cdot PIM) + (NTR - NFS) \qquad (A.10)$$

The price of exports (*PEX*), the price of imports (*PIM*), net factor services (*NFS*), and net transfers (*NTR*) are assumed to be exogenous.

The Government Sector

In this model, government expenditure is exogenous. However, nominal government revenue (*NGR*) is determined by nominal gross national product (*NGNP*).

$$NGR = f_0 + f_1(NGNP) \qquad (A.11)$$

The bank finances a portion of its expenditures through borrowing from the central bank. Net government deposits in the central bank (*NGCB*) are assumed to be a function of current and postgovernmental deficit (*NGEX − NGR*).

$$NGCB = g_0 + g_1(NGEX - NGR) + g_2(NGEX - NGR_{-1}) \qquad (A.12)$$

The Monetary Sector

Increased government borrowing from the central bank increases the monetary base (*BASE*) which in turn increases the money supply. (*BASE*) is defined as the summation of net foreign assets in the central bank (*NFAB*), net governmental deposits (*NGCP*), and other assets (*NOA*).

$$BASE = NFAB + NGCP + NOA \qquad (A.13)$$

Other assets in the central bank (*NOA*) is assumed to be exogenous. Net foreign assets in the central bank of Mexico (*NFAB*) is assumed to be a function of total foreign assets in the country (*NFAT*). A dummy variable (*D76*) has been included to capture the effects of the 1976 devaluation.

$$NFAB = k_0 + k_1(NFAT) + k_2(D76) \qquad (A.14)$$

Net total foreign assets (*NFAT*) is equal to net total foreign assets from the previous period (*NFAT*$_{-1}$) plus the change in net foreign assets (*DFAT*).

$$NFAT = NFAT_{-1} + DFAT \qquad (A.15)$$

The change in net foreign assets (*DFAT*) is equal to net capital flow (*NCAF*) and to the balance of trade (*NBOP*).

$$DFAT = NCAF + NBOP \qquad (A.16)$$

Net capital flow (*NCAF*) is assumed to be a function of changes in the United States short-term interest rate (*RUS*), change in the nominal gross national product (*NGNP* − *NGNP*$_{-1}$), and the exchange rate (*EXCR*).

$$NCAF = l_0 + l_1(RUS - RUS_{-1}) + l_2(NGNP - NGNP_{-1}) + l_3(EXCR) \qquad (A.17)$$

Changes in the United States interest rate (*RUS*) and in the exchange rate (*EXCR*) are assumed to be exogenous.

In this model, the supply of money (*MONY*) is equal to the money multiplier (h_1) times the monetary base (*BASE*). The money multiplier (*h*) is assumed to be constant and is estimated by a regression of the money supply on the monetary base. In addition, a dummy variable (*D76*) on the slope has been included to capture the effects of the 1976 devaluation on the multiplier.

$$MONY = h_1(BASE) + h_2(BASE \cdot D76) \qquad (A.18)$$

Domestic prices (*PDG*) are affected by both domestic conditions through the money supply (*MONY*) and foreign conditions through the price of imports (*PIM*).

$$PDG = m_0 + m_1(MONY) + m_2(PIM) \qquad (A.19)$$

However, the general price level (*P*), which has been used as a deflator, is assumed to be a weighted average of the price of imports (*PIM*) and domestic prices (*PDG*). The weight is assumed to be equal to the historical average value of the ratio of the level of imports (*M*) and the level of gross domestic product (*GDP*).

$$P = n(PIM) + (1 - n)(PDG) \qquad (A.20)$$

The rate of inflation (*INFL*) is defined as the rate of change in the price level.

$$INFL = (P - P_{-1})/P_{-1} \qquad (A.21)$$

Oil Output

Gross domestic product in the oil sector (*GDPO*) is derived in the model as a residual; it is equal to the difference between total gross domestic product (*GDP*) and nonoil gross domestic product (*GDPN*).

$$GDPO = GDP - GDPN \qquad (A.22)$$

The quantity of oil produced (*OILQ*) is equal to nominal gross domestic product in the oil sector divided by the price of oil. We estimate the quantity of oil produced by multiplying real gross domestic product in the oil sector (*GDPO*) by a constant (*t*) which is the estimated ratio of domestic prices to the price of oil. We include a dummy variable (*D74*) to capture the effects of the change in the realtive price of oil in that year.

$$OILQ = t_1(GDPO) + t_2(GDPO \cdot D74) \qquad (A.23)$$

The quantity of oil used domestically (*OILD*) is a function of nonoil gross domestic product (*GDPN*).

$$OILD = r_0 + r_1(GDPN) \qquad (A.24)$$

Nonoil Output

Nonoil gross domestic product (*GDPN*) is assumed to be linearly dependent on the capital stock (*KSO*).[3]

$$GDPN = s_0 + s_1(KSO) \qquad \text{(A.25)}$$

The capital stock (*KSO*) is defined as the capital stock from the previous period (*KSO*$_{-1}$) plus gross domestic investment minus depreciation in the current period (*GDI* − *DEP*). We assume a 5-percent rate of depreciation.

$$KSO = KSO_{-1} + (GDI - DEP), \text{ and} \qquad \text{(A.26)}$$

$$DEP = 0.05(KSO_{-1}) \qquad \text{(A.27)}$$

Gross National and Domestic Products

Gross domestic product (*GDP*) is defined as gross domestic absorptive capacity (*GDA*) plus net exports (*X* − *M*).

$$GDP = GDA + (X - M) \qquad \text{(A.28)}$$

Gross national product (*GNP*) is defined as gross domestic product (*GDP*) plus net factor income from abroad (*FY*). Net factor income from abroad (*FY*) is assumed to be exogenous.

$$GNP = GDP + FY \qquad \text{(A.29)}$$

Nominal gross national product (*NGNP*) is defined as real gross national product (*GNP*) times the price level (*P*).

$$NGNP = GNP \cdot P, \text{ and} \qquad \text{(A.30)}$$

$$GR = NGR/P \qquad \text{(A.31)}$$

The following is a list of the endogenous and exogenous variables in the model:

Dependent Variables

BASE	=	Monetary base
CG	=	Government consumption expenditure
CP	=	Private consumption expenditure
DEP	=	Depreciation
GDA	=	Gross domestic absorption
GDI	=	Gross domestic investment
GDP	=	Gross domestic product
GDPN	=	Nonoil GDP
GDPO	=	GDP from mining and quarrying (a proxy for oil GDP)
GNP	=	Gross national product
GR	=	Government revenue
INFL	=	Expected rate of inflation
KSO	=	Total capital stock
M	=	Imports of goods and nonfactor services
MONY	=	Quantity of money defined as currency plus demand deposits and time and saving deposits
NBOP	=	Balance of payments
NCAF	=	Net capital flow
NFAB	=	Foreign assets to the central bank (net)
NFAT	=	Foreign assets of Mexico (net)
NFS	=	Net factor services
NGNP	=	Nominal gross national product
NGR	=	Nominal government revenue
NGCB	=	Net Central Bank's claim in the government
NTR	=	Net transfers
OILD	=	Oil consumed domestically
OILQ	=	Oil output (millions of barrels)
OILX	=	Value of oil exports
OIQX	=	Oil exports (millions of barrels)
OLX	=	Value of nonoil exports
P	=	Price level
PDG	=	Domestic price level
RINF	=	Rate of inflation
X	=	Exports of goods and nonfactor services

Exogenous Variables

DFAT	=	Change in foreign assets
D76	=	Dummy variable 1976 devaluation
EXCR	=	Exchange rate of Mexican peso

FY   = Net factor income from abroad
NGEX   = Nominal government expenditures
NOA   = Other assets
OILP   = Index of crude oil prices (1970 = 100)
PEX   = Price of exports
PIM   = Index of the prices of Mexican imports (1970 = 100)
RUS   = U.S. rate of interest

Some Methodological Issues

The forecasting model consists of thirty-one equations made up of sixteen identities and fifteen stochastic equations. It is a nonlinear model solved by the Newton-Raphson method with ten iterations.

The system of equations in the model may be grouped under eight blocks as described by table A-1. The equations in the first and second block can be solved without reference to the other blocks. Numbers in parentheses refer to equation numbers in text.

Block 3 is preceded by blocks 1 and 2.

Block 4 is preceded by block 3.

Block 5 is preceded by block 4.

Block 6 is preceded by block 4.

Block 7 is preceded by blocks 2, 5, and 6.

Block 8 is preceded by block 7.

In this model there are ten stochastic simultaneous equations. However, because of having too many exogenous variables relative to the degree of freedom, two-stage least-square estimations of the equations give the same results as ordinary least squares. For this reason, the ordinary least-squares estimations of simultaneous equations have been used for the purpose of forecasting.

Estimation Results

The following are our results for equations A.1 through A.31.

Absorptive Capacity (GDA = CP + CG + GDI,
equations A.1 through A.4)

Table A-1
System of Equations for the Forecasting Model of the Mexican Economy

Block 1	Block 2	Block 3	Block 4	Block 5	Block 6	Block 7	Block 8
(A.27) DEP	(A.4) GDI	(A.26) KSO	(A.25) GDPN	(A.24) OILD	(A.7) OLX	(A.2) CP	(A.21) RINF
						(A.1) GDA	
						(A.28) GDP	
						(A.22) GDPO	
						(A.29) GNP	
						(A.11) NGR	
						(A.9) M	
						(A.18) MONY	
						(A.13) BASE	
						(A.3) CG	
						(A.10) NBOP	
						(A.17) NCAF	
						(A.16) DFAT	
						(A.14) NFAB	
						(A.12) NGCB	
						(A.30) NGNP	
						(A.23) OILQ	
						(A.6) OILX	
						(A.5) OIQX	
						(A.20) P	
						(A.19) PDG	
						(A.8) X	
						(A.15) NFAT	
						(A.31) GR	

$$CP = 13.2 + 0.20(MONY/P) + 0.75(GNP - GR) + 30.96(RINF_{-1})$$
$$(0.49) \qquad (0.44) \qquad\qquad (5.3) \qquad\qquad (0.62)$$
$$R^2 = 0.989; \, DW = 2.74$$

$$CG = -1.51 + 0.40(GR) + 13.77(RINF_{-1}) + 0.56(CG_{-1})$$
$$(-1.2) \qquad (9.8) \qquad\quad (2.3) \qquad\quad (12.6)$$
$$R^2 = 0.99; \, DW = 1.58$$

$$GDI = -33.97 + 0.22(GDP_{-1}) - 28.82(D76) + 0.39(GDI_{-1})$$
$$(-1.3) \qquad\quad (1.93) \qquad\qquad (-2.5) \qquad\quad (0.99)$$
$$R^2 = 0.82; \, DW = 1.96$$

The Foreign Sector (equations A.5 through A.10)

$$OIQX = OILQ - OILD$$

$$OILX = OILP \cdot OILD/P$$

$$OLX = 29.25 - 1.48(EXCR) + 0.61(GDPN)$$
$$(3.97) \qquad (-3.18) \qquad\quad (3.46)$$
$$R^2 = 0.63; \, DW = 1.98$$

$$X = OILX + OLX$$
$$M = -3.09 + 0.14(GDA) - 1.33(PIM/P \cdot EXCR)$$
$$(-0.6) \qquad (11.6) \qquad\qquad (-5.7)$$
$$R^2 = 0.94; \, DW = 1.35$$

$$NBOP = (X \cdot PEX) - (M \cdot PIM) + (NTR - NFS)$$

The Government Sector (equations A.11 through A.12)

$$NGR = -10.24 + 0.133(NGNP)$$
$$(-2.3) \qquad (23.3)$$
$$R^2 = 0.98; \, DW = 1.74$$

$$NGCB = -0.15 + 1.12(NGEX - NGR) + 1.62(NGEX - NGR_{-1})$$
$$\quad\quad (-0.02) \quad\quad\quad\quad (1.9) \quad\quad\quad\quad\quad\quad (2.6)$$
$$R^2 = 0.94; DW = 2.32$$

The Monetary Sector (equations A.13 through A.21)

$$BASE = NFAB + NGCB + NOA$$

$$NFAB = 6.01 + 0.078(NFAT) + 13.48(D76)$$
$$\quad\quad (3.71) \quad\quad (16.7) \quad\quad\quad (13.1)$$
$$R^2 = 0.99; DW = 1.60$$

$$NFAT = NFAT_{-1} + DFAT$$

$$DFAT = NCAF + NBOP$$

$$NCAF = -744.5 + 0.27(NGNP - NGNP_{-1}) - 7.96(RUS - RUS_{-1})$$
$$\quad\quad (-14.5) \quad\quad\quad\quad (4.89) \quad\quad\quad\quad\quad\quad (-2.64)$$
$$+ 60.6(EXCR) - 5.45(D76)$$
$$\quad (14.4) \quad\quad (-1.93)$$
$$R^2 = 0.989; DW = 2.40$$

$$MONY = 1.40848(BASE) + 0.529924(BASE \cdot D76)$$
$$\quad\quad\quad (12.45) \quad\quad\quad\quad\quad (5.09)$$
$$R^2 = 0.97; DW = 1.35$$

$$PDG = 0.305 + 0.00404(MONY) + 0.26(PIM)$$
$$\quad (11.09) \quad\quad\quad (6.45) \quad\quad\quad (3.73)$$
$$R^2 = 0.99; DW = 2.11$$

$$P = 0.103(PIM) + 0.897(PDG)$$

$$INFL = (P - P_{-1})/P_{-1}$$

The Oil Sector (equations A.22 through A.24)

$$GDPO = GDP - GDPN$$

$$OILQ = 75.91(GDPO) + 36.30(GDPO \cdot D74)$$
$$(9.75) \qquad\qquad (3.18)$$
$$R^2 = 0.73; DW = 1.16$$

$$OILD = -296.2 + 0.951(GDPN)$$
$$(-1.873) \qquad (3.51)$$
$$R^2 = 0.92; DW = 1.50$$

Nonoil Output (equation A.25)

$$GDPN = 312.3 + 0.2466(KSO)$$
$$(3.94) \qquad (4.13)$$
$$R^2 = 0.99; DW = 1.61$$

Other Identities

$$
\begin{aligned}
KSO &= KSO_{-1} + (GDI - DEP) \\
DEP &= 0.05(KSO_{-1}) \\
GDP &= GDA + (X - M) \\
GNP &= GDP + FY \\
NGNP &= GNP \cdot P \\
GR &= NGR/P
\end{aligned}
$$

Structural Analysis of the Model

The estimation of the model captures important characteristics of the Mexican economy. The private-consumption function yields a marginal propensity to consume that is high compared with that estimated for other oil-producing countries. This is not surprising because Mexico is a high-absorber country. The mass of low-income people in Mexico results in high levels of consumption relative to income, with most of the saving generated by a small share of high-income families. All of the oil revenue generated in Mexico is used to finance domestic expenditures or to service loans from abroad. Mexico is a net borrower in the world capital markets in contrast with some OPEC members that use oil revenues to accumulate savings and are net investors in international capital markets.

Government consumption (equation A.3) is influenced both by the level of government revenue and by the rate of inflation. With higher rates of inflation the government adjusts its nominal expenditures upward so as to maintain or increase its share in the real resources of the country.

Gross domestic investment (equation A.1) is determined as a distributed lag response to changes in gross domestic product. Because of data limitations we were unable to disaggregate the investment function into separate private and government investment functions. As more oil revenues accrue to the Mexican government, the limitation of the model becomes more serious because of the different factors influencing government investment compared with private investment.

The import equation (A.9) shows Mexico has a much smaller propensity to import than other energy-producing countries. This should not be surprising since Mexico is much further along in terms of industrialization and diversification of their economy than many of the OPEC states. Although it is not self-sufficient in terms of total agricultural consumption, Mexico produces most of its domestic food supply and is a net exporter of some agricultural products.

The government-revenue function (equation A.11) reflects the small percentage of revenue generated by the primitive and inefficient tax system of the country. The monetary equations (A.13 through A.18) are designed to capture the important impact of net foreign assets on the monetary base. The Mexican government has relied heavily on foreign borrowing to finance the development of the energy sector and the rapid pace of development expenditures. Thus, monetary expansion is influenced by the capacity of the government to borrow from abroad as well as at home and then inject those funds into the domestic expenditure stream. The price equations (A.19 and A.20) capture the impact of changes in the price of imports on the domestic price level.

The gross domestic product from the oil sector (A.22) is derived as a residual, that is the difference between total gross domestic product and gross domestic product in the nonoil sector. This endogeneity of the oil sector as opposed to treating oil production exogenously is what distinguishes our macroeconomic model from other econometric models of the Mexican economy.

Finally, the gross domestic product of the nonoil sector (A.25) is estimated using a Leontief/Harrod-Domar-type production function.

Simulation Results

The forecasting model was used in simulation studies for the Mexican economy. Using the forecasting model, the endogenous variables in the model through the forecast horizon 1990 were simulated. The simulation program contains two parts: Sim A and Sim B. Sim A evaluates the structure of the system and determines the order in which the equations are solved. Sim B uses this order system to solve for the endogenous variables based upon projected values for the exogenous variables. Sim B is then used to simulate different scenarios based upon alternative assumptions regarding the exogenous variables.

The forecasting model for the Mexican economy contains thirty-six equations in thirty-six endogenous variables. The model is consistent in the sense that it can be solved for all endogenous variables. There are eleven exogenous variables, the values of which are supplied in order to simulate this model over the forecast period. Although the model is forecast annually from 1978 to 1990, only the estimates from 1980, 1985, and 1990 are reported.

All the simulations are based upon the following assumptions.

1. The structure of the model holds true in the future, and that there are no additional absorptive-capacity constraints other than those reflected in the structural equations of the model. It will be noted that the dummy variables are all effective during the forecasting period.
2. The price of Mexican imports (PIM) is projected upon the assumption that it will follow the time path in 1974-1977, during which period it grew at an annual rate of 16.0 percent.
3. The projected values of other deposits (NOA) in the Central Bank of Mexico for 1978-1990 are constant at the 1977 level of 38.0 million pesos.
4. The projected values of net factor income from abroad (FY), net factor services (NFS), and net transfer (NTR) through the 1978 to 1990 period are based on the corresponding historical rates which are 11, 22.7, and 11 percent, respectively.
5. The projected values of the exchange rate ($EXCR$) for 1978 to 1990 are assumed to be constant at 22.572, the exchange rate after the 1976 devaluation.
6. The difference in the short-term United States interest rate ($DRUS$) has been arbitrarily projected.
7. The projected values of Mexican export prices have been based on the historical rate of 11.5 percent.

The forecast period includes annual observations in the three benchmark years of 1980, 1985, and 1990, and average annual rates of change in the endogenous variables over the entire forecast period.

It is important to note that our forecast period includes most of the years of the Lopez Portillo government and all of the years of the De la Madrid government as well as subsequent administrations up to the year 1990. We construct a control scenario in which the monetary and fiscal policy assumptions approximate those actually pursued by the Portillo government over the forecast period. We then compare the control scenario to alternative scenarios in which we assume alternative monetary and fiscal policies.

During the Lopez Portillo administration, the average annual rate of growth of government spending was close to 30 percent. Therefore we simulated the model over the entire period 1978 to 1990 under these assumptions and refer to this simulation as our control scenario. We then compare our scenario with other simulations based upon different assumptions regarding the rate of growth in government expenditures.

One set of alternative scenarios assumes a lower rate of growth in government expenditures, that is, 20 percent compared to 30 percent in our control scenario. The purpose of this scenario is to examine the impact of a slower rate of growth in government expenditure than that actually pursued by the Lopez Portillo government. This issue of a more or less expansionary fiscal policy is the key element in the debate over economic policy in Mexico at present. The new government of De la Madrid has made a commitment to a policy which, if implemented, will reduce the rate of growth in government expenditures closer to 20 percent. The argument for this shift in public policy is that it will achieve a more stable growth with less inflationary pressures than the more expansionary fiscal policy pursued by Lopez Portillo.

Another set of scenarios assumes a lower rate of increase in the price of petroleum—11 percent compared with 16 percent in the control scenario. Many forecasters predict a slower rate of increase in oil prices in the 1980s compared with the 1970s, while others are predicting a stable or declining trend of petroleum prices. These scenarios provide a sensitivity analysis of our simulated scenarios with respect to changes in the rate of increase in the price of oil.

Four scenarios have been considered based on different levels of government expenditure and different percentage increases in the price of oil.

1. An 11-percent increase in the price of oil with a 20-percent increase in government expenditure.
2. An 11-percent increase in the price of oil with a 30-percent increase in government expenditure.
3. A 16-percent increase in the price of oil with a 20-percent increase in government expenditure.
4. A 16-percent increase in the price of oil with a 30-percent increase in government expenditure.

The Monetary Sector

As we would expect in the Mexican case, a higher rate of growth in government spending is accompanied by a higher rate of growth in the money supply. When government spending increases at the 30-percent rate, the money supply grows 32 percent per year; the lower rate of growth in government spending of 20 percent is accompanied by a 19-percent increase in the money supply. Historically the monetary authorities in Mexico have followed an accommodating policy, adjusting the money supply to support whatever level of desired government spending the administration pursued. The government borrows from the Central Bank in order to finance the higher level of expenditures. Note that bank borrowing from the Central Bank also advances about 32 percent when the money supply is growing at the 32-percent rate, but bank borrowing increases at a 22-percent rate when the money supply grows at the slower rate of 19 percent.

The simulation also captures the impact of changes in monetary and fiscal policy on the price level (table A-2). In the control scenario with government spending increasing 30 percent and the money supply growing 32 percent per year, the rate of inflation is 25 percent. That is very close to the actual rate of inflation during the Portillo administration. In the counterfactual scenario in which government spending increases at the lower rate of 20 percent and the money supply grows 19 percent per year, the inflation rate drops to 16 percent.

The implications of the analysis for the De la Madrid government and subsequent administrations is clear. Reducing the rate of inflation will depend upon the success of the Mexican government in pursuing a slower pace of fiscal and monetary expansion compared with that of the Portillo government.

Changes in the money supply and price level are relatively insensitive to changes in the price of petroleum. The explanation is that higher prices for petroleum enable the Mexican government to generate the same level of revenue with lower rates of production and export of petroleum. Thus, when oil prices are increasing at a faster pace the government can expand oil production and exports at a slower pace without jeopardizing government expenditures. On the other hand, when oil prices are increasing at a slower pace (or falling as in late 1981 and 1982), the government will attempt to expand oil output and exports at a faster pace in order to generate needed revenues. The latter appears to be the policy option confronting the De la Madrid government.

The Oil Sector

The oil sector is very sensitive to the fiscal and monetary policy of the Mexican

Table A-2
Mexico: Four Scenarios of Government Expenditures and Oil Prices—Monetary Sector

Scenario	Rate of Increase (percentage)		Year	Money Supply, M_2 (MONY) (billions of dollars)	General Price Level (P) (index)	Net Government Deposit in the Central Bank (NGCB) (billions of pesos)
	Oil Price	Government Expenditures				
1	11	20	1980	560.19	4.00	310.31
			1985	1,271.60	8.44	1,386.50
			1990	2,892.90	18.24	5,264.40
2	11	30	1980	764.02	4.74	310.31
			1985	2,923.80	14.43	1,386.50
			1990	10,703.00	46.56	5,264.40
3	16	20	1980	560.42	4.00	210.18
			1985	1,274.10	8.45	579.83
			1990	2,910.40	18.30	1,564.20
4	16	30	1980	764.33	4.74	310.54
			1985	2,931.30	14.46	1,391.10
			1990	10,880.00	47.01	5,335.90

government. Higher rates of fiscal and monetary expansion are accompanied by significantly higher rates of oil production and export. Oil revenue is the major source of government revenue, and the Mexican government turns to the oil sector to generate the level of revenue needed to finance higher levels of expenditures. As we have noted, higher rates of fiscal and monetary expansion result in higher rates of inflation. In order for the Mexican government to increase expenditures in real terms, this requires more oil revenues with even higher rates of petroleum production and export. It is in this sense that we can refer to Mexico as an energy-dependent economy. Underlying this dependency is a very primitive tax structure that does not rely heavily on revenue from corporate and personal income as do the more developed countries. Until Mexico broadens its tax base, especially in corporate and personal income taxes, it will continue to be an energy-dependent economy.

Faster rates of increase in the price of oil cause the total production of petroleum to decline. However, this decrease is totally reflected in the quantity of oil exported since the level of domestic consumption remains about the same. The country will still receive the same real revenue from exporting oil at the reduced level because of the higher price of oil. It can be concluded that as the price of oil rises at a faster rate, the cutback in the amount of oil exported is to that point which generates the same amount of foreign exchange as obtained under lower oil prices and higher levels of production for export (table A-3).

Real Output

In contrast to the dramatic impact of higher levels of government spending on the oil sector, we find very little impact in the nonoil sector. The rate of growth in the nonoil sector is virtually the same with a 20 percent increase or a 30 percent increase in government expenditures. As a result the rate of growth in total output is relatively insensitive to monetary and fiscal policies (see table A-4).

An expansionary monetary and fiscal policy is reflected almost entirely in a rising price level that leaves the level of output largely unaffected. Apparently the adjustment of oil output and exports to finance the higher levels of government spending takes place without much effect on the nonoil sector. Thus the model captures a fundamental problem in Mexico that is also evident in other energy-producing countries, that is, the dualism or absence of linkages between the petroleum and nonpetroleum sectors of the economy. In Mexico there has been heavy reliance on imports to supply the factors of production required for expansion in oil production. The petroleum industry is very capital intensive so that the expansion in oil production has not required a significant increase in the supply of petroleum workers.

Table A-3
Mexico: Four Scenarios of Government Expenditures and Oil Prices—Oil Sector

Scenario	Oil Price	Government Expenditure	Year	Total Production of Oil (OILQ) (million barrels)	Real Gross Domestic Product of Oil (GDPO) (billions of pesos)	Total Export of Oil (OILX) (million barrels)	Domestic Use of Oil (OILD) (million barrels)
	Rate of Increase (percentage)						
1	11	20	1980	474.9	9.299	119.3	355.6
			1985	635.1	12.437	193.9	441.2
			1990	964.5	18.887	418.9	545.6
2	11	30	1980	487.9	9.550	132.2	355.6
			1985	814.7	15.950	373.0	441.7
			1990	1,843.4	36.100	1,294.5	548.8
3	16	20	1980	459.7	9.000	104.1	355.6
			1985	576.4	11.290	135.4	441.0
			1990	778.7	15.250	234.0	544.6
4	16	30	1980	470.9	9.220	115.4	355.6
			1985	699.5	13.700	258.1	441.4
			1990	1,248.9	24.460	702.2	546.7

The domestic consumption of oil has grown at a steadily rapid pace as a result of subsidized petroleum prices in the domestic economy. The adjustment to higher levels of oil output has been through higher levels of export rather than through changes in the domestic consumption of petroleum. The oil sector can be seen as a modern enclave that is very dependent on the foreign sector but without close linkages to the domestic economy. Levels of oil production and exports can be adjusted to finance higher levels of government spending without significantly affecting output in the nonoil sector.

The Foreign Sector

The rates of growth in total exports and in nonoil exports are not sensitive to the different rates of oil prices and government expenditure. However, a higher rate of increase in government expenditure generates a higher rate of increase in real imports and may therefore result in a negative balance of payments. It can be concluded that a higher level of government expenditure does not contribute significantly to the productive power of the economy but does contribute to the purchasing power of the economy and hence to its ability to import (table A-5).

Absorptive Capacity

The figures for gross domestic absorption show the effects of higher levels of government spending on the total purchasing power. As we would expect, both real private consumption and real government consumption increase with higher levels of government spending (see table A-6). However, real gross domestic investment is relatively insensitive to higher rates of growth in government expenditures. Most of the increases in government expenditures in Mexico over the last decade have been for expanded social welfare. Some increased government revenue has been channeled into public works such as roads and bridges, and public investment has risen in the energy sector. But private investment has been largely unaffected by these developments in the public sector.

In fact, the increased demands placed on financial institutions to finance higher levels of government spending have tended to crowd out investments in the private sector. This reinforces our view that the petroleum industry is a modern enclave with close links to foreign markets and very sensitive to public policies, but without close links to the rest of the Mexican economy.

Table A-4
Mexico: Four Scenarios of Government Expenditures and Oil Prices—Real Output
(*billions of pesos*)

Scenario	Rate of Increase (percentage)		Year	Nonoil Real Gross Domestic Product (GDPN)	Capital Stock (KSO)	Gross National Product (GNP)	Real Gross Domestic Product (GDP)
	Oil Price	Government Expenditure					
1	11	20	1980	685.71	1,514.2	672.91	695.0
			1985	775.83	1,879.7	750.69	788.3
			1990	885.65	2,325.0	840.65	904.5
2	11	30	1980	685.74	1,514.3	673.19	695.3
			1985	776.29	1,881.5	754.67	792.2
			1990	889.08	2,338.9	801.29	694.7
3	16	20	1980	685.69	1,514.2	672.60	694.7
			1985	775.60	1,818.8	749.31	786.9
			1990	884.60	2,320.8	835.95	789.7
4	16	30	1980	685.72	1,514.3	672.84	694.9
			1985	775.96	1,880.2	752.08	789.7
			1990	886.80	2,329.7	847.36	911.3

Table A-5
Mexico: Four Scenarios of Government Expenditures and Oil Prices—Foreign Sector
(billions of pesos)

Scenario	Rate of Increase (percentage) Oil Price	Government Expenditure	Year	Nonoil Real Exports (OLX)	Total Real Exports (X)	Total Real Imports (M)	National Balance of Payments (NBOP)	Net Capital Flow (NCAF) (nominal)
1	11	20	1980	37.59	54.18	58.72	−99.44	199.6
			1985	43.08	64.94	72.68	−433.68	332.5
			1990	49.77	86.71	89.46	−1,353.00	731.6
2	11	30	1980	37.59	53.70	65.92	−141.79	260.7
			1985	43.11	68.80	91.31	−607.45	703.9
			1990	49.98	97.60	117.78	−1,858.60	2,512.5
3	16	20	1980	37.59	54.70	58.69	−99.70	199.5
			1985	43.07	65.70	72.53	−434.02	332.2
			1990	49.71	88.50	88.94	−1,351.50	729.0
4	16	30	1980	37.59	53.60	65.89	−142.08	260.5
			1985	43.09	68.30	91.01	−608.74	702.1
			1990	49.84	95.10	116.04	−1,585.40	2,484.4

Table A-6
Mexico: Four Scenarios of Government Expenditures and Oil Prices—Absorptive Capacity
(billions of pesos)

Scenario	Rate of Increase (percentage) Oil Price	Rate of Increase (percentage) Government Expenditure	Year	Real Private Consumption (CP)	Real Government Consumption (CG)	Real Gross Domestic Investment (GDI)	Gross Domestic Absorption (GDA)
1	11	20	1980	484.3	77.70	136.94	698.93
			1985	537.3	88.74	168.97	795.04
			1990	597.0	100.0	207.82	904.87
2	11	30	1980	491.02	79.48	137.00	707.51
			1985	552.76	92.22	169.76	814.75
			1990	627.49	105.37	212.47	945.33
3	16	20	1980	484.1	77.68	136.89	698.66
			1985	536.5	88.62	168.64	793.73
			1990	594.0	99.67	206.64	900.32
4	16	30	1980	490.8	79.46	136.95	707.21
			1985	551.1	92.01	169.23	812.37
			1990	618.6	104.19	209.39	932.19

Notes

1. In the Mexican model, all the variables starting with N are in nominal terms. For example, NBOP is the nominal balance of payments.

2. The expected rate of inflation is defined as the lag of the actual inflation rate for the purpose of this model.

3. The Cobb-Douglas Production Function had also been employed but the results of the simulation were not much different from the ones obtained here.

Appendix B:
Econometric Model
for Norway

Over the years, several types of econometric models have been developed in Norway, each with its particular field of application. Four of them in particular have been used as tools for macroeconomic planning: (1) models in the MODIS series (MODIS means MOdel of DISaggregated type) which have been used for short-term and medium-term economic planning; (2) the MSG model (MSG means Multi-Sectoral Growth), which in different editions has been used for long-term projections; (3) the PRIM model (PRice and Income Model), developed for use in incomes policy; and (4) a number of taxation models, designed as instruments for studying how changes in direct and indirect taxation affect public receipts from taxation, personal-income distribution, and the like. This summary focuses on two of them, MODIS and MSG.

Characteristics of MODIS

MODIS as it exists today has developed gradually over a number of years. It was first introduced in 1960. Since then, four different versions have been in use, each new version representing in some way an improvement on earlier versions and drawing always on experiences learned in the past.

There are a few characteristics of MODIS that distinguish this model from some models in use in other countries.

1. The model has been developed as an instrument to be used in the planning process, not as an academic exercise; hence—especially in later versions—much effort has gone into making the model user friendly.
2. Historically, work on the MODIS model grew naturally out of national accounting work. As a result of this, the relationships of the model correspond closely to the accounting structure of the national accounts, and concepts and classifications in the two systems are largely identical.
3. The model may be described as a static, disaggregated, Keynes-inspired model built around an input-output core. Its economic content is not very sophisticated; in its latest version the model includes behavioristic relationships describing consumer demand, taxation, and the formation of prices and incomes, while exports and investments are taken to be exogenous variables and money- and credit-market variables are neglected altogether.

This appendix was prepared with the assistance of Ola Strøm.

167

4. The model is intended for simulation studies rather than for unconditional forecasting.
5. While meager in economic content, the model is at the same time highly disaggregated. For instance, in its latest version it has about 140 production sectors. Hence, when measured by the number of variables and equations the model is by no means small.

As further background, a brief sketch must be given of the planning procedure in Norway as it developed during the pre-MODIS period.

Economic Planning in the Pre-MODIS Period (1946-1960)

Norway formed its first annual economic plan in 1946. Since then, similar plans, called national budgets, have been published every year. Up to about 1960 the national budgets were worked out through a decentralized, administrative procedure. Ultimate responsibility for the national budget document rested, at the civil servant level, with a group of planners within the Ministry of Finance. However, it was left to the various ministries to work out plan proposals for all sectors of the economy under their management and to submit these to the Ministry of Finance. There, the proposed sector plans were combined into a tentative master plan and subjected to a critical examination with respect to internal consistency, economic realism, and political content. Quite often the sector plans were returned to the ministries responsible for them, with requests for revisions. Sometimes this had to be done in more than one round so that the national budget, when it finally emerged, was the outcome of a lengthy administrative process of successive approximation.

But this administrative method (as it has been called) could not guarantee the internal consistency and economic realism of the final plan. Without a formal economic model at their disposal the planners at the Ministry of Finance could do little more than check that all important definitional equations had been respected, that obvious constraints known to exist in the economy had not been violated, and that the plan figures looked plausible.

One particularly important line of development was started in the early 1950s when the Central Bureau of Statistics and the University Institute of Economics used the input-output tables of the national accounts for 1948 and 1950 as a data base for constructing and starting experiments with a thirty-sector Leontief model. From the middle of the 1950s results derived from this model were used by planners at the Ministry of Finance to check that national-budget figures were consistent with what was known about the production relationships existing in the economy. In particular, the planners learned to rely heavily on results from the input-output model, rather than on subjective judgment, in ensuring that projections for imports were compatible with anticipated consumption, investments, and exports. However, throughout all of the 1950s the administrative method remained the main tool for setting up the national budget. This started gradually to change in 1960 when MODIS I, the first model explicitly designed for planning needs, became available.

The Early Quantity Model: MODIS I (1960-1965)

MODIS I might be described briefly as a production-consumption model. It combined information about consumers' behavior derived from demand analysis with a revised input-output model completed by the Central Bureau of Statistics in 1959.

MODIS I was, in some respects, rather detailed. It distinguished some 130 industries, about half of which were assumed to have exogenously determined production levels. However, the economic content of the model was meager. Investment, exports, government expenditures, and government receipts from (net) direct taxation were all considered exogenous variables. The model was a pure *quantity* model, meaning that it had no variable relating to prices. MODIS I, like all its successors, relied on the national accounts as a data base and accepted the definitions and classifications used in the national accounting system.

When used in national budgeting work the model could produce estimates for two successive years, usually the current year (the year when the planning took place) and the following, or plan year. Only one policy alternative could be studied during one run of the model. MODIS I was used in the preparation of five national budgets during the years 1960-1965 and also in the preparation of the government long-term program for the period 1962-1965. To begin with, before the planners through experience had learned to trust the model, it was used in national budgeting work mainly to provide a check on estimates derived, as in the 1950s, by means of the administrative planning method. Later, as faith in the model increased, the model increasingly became the main instrument used in forecasting the real flows of the economy.

Yet, as a planning model, MODIS I had obvious shortcomings. Its economic content was limited. Since it was a pure quantity model it could not be used easily. The effects of credit policy on investment, and through investment on the rest of the economy, had to be analyzed outside the model, more or less intuitively, as before. In addition to its economic shortcomings, MODIS I had operating properties that hampered its practical use.

Yet with all its shortcomings, MODIS I undoubtedly worked and the model represented a great step forward that foreshadowed a complete breakthrough for econometric methods in Norwegian planning.

Extensions with Price and Income Variables:
MODIS II (1965-1967)

The next version of the model, MODIS II, was ready for use in 1965. It represented a considerable improvement on MODIS I in that a price model was added to the volume model. The price model was built around the input-output core of the existing quantity model by classifying industries as either sheltered or exposed and by making assumptions about the price behavior of these two industry groups. For the sheltered industries the model assumed cost-plus pricing. For the exposed industries the model assumed output prices to be determined by the world market and thus to be exogenously given. A third category of industries were industries that had their output prices fixed by government decree; these industries were treated formally like exposed industries.

With these extensions a number of new variables were introduced into the model, notably output prices, wage rates, rates of indirect taxes and subsidies, and other price variables. Furthermore, by combining price and quantity variables, variables such as different types of income flows, tax amounts, and transfer payments could also be defined. A number of new relationships could be added.

MODIS II also represented a great improvement on MODIS I from a technical point of view, in that it was implemented on a much larger computer. The improved computer facilities allowed the model to be solved for ten different policy alternatives simultaneously, each alternative covering two consecutive planning periods (years).

In practice, MODIS II turned out be used less frequently than had been hoped by its constructors. There are a number of reasons why MODIS II was not utilized more extensively. First, it was a lengthy process to prepare the input needed for each run. Second, the model lacked flexibility. Third, it was an exacting task to prepare, in advance of each run, forecasts for each one of the 650 exogenous variables of the model. To ensure consistency in the choice of values for the exogenous variables called for careful work and a high level of competence among the users of the model.

Improved Computer and Programming Technology:
MODIS III (1967-1973)

The next version of the model, MODIS III, dating from 1967, was essentially a reprogrammed and more user-friendly version of MODIS II. It aimed at remedying some of the technical weaknesses of the latter while making no attempt to improve its economic content.

First, and most important, the system for handling exogenous input was greatly simplified. Second, more efficient machine programs reduced to moderate quantities the costs, in machine time and money, of solving the model. Third, the use of parallel solutions was made more flexible so as to allow computations for any number of years, within an overall limit of years by alternatives less than or equal to twenty. Fourth, some of the key classifications of the model were made to depend on parameters the value of which could be chosen by the model user; in this way the planners were given some opportunity to influence the structure of the model.

In an attempt to provide planners and analysts with a tool for working out quick answers to economic problems, MODIS III was used as a basis for computing a set of so-called tables of effects. These tables showed in a systematic way the effects to be expected on endogenous variables of given changes in individual exogenous variables or groups of variables. The table of effects were found by the planners to be a helpful accessory to the model itself.

With these improvements successfully incorporated, the MODIS model became an instrument that planners in the Ministry of Finance found comparatively easy to use. The use of MODIS became a part of the regular routines of the Ministry of Finance for keeping the national budget forecasts up to date. In addition to its place in the national budgeting process, MODIS III was used on some occasions for the analysis of (ad hoc) policy problems.

Revised Data Base and More Flexibility:
MODIS IV (1973-   )

Toward the end of the 1960s it was decided to bring the Norwegian national accounts into correspondence with the revised System of National Accounts of the United Nations (SNA revised). For this purpose a large number of changes were made in the accounting framework, in the definition of variables, and in the detailed specification and classification of variables. It was clear that similar changes would have to be made in the definition and classification of variables of MODIS if the all-important correspondence between the structure of the model and the structure of the data base was to be maintained. Accordingly, work on a new version of MODIS (MODIS IV), adapting the model to its new data base, started in 1969 and was completed in 1973. The opportunity was taken to incorporate into the model certain new features which, it was hoped, would remove some of the weaknesses known from experience to hamper the use of the model as a planning instrument.

Important changes were made in the model structure. First, the new data base allowed the input-output core of the model to be changed from a sector-sector structure to a commodity-activity-sector structure, thereby introducing commodities as a separate category of variables distinct from interindustry flows. This made MODIS a better instrument for analyzing problems of indirect taxation and subsidies. Second, the new input-output structure required consequent changes to be introduced in a number of other relationships. Third, other changes, mostly minor, were needed to adapt the model to the definitions and classifications chosen for the revised national accounts. Fourth, a certain amount of flexibility was infused into the model by arranging for (ad hoc) changes to be possible, without great difficulties, in certain key variables. Finally, steps were taken to integrate fully into MODIS IV certain routines which in relation to MODIS III had been treated as submodels.

None of these changes extended the economic content of the model much. MODIS IV, like its predecessors, remained a comparatively open model. The alterations did, however, have the effect of adding considerably to the number of variables of the model. In its latest version MODIS IV has approximately 2,000 exogenous variables. It is capable of handling simultaneously, if required, between 400 and 500 policy alternatives. It became a formidable task, therefore, to prepare the input needed for even one run of the model.

The solution to this problem was found in an auxiliary program that allowed the model user to present his input in aggregated form if desired. The program accepts forecasts for the 2,000 exogenous variables at any level of aggregation. It then transforms them, in accordance with instructions received, into the disaggregated format required by the main model. The practical consequence is that the model user is given freedom to operate with a level of aggregation of input that he or she may choose according to the needs of the particular problem. A similar flexibility is provided for in the presentation of the output of the model. The number of endogenous (output) variables of MODIS IV is of the order of magnitude of some five thousand and can be made available to the model user in the form of edited tables. The system allows the model user to select from a large number of possible tables exactly those he wants to have, with a specification of detail which he himself is free to choose. Since the model variables are defined in conformity with the variables of the national accounts, it is possible to have the tables set out so as to show model results (forecasts) together with corresponding historical figures. This facilitates the interpretation of the model results and has proved a great convenience.

With the flexibility of MODIS IV and the present ability of the administrative system to avail itself of the model, the days are now past when MODIS was run only a few times each year, whenever a national budget or a four-year plan had to be worked out or revised. The present routine is that, for use within the administration if not necessarily for publication, the national budget is kept permanently updated by means of regular runs of the MODIS model, the planners at each run basing their assumptions on the latest economic information available to them.

A Summary of the Structure of MODIS IV

The structure of the model is outlined in figure B-1. Full-drawn boxes indicate formalized parts of MODIS IV. Dotted boxes indicate still unformalized parts. Other informal models, such as sector models, might be added to the diagram. The connection between informal models and MODIS IV is mediated through exogenous variables and parameter changes. The model is thus, at the present stage, closed at various points by exogenous assumption instead of appropriate additional models. The central part of the model is the conceptual and accounting definitions and the basic relations representing the technological structure and the cost structure of the economy. The technological and cost structures are modeled by using a modified form of the input-output formulation of Leontief.

Apart from the accounting definitions and the basic structural relations, the model consists of a number of parts, or submodels, of which the quantity submodel and the price submodel are primary. At present there are in addition two submodels for direct and indirect taxes, respectively. Figure B-1 also indicates additional submodels that at the present time are not formalized but that reside in the administrative environment. In the further development of the model it is an aim to include in the formal framework all interrelations between the variables of the model. It is almost inevitable, however, that the full model of the functioning of the economy as seen by the user is for some parts too complex or too vague to be included in the computational setup. The envisaged full model is referred to as the *outer model*, while the basic structural relations together with the projections of the outer model into the basic equations will be referred to as the *inner model*. The outer model thus includes the inner model as an embedded part, and the outer model may thus include parts that are not formalized for computational solution. The nonformalized parts of the outer model are represented in the formal structure as quasi-exogenous variables. It is important for the overall consistency of the model results that the logic underlying the estimation of these quasi-exogenous variables is consistent with the other assumptions of the model.

The Input-Output Framework

The core of the MODIS IV is the input-output formulation of the technological and cost structures of the economy. MODIS IV has moved slightly away from its predecessors in that a distinction is now made between *commodities*, *sectors*, and *activities*. *Commodity* means a grouping of goods and services, *sector* means a functional unit of the economy that takes part in the commodity circulation, and *activity* means a subdivision of sectors according to characteristic properties of the type of commodity generation, absorption, or transformation that is taking place. The production activities

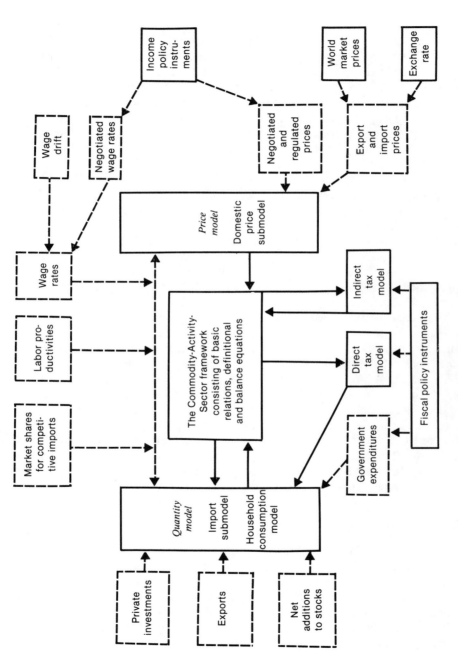

Figure B-1. Structural Map of MODIS IV

normally have both input and output of commodities, while the import and final demand activities have only output and only input, respectively.

Within each activity fixed proportions are assumed between commodity inputs and commodity outputs. This means that, apart from the special treatment of some industries (especially ocean transport and crude-oil extraction), the activity coefficients are assumed to remain constant irrespective of the levels of output (or input) and relative prices. The assumption of fixed coefficients in the original Leontief formulation is thus maintained, but only within each activity. On the production side this means that, for a sector as a whole, changes in the output mix will change the composition of input. On the final demand side the assumption of commodities in fixed proportions is applied to subcategories of the conventional sector classification.

The coefficients are estimated from commodity-by-sector input and output tables for the base year of the model (usually the year prior to the current year). The problem of allocating inputs to a production sector (an industry) among its activities is at present solved simply by classifying each production activity as having either a *commodity technology*, that is, the same input structure as other activities with the same output, or a *sector technology*, the same input structure as other activities belonging to the same sector.

The commodity-activity-sector framework is a mapping of the commodity flows of the economy. The links among the sectors and economic entities outside the commodity sphere are provided by *primary inputs and final outputs* of the sectors. By definition, each sector is balanced in the sense that the value of primary input plus commodity input equals the value of final output plus commodity output.

A production sector has a primary input of labor services (wages), capital services (depreciation and operating surplus), which together with net indirect taxes make up the difference between the value of commodity output and commodity input. The import and export sectors have primary inputs from and to the foreign account equal to the value of commodity output and input, respectively. The domestic final-demand sectors have final outputs equal to the value of the various types of final demand.

The model results consist of sets of prices and quantities, complete and consistent in an accounting sense, with time reference to calendar years. Prices of commodity flows are indexes of the unit values, relative to a given base year, and quantities of commodity flows are measured in unit values of that year. The input-output structure of the economy is modeled both for quantities and prices, the input-output *price relations* being the dual counterpart to the input-output *quantity relations*. The rest of the model system is closely linked to and integrated through these basic structural relations.

The Quantity Model

The quantity model is mainly demand oriented and the supply side is assumed to respond to any real demand for commodities, labor, and capital services. The model distinguishes between commodity demand through household consumption, private investments, government expenditures, exports, and net additions in stocks. Intermediate commodity demand also plays an important role in a rather disaggregated model like MODIS IV. This demand is taken care of through the input-output quantity relations discussed earlier.

Household consumption is dealt with by a system of consumption relations. The main elements of the submodel for household consumption are an aggregate consumption function, and a set of distribution relations. *The aggregate consumption function* determines the total demand for household consumption as a function of real disposable income for three socioeconomic groups: (1) wage and salary earners, (2) the self-employed, and (3) pensioners. The nominal incomes are made up of wages, profits of unincorporated enterprises (including agriculture), and government transfers distributed on the three socioeconomic groups. After deducting direct taxes and deflating by an index of consumer prices, real disposable incomes are arrived at. The *distribution relations* allocate the total demand for household consumption among the household-consumption activities by means of income (Engel) and price (Cournot) derivatives.

The main groups of input variables of the submodel are (1) consumer-good prices, including the appropriate consumer price index (determined in the price model); (2) wage rates (exogenous); (3) industrial employment (simultaneously determined) and government employment (exogenous); (4) profits (simultaneously determined); (5) government transfers (exogenous); and (6) direct taxes (simultaneously determined). Private investments, exports, net additions to stocks, and government expenditures are all exogenously given in the model.

The demand for each commodity is, on the supply side, met by *domestic outputs* and *imports*, the distribution between these two sources being dependent upon the demand composition for the commodity. Imports of commodities are divided more or less conventionally into competitive and noncompetitive commodities. The noncompetitive imports are directly determined by demand. The import relations for competitive commodities are built around a matrix of import shares for the input of each commodity to each activity. However, it is possible to change these import shares exogenously. The matrix of import shares (specified by commodity and receiving activity) reflects the fact that the import content of a given commodity will differ between receiving activities, especially between export and domestic demand. The distribution of domestic production of a given commodity among its various suppliers is dealt with through fixed market shares.

Value-added production functions in inverted forms are used as labor-requirement functions. In these functions *industrial employment* is linked to the domestic production level through exogenous productivity estimates. Industrial employment is thus also demand-determined in MODIS IV. The numbers of self-employed and government employees are exogenously determined.

The Price Model

The price side of MODIS IV is, as in the earlier versions of the model, strongly supply (cost) oriented. The far-reaching changes in the actual formulation of the price relations are mainly a consequence of the new commodity-activity-sector approach, but some new elements have been added.

The commodity prices are the most important variables in the price model. The price of a given commodity flow is assumed to differ depending on whether it is imported or domestically produced and on whether it is exported or delivered to the domestic market. Each commodity may, accordingly, have an import price, an export price, and a domestic price. The import and export prices are exogenously given through forecasts for the world market prices and of the exchange rate.

Reflecting the openness of the Norwegian economy, an important feature of the price model is the distinction between *exposed* and *sheltered* domestic prices. The exposed domestic prices are prices of commodities produced and marketed domestically under strong foreign competition. In the model it is assumed that the exposed domestic prices normally are adjusted to the corresponding import prices. The sheltered domestic prices, on the other hand, are prices of domestically produced commodities sold in domestic markets and sheltered to a greater extent from foreign competition. For the latter commodities the model assumes two different kinds of price formation, *regulated and negotiated prices* and *cost-determined prices*.

The regulated and negotiated prices are those which are either fixed or regulated more or less completely by public bodies or determined through negotiations between the government and producer organizations (agricultural prices). The cost-determined prices are assumed to adjust to changes in the costs of producing the commodities. Wage costs per unit of production are given by the exogenous estimates for labor productivities and wage rates. In normal use of the model the exogenous markup rates are adjusted so that the share of gross profits (depreciation and profits) in factor income in the production for sheltered domestic markets is left more or less unaffected by changes in costs. The necessary parameters for the computation of the indirect tax costs are determined in the indirect tax model. The price propagation process that follows from the fact that higher output prices of commodities from one production sector means higher input prices, that is, higher costs, in other words, is dealt with by the input-output price relations.

The Interactions between the Relationships

From this short description of the formalized parts of the quantity and price sides of MODIS IV it follows that supply conditions determine prices independent of demand. It is possible to illustrate this by the simple supply-demand situation shown in figure B-2. The supply curves, with commodity prices as arguments, are infinitely elastic or horizontal, since the price model is solved independent of final demand. The demand curves have downward slopes because of the commodity-price influence on household consumption. It follows from this that the price model can be solved before the quantity model. Apart from some minor obstacles, this is the actual solution procedure followed in MODIS IV.

This recursive structure of the price and quantity models of MODIS IV resembles that of a general equilibrium model in which production takes place under constant returns to scale and primary input prices are given. Both of these assumptions are also made in MODIS IV. It should also be noted that the horizontal supply curve is supposed to be a reasonable approximation to the actual one only in the area close to the desirable equilibrium point (near full employment).

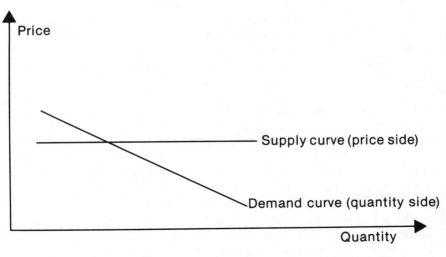

Figure B-2. The Supply and Demand Curves of MODIS IV

In explaining the interactions within the quantity and price sides of MODIS IV, we shall present the major closed loops of the model. We define a *closed loop* as one where the relationships feed back upon themselves so that any solution of the model satisfies the set of relationships in the loop. As noted earlier, much of the interpretation and operational meaning of the model is provided by the unformalized parts of the outer model. In actual use the model thus also contains many open loops, not specified here, in which imbalances can arise. The imbalances may be caused by differences between target values and model-calculated values, in which case the policy instruments must be changed, or by informal or formalized behavioral relationships not formally included in the model, in which case the model user must change the exogenous variables in such a way that the model results also are in accordance with these relationships.

The three main closed loops are (1) the input-output domestic-production loop, (2) the household consumption-income loop, and (3) the input-output domestic price loop. (1) and (2) are both parts of the quantity model while (3) forms the core of the price model.

The input-output domestic-production loop is presented in figure B-3. Intermediate demand together with household consumption and the various exogenous final demand items add to commodity demand. The domestic part of commodity demand determines industry output. The link between industry output and intermediate commodity demand closes the loop.

As indicated in figure B-3 there is also a link between industry outputs and household consumption. This household consumption-income loop is presented in figure B-4. Here household consumption is related to real disposable income for the various socioeconomic groups and to relative consumer-good prices. Household consumption results in commodity demand and industrial outputs. Through the wage relation (which includes exogenous estimates for industrial labor productivities, government employment, and wage rates) and through the profit relation (which includes results from the price model), industry outputs generate wage income and profits of unincorporated enterprises. These incomes, together with government transfers, are distributed to the various socioeconomic groups. By deducting direct taxes (the parameters given from the direct-tax model) and by deflating by the consumer price index (given from the price model) real disposable incomes are generated. This closes the loop.

The input-output domestic-price loop (see figure B-5) is the counterpart on the price side to the input-output domestic-production loop. Wage costs are determined by the exogenous wage rates and industrial labor productivities. Gross profit costs are given by the exogenous markup rates. The parameters necessary to determine the indirect tax costs are given from the indirect tax model. Intermediate inputs are partly import-priced and partly domestically priced, the distribution being determined by the import market

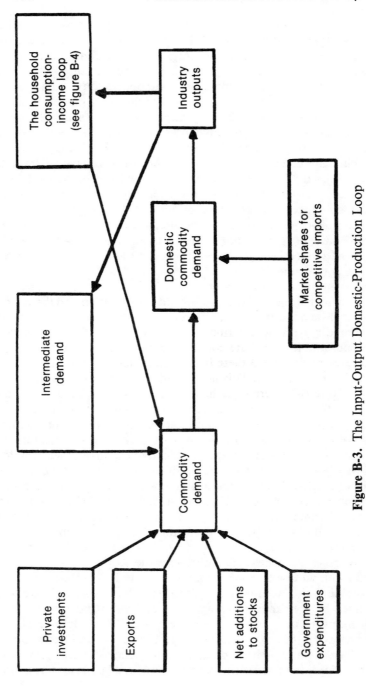

Figure B-3. The Input-Output Domestic-Production Loop

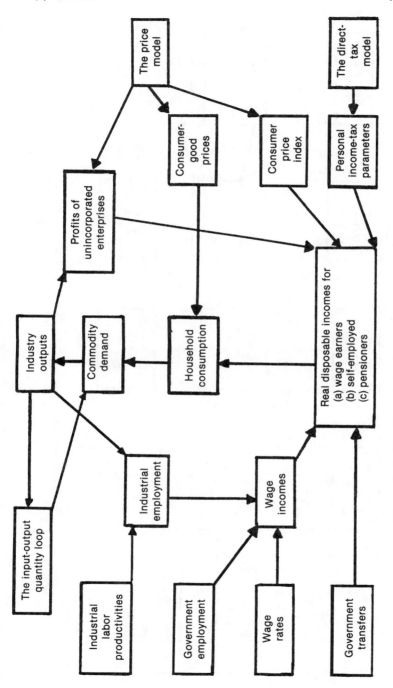

Figure B-4. The Household Consumption-Income Loop

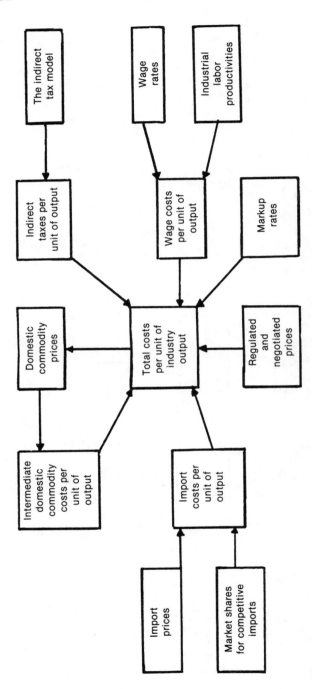

Figure B-5. The Input-Output Domestic Price Loop

shares. Total unit costs generate domestic commodity prices and the loop is closed.

Taxes, Transfers, and Fiscal Budgeting

The treatment of fiscal items in MODIS IV is intended to serve a threefold purpose. First, while remaining within the macroeconomic framework of the model, the specification of exogenous variables relative to fiscal budgets is made to correspond closely with fiscal instruments as determined by law or regulations. Second, for the purpose of fiscal budgeting it sees that each fiscal item in the model belongs to one and only one of the general government accounts. Third, arrangements have been made to allow a thorough treatment of the interrelations between the various fiscal items on the one hand and commodity flows and income categories on the other.

The direct-tax model distinguishes among the three socioeconomic groups of households, and the income distribution by income intervals within groups is represented in the model. The proceeds of some of the specified types of direct taxes are wholly exogenous. For the others, the tax-assessment rules are represented in a very detailed way in the nonstochastic tax functions within the microeconomic portion of the model. The microeconomic part can be run as a separate model that requires input of forecasted growth of income, number of wage earners, self-employed, pensioners, and so on. As a part of MODIS IV this portion is used to estimate parameters of macroeconomic tax functions that enter into the household-consumption submodel and therefore into the simultaneous solution of the quantity side of MODIS IV.

The design of the *model for indirect taxes* (and subsidies) is strongly influenced by the general framework of MODIS IV. The disaggregated representation of the commodity flows has opened up the possibility of establishing rather close connections between the indirect-tax parameters of the model and the kind of information contained in tax rules. Each indirect tax is classified as either a commodity tax or an industry tax. The proceeds from industry taxes are exogenous. The proceeds from commodity taxes are endogenous in the model. Each commodity tax is further classified according to the tax base and the taxpayer. The tax base of a commodity tax is either the quantity or the current value of one or more commodities. The tax rate for each commodity is given by a vector. The vector gives the tax rate on commodity flows *to* each activity. In this way the model reflects the fact that the tax rate of a commodity tax may differ among the receivers of the commodities on which the tax is levied. Typically, the tax rate will be zero on deliveries to export, but the tax rate may be differentiated on deliveries to other receivers as well. As for direct taxes, the assessment rules are thus represented by very detailed tax functions.

For use in *fiscal budgeting*, the revenue models for direct and indirect taxes play a central role. There is no corresponding model covering the fiscal expenditures (apart from subsidies included in the indirect-tax model). As a preliminary for such a model, efforts have been made for a specification of fiscal-expenditure items in the model to link the national-accounts data to the fiscal budget. Expenditures for goods and services are specified by government purposes; by government production sectors; by government account (institutional sector); and by type (wages, goods, services). Transfer expenditures are similarly classified by kind of government purposes, by type of government, and by socioeconomic groups. Sales of government services to the public are also specified to fit into this classification.

The Input-Output Framework of MODIS IV

MODIS IV is basically an input-output model. Its input-output framework differs, however, from the traditional Leontief-type square matrix of input-output coefficients for industry-by-industry transactions with a set of conversion coefficients connecting industry flows and final-demand categories.

The Commodity-Activity-Sector Approach and the Basic Quantity Equation

The three central concepts of the input-output framework of the model are *commodity, sector,* and *activity.* These concepts distinguish among three different aspects of absorption and generation of goods and services, namely, what is absorbed or generated (the commodity concept), where the absorption or generation is taking place (the sector concept), and how the goods and services are absorbed or generated (the activity concept). The number of commodities of the model, which are aggregates of the commodities of the national accounts, is about 200. Nearly 190 of these are industry commodities while 10 are *marketed* government services.

A sector may generate commodities or absorb commodities, or both. The most important group of sectors are the industries which, together with the general government production units, form the production sectors. The production sectors transform input flows of commodities into output flows of commodities and thereby absorb some commodities while generating others. The other main sector groups, which either generate or absorb commodities, are the import sectors, export sectors, the houshold-consumption sectors, and the gross-investment sectors.

By *activity* is meant a subdivision of sectors according to characteristic properties of the type of commodity generation, absorption or transformation which are taking place. The subdivision of sectors into activities carries a different meaning for each type of sector. The commodity flows among activities include all generation and absorption of commodities except changes in stocks. Within each activity there are assumed fixed proportions between commodity inputs and commodity outputs. The main purpose of subdividing sectors into activities is to avoid having to assume fixed proportions between commodity inputs and commodity outputs for the sector as a whole. The subdivision also makes it possible to distinguish among different ways of generating or absorbing a certain commodity within the same sector.

To describe the commodity-by-sector flows of the economy we introduce the following definitions and balance equations:

S_{ij}^+ = output of commodity i from sector j,

S_{ij}^- = input of commodity i from sector j,

S_j = net output of commodities in sector j
   = *sector level* of sector j.

$$S_j = \sum_i S_{ij}^+ - \sum_i S_{ij}^- \qquad (B.1)$$

X_i = net addition to stocks of commodity i.

$$X_i = \sum_i S_{ij}^+ - \sum_i S_{ij}^- \qquad (B.2)$$

Balance equations similar to those given for the *sectors* in equations B.1 and B.2 will also hold for commodity flows into and out of activities:

A_{ij}^+ = output of commodity i from activity j,

A_{ij}^- = input of commodity i to activity j,

A_j = net output of commodities in activity j
   = *activity level* of activity j.

$$A_j = \sum_i A_{ij}^+ - \sum_i A_{ij}^- \qquad (B.3)$$

$$X_i = \sum_j A_{ij}^+ - \sum_j A_{ij}^- \qquad (B.4)$$

By the concepts of sector and activity levels is meant a measure of the net commodity generation and absorption that take place in a sector or an activity, respectively. The values of the activity levels within each sector add up to the sector level. As for the sector and activity concepts themselves, the activity level and sector level carry different meaning for each type of sector.

The basic quantity equation of the input-output framework is

$$\Lambda A = X \tag{B.5}$$

where

Λ $= \{ \lambda_{ij} \}$ is a commodity-by-activity coefficient matrix
in which the element $\lambda_{ij} = (A_{ij}^+ - A_{ij}^-)/A_j$
(positive or negative) gives net output of
commodity i per unit of activity level j,

A is a vector of activity levels, and

X is a vector of net additions to stocks (by commodity).

Equation B.5 follows directly from manipulations of B.4 by inserting the expression for λ_{ij}.

The basic assumption of the quantity input-output model of MODIS IV is that the quantities of commodity inputs to and outputs from an activity are related by fixed proportions, i.e., that all elements in Λ are constants.

In general, the elements in Λ are estimated from the national accounts for the base year of the model, usually the year prior to the current year. This means that quantities of commodity flows are measured in unit values (prices) of the base year, constant values. The system of commodity flows is closed with regard to all generation and absorption of commodities except changes in stocks. The excess of commodities generated over commodities absorbed is thus defined as net additions to stocks.

Value Concepts and the Basic-Price Equation

The principal concept for evaluating commodity flows in the model is *basic value*. In terms of the more commonly used concepts of producers' value and purchasers' value, the basic value of a commodity flow is defined as the producers' value less commodity taxes, net, in respect of production, or the purchasers' value less trade margins and commodity taxes, net, in respect of production and trade. In the national accounts, each commodity flow is broken into several different value components, that is, basic value and commodity taxes, net, in respect of production, which add up to producers' value, and trade margin (in basic value) and commodity taxes, net, in respect of trade, which together with the producers' value add up to purchasers' value. In addition, the commodity taxes, net, for each commodity flow, both in respect of production and trade, are further split between general purchase tax (VAT), other commodity taxes, and commodity subsidies.

The basic-value concept is preferred to producers' value or purchasers' value because the trade margins (which include transport charges), and commodity-tax rates may vary among receiving sectors for some commodities and may change over time. (This will be the case even with a more disaggregated commodity classification than that of MODIS IV.) The aggregation of microeconomic commodities to industry commodities of the model implies the assumption of one and only one price for each commodity in the base year. The choice of basic values as the concept for evaluating commodity flows increases the realism of this assumption. The importance of this for the model computations in constant values is easily seen. If the relative shares of buyers of a commodity with differentiated trade margins or commodity-tax rates deviate from those of the base year, this will in itself appear as a change in demand of the commodity as measured in producers' or purchasers' values. In input-output models it therefore seems advantageous to use the basic-value concept for measurement of commodity flows.

It is important to have in mind that apart from trade margins and commodity taxes there may be genuine price differentiations in the base year. This implies a bias in the base-year values used as weights for quantity summation and, thereby, a source of errors in the model computations. All model computations start from a chosen base year. Quantities of commodity flows are measured in the unit basic values of that year. Prices of commodity flows are indexes of unit basic values relative to the base year.

The activity levels for internal activities are defined as the values of net commodity output of each activity. The activity levels are not, however, evaluated in basic values but in market values. The use of market values in the definitions of activity levels gives the valuation scheme of the model framework a hybrid form, combining commodity flows in basic values with activity levels in market values. Activity or sector levels measured in basic values is a concept that can hardly be said to exist outside the model. It seems desirable to remain within the accounting framework of the environment at the expense of some awkwardness in the price relations. The market value of internal-activity levels is computed as producers' value of commodity outputs less purchasers' value of commodity inputs. The addition to stocks (by commodity) is on the other hand evaluated, as in the national accounts, in basic values.

In accordance with these principles of value evaluation, the vector of internal activity levels may be written as

$$A = A_X + A_T,$$ (B.6)

where

A_X is a vector of net output of commodities by activity in constant values computed as basic value of commodity outputs less basic value of commodity inputs, and

A_T is a vector of commodity taxes, net, by activity in constant values, computed as commodity taxes, net, on commodity outputs less commodity taxes, net, on commodity inputs.

Both A_X and X represent the basic value of net output of commodities from the internal activities by activity and by commodity, respectively. The totals of these two vectors must accordingly be the same:

$$e'A_X = e'X. \tag{B.7}$$

By combining B.5 and B.6 the basic quantity equation may be written as

$$\Lambda \; (A_X + A_T) = X. \tag{B.8}$$

Since the input-output coefficients for commodities (the elements of Λ) are assumed constant, it follows that the proportions between corresponding elements in A and A_X and thereby also in A and A_T will be fixed. This means that the constant values of commodity taxes, net, by activity are computed as fixed shares of the activity levels.

Conceptually, this result may be arrived at in two steps. The first step is the computation of commodity taxes, net, by commodity and sector by means of tax rates given from the base year. This is in accordance with the definition and the computation of commodity taxes in constant values in the national accounts and it involves no assumption of fixed coefficients. The second step is the combination of the tax rates from the base year and a set of input-output (activity) coefficients which together imply that the constant values of commodity taxes, net, by activity are in a fixed proportion to the activity levels in constant market values. The constancy of the input-output coefficients is, of course, a specific model assumption.

As discussed earlier, prices of activity levels are indexes of unit market values, relative to the base year. Corresponding to the decomposition of activity levels in constant market values in equation B.6, the prices of activity levels may be written as

$$P_A = b_{AX} + b_{AT}, \tag{B.9}$$

where

P_{AX} is a vector of price indexes of activity levels in market values

b_{AX} is a vector of net output of commodities in current basic values by activity per unit of activity level, and

b_{AT} is a vector of commodity taxes, net, in current values by activity per unit of activity level.

With the prices of commodity flows defined as basic values relative to the base year, it follows from the definitions of b_{AX} and the activity coefficients Λ that

$$\Lambda' b_X = b_{AX}, \tag{B.10}$$

where b_X is a vector of commodity price indices in basic values.

By combining B.9 and B.10, the basic price equation, which is the dual of B.5 can be written as

$$\Lambda' b_X = p_A - b_{AT}. \tag{B.11}$$

The overall equilibrium condition in the input-output framework outlined here is that the total (algebraic) value of all activity levels is equal to the total value of net additions in stocks. By evaluation in basic values the equilibrium condition follows directly from the basic equations.

More relevant is evaluation in market values. It is easily derived from the basic equation B.5 and B.11 that

$$p_A' A = b_X' \ \Lambda A + b_{AT}' A = b_X' X + b_{AT}' A. \tag{B.12}$$

The overall equilibrium condition is thus satisfied if and only if

$$b_{AT}' A = 0, \tag{B.13}$$

that is, the net value of commodity taxes over all activities is equal to zero.

A Brief Outline of MSG-E

The MSG-model (Multi-Sectoral-Growth model) was originally developed by Professor Leif Johansen at the University of Oslo in 1960.[1] It was primarily an academic piece of work. Since then, the model has been further developed and each new version has been more user-friendly and suitable for planning purposes. The model is being used to an increasing extent as a tool in medium-term and long-term economic planning.

The MSG-model takes as exogenously given the growth in productive capacity for the economy as a whole, summarized by the growth in labor force, capital stock, and the trends of technological progress. The main strength of the model is its ability to trace out the long-term-growth paths of the economy, especially the distribution of labor, capital, and production over a disaggregated set of industries, the changes in the household-consumption patterns, and the development in the corresponding equilibrium prices. The major changes compared with the previous MSG version are partly determined by the energy orientation of the MSG-E model. A general presentation of the MSG-E model is given here, emphasizing the main behavioral relationships.

A system of partly nonlinear, simultaneous equations forms the core of the model. It is often a somewhat dubious task to explain the economic logic of a simultaneous system. One has to start somewhere and reason through, but inevitably one needs some loops back since the model has no head or tail. A simplified diagram of the structure of the model is depicted in figure B-6.

In figure B-6, assume that all sectors produce at constant returns to scale, minimize costs, and set prices equal to unit costs. Start in the upper left-hand corner of the diagram and assume given wage rates, trends of technical change, and returns on capital. The producers then have enough information to choose the cost-minimizing technique in terms of input coefficients and to determine prices that cover costs.

For given final demand, the scale of production by industry is determined as in simple traditional input-output models. Industry demand for capital and labor services is also derived. Imports are calculated from import shares, differentiated by commodity and by purchasing sector. Actually, final demand is partly exogenous, such as exports and government expenditures, and partly endogenous, such as private gross investments and household consumption.

Private gross investments are determined in a closed loop with the scale of production by industry. The scale of production by industry determines capital service and capital stock by industry and by kind of capital goods. This again determines private gross investments by commodity. For given prices the commodity composition of household consumption depends only upon total household consumption, which is determined in such a way that full-capacity use is ensured. The total productive capacity for the economy as a whole is determined by the exogenous total labor force and total capital stock and the given production efficiency.

This description may be regarded as the first iteration step in solving the equation system. Starting with arbitrarily chosen rates of return on capital and wage rates, the techniques chosen and the prices determined would generally not lead to an equilbirium solution. When producers optimize their use of labor and capital services for given remuneration to factors, their total factor use will not equal given factor supply. Consistency may be achieved, however, by letting the index of overall returns on capital be endogenous. Gradually adjusting returns on capital imply changes in prices and input coefficients. The final iteration will trace out a balanced picture of the economy with neither shortage nor surplus of commodities, labor, and capital.

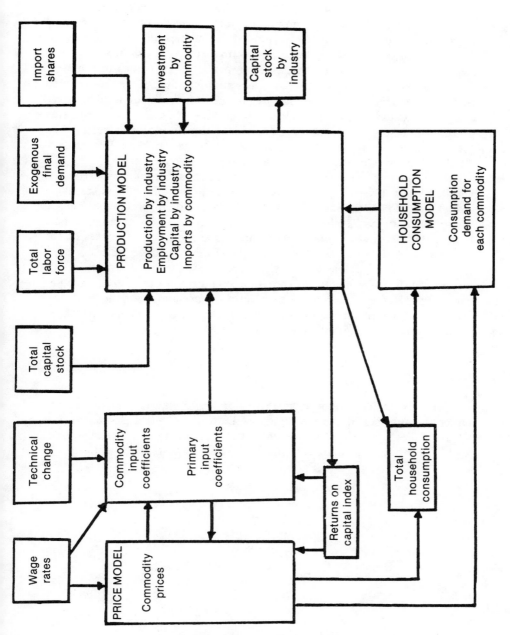

Figure B-6. Structure of MSG-E

The MSG-E model also includes submodels for capital depreciation, indirect taxes, and changes in commodity stocks. Special options to control the model results for the deficit/surplus of the balance of trade (such as adjusting the import shares or the export estimated) are introduced. In some sectors, mainly primary industries, decreasing returns to scale are assumed. This imposes another link between prices and quantities since unit costs in these sectors depend upon the scale of production. Some commodity prices are given outside the model, and the production levels and/or investments of some industries are exogenous. Some of the special cases referred to (decreasing returns to scale exogenous prices, exogenous estimates for production and investment) apply to the energy-producing sectors.

A complete representation of technological and behavioral relations within households and industries would exceed the limits of a manageable model. In MSG-E the interplay of sectors in a growth process is focused upon; behavior and technology within sectors are given a rather simple representation. It should be noted that several general weaknesses of the previous MSG-version are inherent in MSG-E. For instance, all exports are exogenous. Energy-intensive industries are major export industries, which means that the assessments of exports directly influence the development of energy use. However, several ongoing projects are aiming at the modification and improvement of various parts of the model. Results from these projects will gradually be implemented in MSG-E.

Note

1. This model developed by Professor Leif Johansen was carried out under the auspices of the University of Oslo, the Central Bureau of Statistics of the Norwegian government, and the Ministry of Finance of Norway. The model is available through the Ministry of Finance in Oslo.

Index

193

Mexico: *(cont.)*
20-21, 23, 25, 30, 49-50; energy
policy, 20, 21, 24, 30, 47-48, 49, 50;
federal budget, 46, 50, 53-55;
Federal Electricity Commission
(CFE), 37; foreign policy, 60-61;
foreign trade, 13-17, 32, 144-145,
152-153, 162; Global Plan and
Energy Program, 6, 47-48, 49,
50-56, 142; government sector, 145,
153; In-Bond Program, 37; Law to
Promote Mexican Investment and
Regulate Foreign Investment (1973),
18, 37-38; legal system, 59;
monetary sector, 146-147, 153,
158-160; National Congress, 57-58;
National Indian Institute, 59; oil
imports, 19, 23; oil subsidies, 20,
21, 25, 29-30; organization of
government, 57-58; presidential veto
power, 57, 58, 61, 64; real income,
41, 42; real output, 161-162;
redistribution of income, 34, 53;
religion, 59; Secretaria de Educacion (SEP), 40; state development
bank, 17, 41, 47, 55; Supreme
Court, 57; tourism ministry/day-
light savings time, 50
Mexico City, 9, 38, 39, 61, 65, 66, 68
Mineral resources/mining; Mex., 9, 35;
Norw., 79, 97
Mobility, occupational/regional:
Norw., 84, 111, 112, 121-122,
132-134
MODIS (Model of Disaggregated type),
167-189
Monetary and fiscal policies:
Mex., 24, 40-50, 51; Norw., 126
Monterrey, Mex., 9
MSG (Multi-Sectoral Growth) model,
167, 189-192
Multinationals. *See* Oil companies,
foreign

Nacional Financiera, 17, 41, 55
Nafinsa, 47
National Railways, 38
Nationalization: Mex., 1, 2, 18, 19, 20,
21, 22, 25, 26, 60; Norw., 85, 86
Natural gas: Mex., 23-24, 48-49;
Norw., 103

Nonoil sector: Mex., 148, 154; Norw.,
3-4, 82, 91-94, 95, 98, 100, 109, 130
Norway: capital export, 136, 137;
countercyclical policy, 87-88, 98,
100, 102, 112-113, 127; economic-
interest organizations, 82-83;
Employers' Federation, 88; foreign
competition, 78, 85, 88, 89, 90-91,
94, 97, 98, 100, 102, 109, 113, 114,
116-117, 128, 129; gross investment,
97; industrial exports, 101, 114; industrial imports, 82, 120; Long-Term
Program, 87, 89; managerial competence, 109-110, 111, 112, 120, 125,
131; manufacturing subsidies, 87,
112, 127, 128, 133; organization of
government, 82; Petroleum Direc-
torate/ministry for oil and energy,
104; service sector, 81, 123-124;
transfer of income, 77, 78, 101, 102
Nuclear power, 39, 62

Oil, crude, 13
Oil and Gas Journal, 19, 142
Oil and gas reserves: Mex., 19, 21-22,
27; Norw., 78-79, 103
Oil companies, foreign: in Mex., 1, 2,
5, 25; in Norw., 1, 2, 5, 104, 105,
120, 127
Oil development: Mex., 22-23, 24, 25-
26, 44, 46, 50-51, 54, 56, 68, 71;
Norw., 3, 85-86, 87, 88, 94, 97-98,
100, 129-130
Oil exploration, 20, 21, 22, 24
Oil exports: Mex., 13, 21, 24, 29, 44,
48, 49, 147; Norw., 3, 78, 94
Oil extraction costs, 104
Oil glut, 27, 31, 45, 48, 49, 56, 71
Oil-importing countries, 3
Oil pricing, 2; Mex., 5-6, 20-21, 25,
27-30, 45, 71; Norw., 88, 94
Oil productivity: Mex., 19, 27, 35, 70;
Norw., 105-106
Oil revenues: Mex., 2, 3, 19, 29, 31,
44, 49, 53, 56, 64, 71; Norw., 1-2,
3, 77-78, 85-86, 87, 88, 89, 90-91,
100, 101-103, 106-107, 109, 114-116,
134-135
Organization for Economic Coopera-
tion and Development (OECD), 4,
82, 130, 134

About the Authors

Ragaei El Mallakh is professor of economics at the University of Colorado, Boulder, executive director of the International Research Center for Energy and Economic Development, and editor of the *Journal of Energy and Development*. He has written or contributed to some fourteen books, including *Economic Development and Regional Cooperation: Kuwait*, and *Saudi Arabia: Rush to Development*, and he has published over eighty articles and reviews in the *American Economic Review, Journal of Economic Literature, Kyklos*, and *Land Economics*, among others. He has given papers to such bodies as the Oxford Energy Seminar (England), the National Autonomous University of Mexico, and the University of Riyadh. Dr. El Mallakh has been a consultant to or a member of the World Bank, the Joint Economic Committee of the U.S. Congress, and the U.S. National Committee on World Petroleum Congresses.

Øystein Noreng is a professor at the Norwegian School of Management, Oslo, and also research director of the Institute of Energy Policy. He holds the Ph.D. from the Sorbonne in political science and international affairs, and has been a fellow with The Rockefeller Foundation. His earlier positions included working as a counselor with the Planning Department, Norwegian Ministry of Finance and Research, and as planning manager with the Marketing Department of Statoil. Dr. Noreng's publications include *The Oil Industry and Government Strategy in the North Sea*, 1980, and *Oil Politics in the 1980s*.

Barry W. Poulson is professor of economics at the University of Colorado, Boulder, has been a Fulbright Professor at the Universidad Autonoma de Guadalajara, and has edited a number of books, including *U.S.-Mexico Economic Relations*, and *El Dilema de Dos Naciones: Relaciones Economicas entre Mexico y Estados Unidos*. His articles have appeared in such publications as *Review of Business and Economic Research, Journal of Economic History, Oxford Economic Papers*, and *Southern Economic Journal*. Dr. Poulson has served as director of the International Economic Studies Center of the University of Colorado's Department of Economics.